After the Locusts

D1468999

After the Locusts

Letters from a Landscape of Faith

DENISE M. ACKERMANN

William B. Eerdmans Publishing Company
Grand Rapids, Michigan / Cambridge, U.K.

David Philip Publishers
Republic of South Africa

© 2003 Wm. B. Eerdmans Publishing Co.
All rights reserved

Published jointly 2003 by
Wm. B. Eerdmans Publishing Co.
255 Jefferson Ave. S.E., Grand Rapids, Michigan 49503 /
P.O. Box 163, Cambridge CB3 9PU U.K.
www.eerdmans.com
and in South Africa by
David Philip Publishers
an imprint of New Africa Books (Pty) Ltd
P.O. Box 46962, Glosderry 7702, Republic of South Africa

Printed in the United States of America

08 07 06 05 04 03   7 6 5 4 3 2 1

Library of Congress Cataloging-in-Publication Data

Ackermann, Denise M.
After the locusts: letters from a landscape of faith /
Denise M. Ackermann.
p.   cm.
Includes bibliographical references.
ISBN 0-8028-1019-5 (pbk.: alk. paper)
1. Feminist theology — South Africa.
2. Christian life — South Africa.
3. Ackermann, Denise.   I. Title
BT83.55A28   2003
230′.3′092 — dc21

2003044357

David Philip ISBN 0-86486-604-6

For Laurie

Contents

Foreword

When I was much younger, I asked a professor at a leading European university if I could do a Ph.D. on Black Theology. He replied, quite seriously, "What is black theology?"

He asked the question in a tone of voice that made it clear he had no doubt at all that it was obvious there could be no such entity. He had the unconscious arrogance of one who expected everyone to know that there really was only one kind of theology and that was theology as practised by himself and those like him, Caucasian and overwhelmingly male. It was easy to have fallen into this way of thinking, for in the history of the church until the '60s of the twentieth century there had been relative theological homogeneity. Those who theologised up to then had almost exclusively been male, and if they were not Caucasian certainly shared the same thought forms, worldview, and point of reference and had been dealing with communities that shared a great deal in common. There might have been distinctions that characterised ethnic and geographical entities, but broadly speaking, it could be said that they belonged under one class. Everything that did not fit this classification was an aberration and was ruled out of court in principle.

It is very odd that it should have taken so long to establish the fact that an authentic and relevant theology by definition almost had to be particular, avoiding a premature and almost certainly invalid claim to universality like the plague. It had to be contextual, being spatio-temporally conditioned, made relevant precisely because it was answering the specific questions and concerns of a definite and specific community, the ultimate reference point being Jesus Christ, the same yesterday, today, and forever. It is passing strange that it should have taken us so long to recognise a verity that stuck out as prominently as a sore thumb for any diligent reader of the bible. There we are confronted by a plethora of theologies seeking to make sense of the experiences of specific faith communities who had particular perplexities to sort out and who could be reached in any meaningful way only through categories, thought forms, and vocabularies that had currency in their particular settings — their *Sitz im Leben*.

We should have been glorying in what could be described as the inbuilt obsolescence of proper, authentic, and relevant theology, for the settings and circumstances giving rise to it are always in flux and the questions and perplexities that have to be dealt with change. The theologies must change too, to be useful.

I am amazed how easily I learnt splendid answers in England to questions no one in my black community was asking at home in South Africa. I had become adept at dealing with what might have been issues of concern among Christians in the northern hemisphere who appeared to be concerned with the grammar of belief — what did theological assertion actually say or purport to say? Now the existential issues for our people were not doubt about God's existence or puzzlement about what you meant when you asserted that God loved us. For them the critical issues were seeking an explanation for the anguish and agony they were suffering under a vicious system of injustice inflicted not by pagans but by those who claimed to be fellow believers. The questions were, "God, on whose side are you?" "Do you love us blacks as you do other people, or are we really just your stepchildren?" In the southern hemisphere there could be no final theology, for often these questions had been dealt with when the context that gave rise to them had passed, and the relevance of that theology had passed with it — as has happened with the defeat of apartheid and the emergence of democracy and freedom.

Of course, it was possible and indeed likely that in dealing with the particular context those theologising might uncover insights and verities that could have relevance for other possibly similar contexts, that there would be as it were contextual and temporary relevance and application. But the point being stressed is that this latter result was not the primary *raison d'être* for the original theologising.

Denise Ackermann has made a telling contribution, almost a unique contribution. Hers belongs to the *feminist* theology genre, but it comes from someone who is part Afrikaner, a member of a community that gave the world the ghastly system of apartheid.

She wants to make sense for herself and her family, for her community, and really ultimately for all of us, her fellow Christians, just how it was possible for all the awfulness of apartheid to come from a people so deeply religious and devout. She wants to come to terms with what it has meant to share in the privileges of power, even if she herself had repudiated them, privileges that came just because of her ethnicity and her skin colour.

It is a deeply moving account of a very special person, remarkably courageous: she and her lawyer husband, now a judge in our Constitutional Court, have paid heavily for holding to their beliefs and principles which put them at odds with the majority of their community. None of us can be too comfortable with power and influence, nor can we afford to be smug, for we stand under the judgement of the cross of Jesus who emptied himself and took on the form of a servant and was obedient even to death, yes, death on the cross. Only so could he then be highly exalted. There is no other way for us his followers.

DESMOND M. TUTU
Archbishop *emeritus*

Introduction

One morning in October 1999 I woke up with a simple conviction. I had a six-month sabbatical ahead of me. I planned to write a book on a feminist theology of healing praxis in the South African context. But I felt increasingly uneasy. Something was not right. That morning I knew. I was not, once again, going to write for the limited inner circle of the academy. I had spent years doing precisely that. No more! Now I wanted to write for the general reader, for people in the churches, as well as for anyone else who might be interested in the theological reflections of a white South African woman on the life of faith. I immediately felt daunted. Changing gears put me in a pickle. I am not a creative writer. I felt like a mole emerging into the bright sunlight — blind and groping, out of my habitat. Writing for the academy gets one into bad habits. We theologians use our own kind of jargon. We know the rules and how to play the game. I had no idea of how to shift gears. I went through a period of great uncertainty. Would I manage to let go of the comfort blanket of academic speak? I talked to friends. I thrashed around. Eventually on a sunny December day I found what I wanted, a vehicle to keep me from academic excesses. I would write letters to people who matter to me, about the themes that have been at the core of my search for healing and freedom.

After the Locusts is about my efforts to discover what is worth living for in the midst of troubled times. This book has been a risky venture. Taking complex theological doctrines and philosophical concepts that are at present central to debates in the academy and attempting to make them simple and straightforward lays me open to charges of reductionism, of dishing up well-known ideas like boiled rice, without garnishes or subtle sauces. Many a day G. K. Chesterton's warning that "[a]nyone who wants to write should first contemplate the majesty of the empty page" has reverberated in my head. A few beliefs have kept me going. I believe that theology should be rooted in its social and political context. I have little interest in theologies that appear to fall from above like some great received deposit of wisdom. The seedbed of my theology is my understanding of the bible and Christian tradition in dialogue with the recent turbulent history of South Africa as seen through my experiences of living here through the second half of the twentieth century. This I want to write about. I am also passionate about theology. I believe in its potential to change people, to deepen faith and understanding, and to heal our wounds. That is why it cannot be limited to the inner circle of the theologically trained. It should not be some inward-looking academic game, untried by those outside its cloisters who struggle to live the life of faith in a world that is often unwelcoming, if not antagonistic.

The title of this book, *After the Locusts,* comes from the Old Testament book of Joel. Joel, a Hebrew prophet, lived sometime between the late sixth and early fourth centuries B.C.E., at a time when an ecological disaster had struck the land of Judah, the southern kingdom of Israel. A plague of desert locusts had devastated the countryside, laying waste the vines, stripping the fig trees, and destroying the fields of grain. After vividly describing the effects of the plague, Joel calls the people to lament and repent "for the day of the Lord is coming, it is near." Together with the priests, they are to return to God by fasting, weeping, and mourning; they are told to "rend your hearts and not your clothing." Then Joel recounts how God will have pity on the people. His tone changes from the gloom of disaster to the hope of salvation. The armies of nations gathered against Judah will be judged and defeated just as the armies of locusts that have invaded Judah will be destroyed. God will remove the "northern army far from you, and drive it into a parched and desolate land. . . . The threshing floors shall be full of grain, the vats shall overflow with wine and oil." And finally the promise: "I will repay you for the years that the swarming locusts have eaten. . . ." Two very different tones in the book of Joel are united by one single concern: God's ultimate vindication of Judah.

I remember reading this book during repressive times in South Africa.

The locusts became a metaphor in my life for the ravages of apartheid as well as for my own personal demons. The idea that God would repay the years that the locusts had eaten stayed with me. The destruction wrought by the locusts would be restored and "God's people would never again be put to shame." This thought drifted down into my subconscious, like a small red autumn leaf. In troubled times I would retrieve it, hold it, and feel comforted. Most of my life was lived in the time of apartheid. I went to university, married, had children, worked, and then became a theologian during those turbulent times. Childhood experiences of feeling an outsider translated into an adult passion for justice. Life became troubled, fraught with daily decisions about what to do, what to believe, how to act as a white person, as a South African, and as a woman. Sorting out the good from the bad was easy on the big issues such as racism. It became more complicated when one's culture, one's family, and even one's faith appeared to be at odds with one's convictions.

As I struggled to come to terms with my responsibility as a white South African, and as we lived through one state of emergency after another, reeling under the excesses of the security forces and the preposterous lies of politicians, I would remind myself of the locusts and how Joel's story ends. Eventually the racist locusts became a spent force, trapped in the morass of immoral ideologies. The war on our borders was lost, sanctions had bitten deeply into the South African economy, and the momentum for change generated by the United Democratic Movement had become a tidal wave. Finally it was over. Today South Africans live with the ravages of the locust years while yearning for the restoration and healing of our land. The book of the prophet Joel binds together the central theme of this work, the longing for healing and freedom.

Life under apartheid is only a part of this story. I am troubled by the present loss of direction in many of our religious communities. People seem fatigued, even helpless, when violence, increasing poverty, corruption, or HIV/AIDS is mentioned. I am equally troubled by the uncritical stance of some churches on present state policies that are having devastating effects on people's health, education, and safety. Questions are asked about the future of our fragile democracy in the face of overwhelming problems. Equally disturbing is the sense that academic theology has lost its way. Scholars write for scholars and students, and the churches look elsewhere for nurture. They try new tricks: self-discovery and community-building programmes, groups for this and that, services dominated by popular speakers and performing artists. Unsure of their theological grounding they try to keep the faithful from becoming restless. I am not deriding these efforts. I believe that a church that is open to society should include all these activities and more. My concern is that theology no longer has the ear of the institutional church. This saddens me. We theologians must shoulder the blame. Have our theologies been alive with the conviction that God's love and redeeming power will make us and the entire creation whole? Have they grappled unceasingly with the everyday concerns of people of faith like poverty, justice, death, family, and so on? Have they found new understandings of God's omnipotence and love in the face of the death of millions from AIDS-related diseases? Have they offered friendly frameworks for people of different social, ethnic, and cultural groups to speak about their faith? Have they been more interested in method than in people? No wonder we are outside the church door. I realise that asking these questions is akin to setting myself up. I too have failed to be sufficiently critical of my own theology. We need a new theological language if we are to make the church doors swing open and welcome us once again.

I do not apologise for writing letters. Knowing that I am addressing someone I care for has helped to keep my feet on the ground. A blind mole needs help in navigating the world above her burrows. I have found my way by making an imaginary sketch of the landscape I have tried to travel. This device, more geographic than artistic, has kept me focused on the terrain I have traversed in my efforts to chronicle a theologian's journey of faith.

As a woman theologian, I believe that the method I choose for communicating is in fact part of the kind of theology I am committed to. Our methods uncover our moral and religious commitment. They also reveal what in essence we think about how knowledge is acquired and transmitted, and which categories of thought are more important than others. Although this book attempts to reach a wider reading public, it remains the work of a theologian and as such it follows a certain theological method. Augustine said: "I believe in order to understand." My point of departure is my faith as a Christian. My method draws from experience that is submitted to critical scrutiny and tested within the social and political milieu in which it is shaped. I believe that feminist theology — for that is what I write — is a kind of liberation theology. Liberation theology is committed to participating in solidarity with all who struggle to find healing and freedom. The cries of the prophets in the Old Testament and the life and ministry of Jesus Christ as told in the New Testament converge around the themes of justice and love as God's intention for the world. This kind of theology therefore starts by looking at social reality — a move that entails analysis as well as the recording of stories. Narrative is the lifeblood of this kind of theology, for it is in stories that the validity of a host of very diverse experiences is found. The next step is to allow experiences and stories to engage critically with our biblical and theological traditions. Throughout the letters in this book my stance is one of critical questioning within my own faith tradition. This leads me to the next step in the way women go about doing theology. Out of experience and critical questioning the search for clues for transformation emerge that can translate into actions on behalf of healing and freedom.

Not surprisingly, given the method I have just described, these letters have drawn me into writing about myself. Being personal means being vulnerable. I cannot hide behind the tricks that govern academic writing. Beside that, letters to people I care for can hardly be impersonal. As this book took shape, I found that the locusts are as much a metaphor for the personal demons that have dogged my efforts to live the life of faith as they are for the ideological destructiveness of sexism, racism, and nationalism that have blighted the history of South Africa. The letters in this book do not separate the private from the political. I simply do not know how to maintain this kind of separation. Personal and public themes are woven into the fabric of our lives, and together they tell the story. At a session of the Society for Biblical Literature in 2001, Walter Brueggemann generously described my paper together with that of two other participants as the work of organic intellectuals (à la Gramsci). Without pushing the point, I believe that theology should be an "organic" enterprise, one that is close to the ground, that can nurture the fragility of our lives as we struggle to put out shoots of new growth. In the search for meaning we need to test the evidence "from below" in the contestation of truth. I also admit that this work is something of an apologia. Those who stand outside communities of faith may just be sufficiently curious to pick it up. Throughout the time of writing, Nietzsche has cast a shadow over my computer screen. Apart from the obvious enjoyment provided by his scintillating, trenchant writing, his searing critique of Christian practices has been a dialogue partner in writing these letters. While disagreeing deeply with Nietzsche on many scores, I am always grateful for the response he provokes.

The order of chapters in this work emerges out of my efforts to sketch my landscape. Although they deal with separate themes there is a sequence to their ordering that makes sense to me as I try to plot my landscape of faith. Chapter One sets the scene by telling something of my own story around issues of context, identity, boundaries, and the life of faith in a letter to my two granddaughters, one of whom is being raised as a Christian and the other as a Jew. Chapter Two arises out of a question my mother asked me many years ago: "What *is* theology?" What I understand by theology, what kind of theology I am drawn to, and how I deal with the bible, the church, and ideologies that crop up along the way, are tackled in this chapter. Chapter Three is about embodiment. This theme is not only central to feminist theological thought but it is pivotal to understanding what it means to have lived through apartheid as a white woman in a country that now faces a future blighted by the scourge of HIV/AIDS. Chapter Four is for my children, who have all had their share of anguish. There is no answer to the ever-present question of human suffering, but in the language of lament we can find means of coping with its unrelenting nature. Chapter Five draws together the themes raised in the previous letters under the rubric of spirituality. Struggles with despair about "the state of the world," struggles with prayer, thoughts on ageing and death, and the wisdom of Julian of Norwich have all been part of the conversations I have had over the years with my spiritual director. This letter is addressed to him. The final chapter, which is no more than a brief postscript to my "ready-made" grandson, is about the wonder of seeing the small things; how God is to be found in the details. At the heart of all these letters is the longing for healing and freedom that has shaped my theology and the practise of my life of faith and has given rise to the question: What makes life worth living? Each chapter has a series of end notes that give brief biographical information on the addressees, clarify terms, amplify theological points, and provide bibliographical material for the more serious student. Some letters have excessive bibliographical details, but their purpose is to provide a ready-made reading list for those with an academic interest in the issues discussed. Throughout, quotations from scripture are taken from the New Revised Standard Version.

Thanking those who have been part of this project is a satisfying task. I am allergic to the ritual of mentioning every single person who in fact deserves thanks. While I type away, I see the faces of my theological friends and colleagues both in my own country and abroad — all of whom have helped shape my thinking. You are remembered! In particular, I want to thank Archbishop *emeritus* Desmond Tutu for his gracious foreword. Looking back on the years I have known him, I find there is much for which to thank him. I want to single out two abiding lessons he has taught me. Desmond Tutu's ability to see the humanity of all people as precious and worthy of respect has made deep tracks on the lives of many who know him. I also want to thank him for his unshakeable trust in a God who never ceases to woo us, cherish us, and guide us, despite the vicissitudes of life. And Arch, thanks too for the jokes and the joy! I owe the Center of Theological Inquiry at Princeton profound thanks for allowing me to work there in great comfort, surrounded by unparalleled resources. In particular, my thanks go to the director, Wallace Alston, for repeated invitations to the Center and to Kathi Morley, who administers the Center with concern and care. Francine Cardman has been my partner in conversation about this project from its inception. She has provided me with hospitality and critical feedback as well as support when my enthusiasm and confidence lagged. For this I thank her. I also want to thank Elfriede Bremer for her help with the manuscript of this book, Cassandra Parker for her meticulous and critical reading and for very valuable suggestions, and Angelika Alberts and Tessa Ackermann for their scrupulous and imaginative reading of the manuscript. Finally, there is one person missing from the letters in this book, yet without whose interest and encouragement it would not have seen the light of day. I want to thank my spouse Laurie, not only for reading numerous versions of this book, but most of all for his generous and unflagging support of the process I had to go through in writing this book and for trusting in me to get through it. I dedicate it to him with gratitude.

Cape Town
April 2003

CHAPTER I

To My Granddaughters

on the Vexed Questions of Identity, Difference, and Faith

Then afterward I will pour out my spirit on all flesh;
your sons and your daughters shall prophesy,
your old men shall dream dreams,
and your young men shall see visions.
Even on the male and female slaves,
in those days, I will pour out my spirit.

JOEL 2:28-29

Dear Rachel and Jo,

Why am I writing this letter to the two of you long before you are able to read, in a book you may never see? The answer to this question has two parts. First, you are growing up in times of uncertainty and challenge, in a country possessed of blessings and blight. You will have your own questions and views about your native country. I want to tell you how it has been for me. Second, as I tell you parts of my story, I am aware that this is

---

An earlier, somewhat different version of this letter entitled "A Letter to My Granddaughters on Matters of the Heart" appeared in *Claiming Our Footprints: South African Women Reflect on Context, Identity and Spirituality,* ed. Denise M. Ackermann, Eliza Getman, Hantie Kotzé, and Judy Tobler on behalf of the Cape Town chapter of the Circle for Concerned African Women Theologians (Stellenbosch: EFSA, 2000).

also a letter to myself. Writing about our history, our identities, and our differences takes me to the question at the heart of this book: What is worth living for? Or, put differently: What have I found to be life-affirming and what has been harmful, even poisonous, in my struggles to live fully in this place?

To help me find my way through many questions, doubts, and discoveries, I want to imagine that I am sketching a landscape. Unlike professional cartographers I do not want to be tied down to the certainty that, provided the measurements are right, this sketch will be a reliable guide in all circumstances. This is not an accurate map. It is really like a giant picture with different landscapes and figures, swarms of locusts and fields of flowers, different colours and symbols; it requires imagination, even guesswork, and it is always provisional. I know that writing to you like this will take me into unexplored territory. So, as I go, I shall have to modify, update, and improve my sketch. As the next generation you will, I hope, make your own kind of picture map. Do look for the markers on mine. They are clues to understanding the connections between my life and yours, between thinking and feeling, between beliefs and actions. These markers are not selected at random, neither are they complete. The place and the time in which I write have chosen them for me. Times change. Guided by a memory that often fails me, I want to mark our different histories and identities and what they mean for me as your grandmother. Memory is not fiction, yet once I begin to recall emotions, events, and places, I wonder — is that true? How much of memory is invented or rearranged? Did that happen or am I remembering being told it did? Fragments, tainted memories, stories retold too often are all I can offer. What will you make of them?

I have waited for grandchildren longer than almost all my friends. Now, somewhat unexpectedly, there you two are, so different, yet both members of the same family. It is your apparent differences and your shared sameness that freshly and immediately raise questions of identity. You may have questions yourselves about these themes when you grow up. If I were there, what would I have to say to you?

I would begin by affirming that we are a family of hybrids. The dictionary defines a hybrid as a person of mixed descent or mixed ancestry. That is who we are, a *"Mélange,* hotchpotch, a bit of this and a bit of that . . ."* in Salman Rushdie's words. Your *oupa* Laurie's family was of German, French

Huguenot, and Dutch descent. He grew up speaking both English and Afrikaans, familiar with both cultures. This was important to his parents despite the fact that their parents had lost all their possessions in the Anglo-Boer War, had known exile, and had children perish in the British concentration camps. They were remarkable people. Never did they succumb to the temptation to base their identity on a sentimental memory of being the victims of British imperialism. They were firm believers in crossing cultural barriers, and they eschewed a narrow view of history or any thoughts of vendetta.

My father's family, the du Toits, were French Huguenots who came to the Cape in 1686 and mixed with the local population and with the Dutch settlers. The Huguenot history was one of religious persecution, of being refugees, of having to forego the French language and French Protestantism under the strictures of the Dutch authorities and of eventual capitulation to a narrow form of Afrikanerism. My mother's family, the Fichats, were also descended from French Huguenots who fled to Ireland and then England, and eventually sailed to the Cape in 1807. They were farmers and, at one time, slave owners. The Fichats became members of the English-speaking South African community with its own cultural history. I grew up speaking only English to my mother and only Afrikaans to my father — a cultural hybrid, between two heritages, trying to find that place in between two opposing histories, where my identity would no longer be confused, but new.

This initial sense of being many selves was intensified by the fact that my father became a diplomat just after the Second World War and I went to school on three different continents. My first eleven years were spent in South Africa, followed by two years in Sweden and then Argentina for my last three years of high school. Soon two languages became five and, as I learned a new one, I promptly buried the previous one. After my English/Spanish high school years, I was sent to Stellenbosch, an Afrikaans-speaking university. I have many memories of being the alien, a foreigner at school and, on returning from abroad, a stranger in my own country, even among my cousins. Being a hybrid meant being an outsider.

Am I my language? If so, which one? I am told that I first spoke Afrikaans, itself a mélange of Dutch, Malay, and slave patois. English became dominant during those formative years at high school. Throughout history people have switched languages as a way of surviving. In the midst of war and destruction, writes Chilean Ariel Dorfman, "barely a bit behind the fist holding the sword, is the verb. A captive always ends up being the captive of somebody else's words." Survival often means deciding to learn the language of those who have power over us. I did not switch in the same way as Dorfman did when, as a child in New York, he decided never to speak Spanish again. I had to speak to my parents. I learnt that being bilingual was a means of remaining alive in a divided family. I had no choice but to be "double", a hybrid who, in Dorfman's words, knew "the anxiety, the richness and the madness of being double." I still wonder whether I ever truly had a first language. Were there ever those words that are alive, warm, and close to the core? I am telling you this because you are growing up in a country that has eleven official languages, and you will doubtless learn to speak several of them. How will language "speak" your identities?

Rachel, you will probably never know much about your biological grandparents. How important will this be for you as you grow up? Your mother came to us as a baby of eight days. Her heritage is a mixture of Italian and Austrian. Her battles to establish an identity have been long and painful. Her situation is one that has no satisfactory answers. Your father's parents are no longer alive and his experience of them seems distant and not without *angst*. His father was a German Jew who fled from Germany to England during the rise of National Socialism in the 1930s, and his mother was an Englishwoman. That is all I can tell you. Here you are, so perfect, eyes like the sea on a sunny day, responsive and vital — a hybrid of mystery.

Jo, you too are a hybrid, like a small cross-pollinated plant, my Jewish granddaughter. Your mother and her parents are the descendants of northern European Jews who came to this country from Lithuania a couple of generations ago. The people of the Old Testament are your history. In your veins there is also the blood of those French Huguenots and their ambiguous story. Your identity will be forged by shabbat gatherings on Friday nights, by Rosh Hashanah, Hanukkah, and other defining moments in Jewish history and culture, as well as by sorties into the African bush with your father and Christmases spent with us. You, with your wonderful Mediterranean looks, burnished olive skin, engaging smile, and mop of black hair — what will your questions be when you grow up?

Perhaps you will wonder one day what it was like growing up white and privileged in apartheid South Africa. Frankly, I never thought about being white or privileged when I was a child. The years abroad insulated me further from questions of race and only served to emphasize that I was an outsider. Today, I know that being white meant not questioning a comfortable home, good medical care, good schooling, holidays, travel, and — had I needed it — better treatment by the law. My parents were not wealthy. They were frugal with what they had but we lived comfortably. I accepted without question a host of concepts and ideas about race, about tradition and culture. I was an ordinary privileged white girl growing up in the late 1930s and '40s in South Africa. Only when I left to live abroad did I begin to experience other realities.

My earliest memories are ones of a struggle to find my place in a patriarchal family. My father was powerful, shrewd, charismatic, and never wrong. He, your great-grandfather, was proud of his Huguenot heritage, unwavering in his conservative worldview, and a vigorous patriarch who believed that a line of sons would establish his "name" and his values. As his only daughter, my earliest experiences in my family were, at best, ones of being an onlooker, and at worst, of painful discrimination. My mother was less conservative than my father in her beliefs, but her concept of what it meant to be a wife and mother was nonetheless traditional. She too knew her place. As I grew up, I understood instinctively that patriarchy was about power and that power was for men. At the same time I was trying to cope with the cultural confusion of my home. My father had no truck with the Allied cause during World War II because he was not partial to the English. My mother's family were joining the South African army and dying in the North African campaigns. The war was fought in our home. Daily news reports fuelled the battle between "Boer and Brit". I did not confront or question my parents about these clashes. Like Edward Said, the Palestinian activist and academic who did not confront his father with the loss of Palestine in 1948, "I had no available vocabulary for the question."

I first became aware of my privilege in postwar Germany. This is not strange. My childhood in a comfortable white suburb of Cape Town, with occasional excursions to District Six where my mother had a seamstress, had largely inured me to the life and circumstances of South Africans who did not live as I did. I was eleven when my family went to live in Sweden. On a visit to Hamburg in 1947 and in defiance of my parents' express instructions to stay indoors, I wandered off down the street, lined with the

ruins of bombed houses. An emaciated German child wearing a long tat-
tered raincoat crept out of a heap of rubble and stared at me with hungry
eyes. I offered the child my banana. Grabbing it from my hand, the child
devoured it, skin and all. Shame, guilt, and an unarticulated anger overwhelmed me. I ran home.

After Sweden we went to live in Buenos Aires. It was the time of Eva
and Juan Peron. I remember standing on the Plaza de Mayo, watching a
throng of enthusiastic Peronistas chant: "Evita, Evita!," until she appeared
on the balcony of the *Casa Rosada* to greet them. I saw her one other time.
It was at the Colón Opera House. An hour and a half late for the performance (which had to be delayed), she was wearing a sheath-like, strapless
white satin dress, a collar of diamonds and aquamarines, draped in a cloak
of pale blue shimmering ostrich feathers. I also remember having to read
extracts from her book *La Razón de Mi Vida (The Reason for My Life)* before
school every morning. I remember fear in the air, people whispering on
the train, the arrogant police. My privilege as a diplomat's child protected
me; it was different for some of my friends at school whose relatives lost
their possessions and were imprisoned during the regime of the Perons in
the Argentine. I learnt the smell of dictatorship, an experience that later re-
curred as apartheid tightened its grip on South Africa.

In 1951 I returned to South Africa to go to University in Stellenbosch. I
was too young, too confused, and too much a stranger in my own country
to benefit academically from those years. My generation of young postwar
whites was singularly uncritical of our social and political environment.
We did not question, we had no real "causes". My primary goal was to pass
my courses because I knew that if I failed I would be sent home — home at
that time was Portugal. I do remember chafing at the stifling "we know
what is good for you" authoritarianism of the Stellenbosch *broeders* and being offended by the easy attitudes of racist condescension. My feelings
about the racism of my own people crystallized in 1956 when I was working in Stellenbosch. After a drawn-out process of political trickery, the Nationalist government removed the coloured people from the common voters' roll. You will learn more about this at school one day. One night I
attended a political meeting in the Stellenbosch town hall where the local
Nationalist politician explained the rightness of his party's actions. I was
incensed and said so. That night a brick was thrown through the window
of my room. I knew that something irrevocable had happened. Not only

had the history of our country been changed, but the course of my life had been affected. I did not analyse enough or understand enough; I was too caught up in finding out who I was and what I wanted to do with my life to become overtly political. But this awareness of what apartheid was doing fuelled my opposition to Afrikaner nationalism.

I wanted to tell you about these experiences, as different and as separated by years as they are, because they all played a role in shaping my identity and, sadly, in my progressive alienation from my family. My subsequent involvement in organizations that opposed apartheid cost me dearly with those members of my family to whom such behaviour was traitorous. Looking back, I do not know that it could have been different. But I still mourn the alienation. Perhaps now you can see why identity is an important marker on my landscape. Both of you may question the relevance of dwelling on matters of history, culture, and identity. I hope you will be spared the pressures, problems, politics, and ideologies that can thwart your personal efforts to know yourselves. You will, however, have to learn to live with different, often conflicting, ideas about race, class, gender, and culture. Questions of identity will not disappear.

You are both born South Africans. I wonder what this will mean to you when you are my age? For me, being a South African has been like riding a roller coaster. Why? We live in a country fraught with extremes: rich and poor, love and hatred, ugliness and great beauty, flood and drought, desert and forest. A country described as pluralistic, multicultural, as a rainbow nation or as the *Groot Gariep*.

Our history as white people in this country is not necessarily one of sameness. It is a history of contradictions, disputes, clashes, anomalies, and absurdities. It is also one of inclusion and exclusion, as I found out in the days of the struggle against apartheid. Not all whites were Afrikaner nationalists. Not all Afrikaners were supporters of the Nationalist Party, a party that received considerable support from English-speaking South Africans. All whites were, however, beneficiaries of apartheid, even those who opposed it. Sadly, you are heirs to a history of discrimination and injustice, no matter where your parents and grandparents stood on the issue of white dominance. You may, therefore, be tempted to say: "We have our own problems and our own challenges; we have to get on with our own future, however instructive you may think your past is." As young women you may well tire of the insistence to remember the past. Danish philosopher and religious thinker Søren Kierkegaard said that the problem with existence is that it has to be lived forward and it can only be evaluated or reviewed, so to say, backward. That is my dilemma and it will be yours too.

A painful history can cripple human memory in two ways: you can either forget the past or be imprisoned by it. I wish neither on you. Your understanding of our past will enable you to deal with your future. Understanding the past will also help you to recognise — both in yourselves and in those who will govern you — the inclination to harm and destroy. I shudder as I write this, for you are still so innocent. You will encounter a world in which injustice and unkindness abound and in which you too will have to recognise things about yourselves that are not good news. You will hear your share of lies and you will be tempted to bury the truth. I wish for you both the ability to accept that we human beings make history and that we are all responsible in some way or other for the circumstances in which we live our lives. I know that there are many conditions that humans themselves cannot control. I know too that we are not necessarily directly responsible for all that is wrong around us. What I am talking about is an attitude of mind that knows that our ability to recognise and to lament what is harmful depends upon our belief that at some point it is worth opposing.

If, on the one hand, you believe yourselves to be immune to the evils perpetrated by previous generations, you will be more vulnerable to evil. If, on the other, you believe yourselves to be the victims of history, you will forego the opportunity to emerge from self-exoneration into the more turbulent but rewarding waters of self-knowledge. To help you understand what I am talking about, you could well look at the records of the Truth and Reconciliation Commission one day and borrow Antjie Krog's book *Country of My Skull* and Desmond Tutu's *No Future without Forgiveness* from your local library. So my prayer for you both is that you will not shirk the clamour of history, while at the same time you will not be burdened by it to the extent that you feel helpless to act.

I am writing this at the beginning of a new millennium. Speculation about the future of the human race is rife. How will the world be fifty or one hundred years from now? I think that in some respects it will be very different and, in others, achingly the same. No doubt you will learn technological skills I cannot conceive of. You may well become so familiar with the dazzling images of the Hubble Space Telescope — the stellar nurseries and the bubble-like nebulae of gas — not to gasp as I do when I see its pictures.

The secrets of the black hole that is supposed to lie at the heart of our galaxy might well have been revealed. I cannot fathom what it means to look back eleven billion years and see galaxies forming two billion years or so after the creation of the universe. I wonder how our expanding image of the universe will affect our ancient conviction that our role is all-important, and what this might mean to you. We are already beginning to realise that our planet is an infinitesimal speck circling around an unremarkable star far out on an arm of the Milky Way, and that beyond us lie a hundred billion galaxies. What does this mean for our idea of God? The biological sciences are unpacking the mysteries of all living organisms. We know that we are made of stardust. As the secrets of our genes are unravelled, you might well one day be introduced to your self in your DNA. What does this mean for our understanding that we are made in the image of God?

Yet, despite all these wonders, all is not right. The global civilisation that is fast becoming the order of the day fills me with unease. One of the few world leaders I find worth quoting describes it well. Commenting on a global civilisation, the Czech president and writer Václav Havel says that it is "no more than a thin veneer over the sum total of human awareness. . . . [T]his new single epidermis of world civilization merely covers or conceals the immense variety of cultures, of peoples, of religions, a world of historical traditions and historically formed attitudes, all of which lie 'beneath' it." The terrible tension that is building up at the moment between this single global civilisation with its greedy economic system and "the cry in every valley" for independence gives rise to war and destruction. Poet David Jones describes the current world power as

> detailed to beat
> > to discipline the world-floor
> to common level
> > till everything presuming difference
> and all the sweet demarcations
> > wither
> to the touch of us
> and know the fact of empire.

I wonder how it will be when you are adults. Can we save ourselves? Will we humans truly accept our responsibility for this world? Will the ozone gap grow smaller? Will the air and the water be cleaner? Will there still be forests around the equator? Will the scourge of AIDS have been conquered? Will the millions of poor have food and the millions of privileged be content with less? Will your age be more sane? Will conscience have caught up with reason?

Let me shift from the mysteries of the universe to an ever-present concern. I wish I could be sure that you will grow up in circumstances in which you will not experience the blight of sexism. In some respects, things are better than they were. In South Africa we have a bill of rights that explicitly protects women's rights. Increasingly, women are raising their voices and are more visible in the professions, academic life, business, and in some religious bodies. Yet this war has not been won. Gender discrimination has a great deal to do with the abuse of power. So does the endemic violence against women that we are presently experiencing. My heart chills when I think about your vulnerability as young girls growing up in this country. I pray for your safety. I pray that you will have the strength to pursue justice for yourselves, for your daughters, and for other women.

My last thoughts on living in our country are quite different. Many white people of my generation have watched their children leave South Africa. Their grandchildren are growing up in faraway places. I have been spared this pain, at least so far. Like me, your parents seem to share a deep attachment to this land. What is the source of this bond? Is it possible to describe it otherwise than to say quite simply: "This is my place"? I am not sure that I can or want to analyse it. All I can say is that it is an affinity that has a million facets. It is in the air, the softness of the Cape spring, the south Atlantic storms, the vastness of the Highveld skies; it is in the looming presence of the mountain behind me as I write; it is in the salt of the cool seas in summer; in the miracle of the blooming desert of Namaqualand, the *fynbos,* the tortoise crossing the road, the jokes, the endless acronyms, the taste of a spicy curry, *snoek, melktert,* or apricot jam — and much, much more. It is in an awareness of history, my history and ours. It is in the people — our different accents, different colours, different customs — people who belong to this place, and who, when we hear its name, feel a throb and know, "This is my place". I pray that you will have great joy from the beauty of this country and its people, that you will travel its length and breadth and have a great deal of fun doing so, and that your spirits will be wiser for having lived here.

To return to the issue of identity and difference. Identity as a concept has a fraught history in our country. In the days of apartheid it was used to justify keeping people of different races separated. The edifice of apartheid rested on the notion of separate identities, each sovereign in its own sphere. This idea gave rise to "separate development", which in fact was no more than the forced separation of peoples. The will to claim identity is the cause of conflict all over the world and on our continent. When cultural identities merge with religious identities, "holy" wars can ensue. So you see, identity can quite simply be the word that describes who each one of us is, or it can be a charged, painful trap. I also ask myself: Is it a concept worth pursuing in a family such as ours? Can a hybrid identity really be described? Is it not harmful to those who may feel "outside" to have too much importance attached to an identity that has certain familial, racial, or national characteristics? To what extent do our identities bind us together or separate us? I shall not try to answer all these questions, but I cannot duck the fact that identity as an issue will not disappear.

What is identity? Philosopher Charles Taylor describes identity as follows: "It is who we are, 'where we're coming from'. As such it is the background against which our tastes and desires and opinions and aspirations make sense. . . . [M]y discovering my own identity doesn't mean that I work it out in isolation, but that I negotiate it through dialogue, partly overt, partly internal, with others." I like this understanding. It is simple and it introduces the important rider that identity is shaped in ongoing dialogue with others. As I understand it, my identity is partially shaped by being in conversation with you. After all, you have made me a grandmother! But I am also other things, shaped by other conversations. Is there also a part of me (and of you) that is wholly ours, perhaps mysterious, even to ourselves? However we answer this question, it is clear that we discover our identities through others.

What has not been said is that the term "identity" actually means sameness, yet it is often used to define our differences. In fact it has a double meaning. It means sameness as in "identical" — a person's identity as a woman or a Jew means belonging to the same identifiable group. But this term is also used to say how we are different from one another — a woman is different from a man, a Jew from a Muslim. So identity can mean both sameness and difference. A word of warning — identity becomes a danger-ous issue if we give our identity a higher value than anyone else's.

Identity can be more than a bond. It can be a bondage, a tie that holds me captive to criteria that exclude others. This was a common experience for Afrikaners who opposed Afrikaner nationalism. As mentioned before, I learnt this in my father's family. Identity can also be a shackle to keep me in, even when I do not want to remain in. This it does, for instance, by in-sisting on an essential racial or cultural character or simply by requiring solidarity. You will doubtless find examples of this in your own lives.

There are clearly chosen aspects to identities. We can, within the limits of possibility, make choices about our cultural affiliations. We can make bad choices. If I take myself for someone else and come to think of myself as that other, then I have, as it were, broken faith with myself. The tempta-tion is either to take on the identity of one's family or culture uncritically or to adopt a full identity from an alternative culture with equally little self-reflection. Both are hideous mistakes. We cannot turn our back on our cul-ture of origin; neither should we be its slave. We do not choose when, where, and to whom we are born. So both a sense of distance as well as a sense of belonging are necessary. Belonging without distance is destruc-tive. It says: I am exclusively a white South African and everybody and ev-erything must be shaped to conform to my image. Distance without be-longing isolates us. It says: I deny my own roots and my culture. In so doing it sets me up for finding a false identity because I cannot live without one. We live as people who belong, while at the same time we need dis-tance, not in order to deny our identity and culture, but to live well with it. Should parents determine children's cultural identities? Not wholly. Family stories *do* cement cultural identities. But I am confident that you will be raised with enough freedom to enable you to think critically and to make your own judgments when you grow up. You are both smart enough to know that what is volunteered is not so much worth prizing as the unspo-ken moments — the snippet of conversation or the scenes overheard, that one day suddenly make sense as you put together the fragments of your own mixed heritages. I shall watch with great interest the choices that you make from your hybrid backgrounds.

Now a word of caution. I mentioned the link between identity and dif-ference. The differences between us, and the ways in which we deal with the question of difference, shape our identities. By "difference" (often called "otherness") I mean the fact that we are not alike, that while humanity is marvellously diverse, we find difference problematic, often threatening or even alienating, and we do not always live easily or well with it. For example, we often speak of "the other" in a way that mistakenly assumes she is just like me when, in fact, she is not like me at all, or conversely, we perceive "otherness" as totally foreign and are then surprised to find that we share common interests or feelings. To speak of otherness is also to be open to otherness within myself, to the possibility of a foreigner within my own unconscious self. To speak of difference and otherness is to speak of gender, of race and class, of poverty and justice, of human sexuality, of history and tradition. To speak of difference is to acknowledge difference even in one's own family.

As I have said, we do not always live well with difference. Sometimes we fail to see those who are "other" as real persons. We treat them as clean slates, people without histories, rather in the way that certain Christian missionaries in the past viewed people in Africa. Those intrepid souls came to "darkest" Africa to bring the light of the gospel. On encountering the indigenous people whom they clearly found to be very "other" — that is, other than themselves — they failed to see them as people with their own local stories, cultures, and traditions. Those missionary colonists simply brushed aside differences. Everyone was to be the same, which really meant that everyone was to be an image of the missionaries themselves. What they were in fact implying was: "You should be like me. I am the centre, the fixed point by which you will be defined." This is nonsense. There is no one centre. There are many centres because of our differences.

Another failure to deal with our differences happens when we view those who are different as a threat. This reaction to difference underlies much of our intolerance. It is what *apartheid* was about, it is what leads to genocides and to racist and sexist attitudes. Those who have power say: "Only we have the truth and those who are different are our enemy." When "the other" becomes a threat, the strategy is to separate people and then, increasingly, to dominate, to demonise, and even to exterminate them.

There are still other problematic responses to difference. Sometimes "the other" is seen as some exotic, romantic being who does not have to be taken seriously since she or he is so different. No wonder that in the eighteenth century the idea of the "noble savage" was batted about in intellectual circles in the West. At other times, those who are different are lumped together as some sort of universal person with no particularity. In more recent times this happened in the early days of the women's movement. Unthinkingly, some of the early writers spoke about women as though we were all alike. Our different experiences, cultures, and histories were ignored. Neither of these views, indeed, not any of these problematic responses to difference, affords "the other" the dignity of being treated as a real person in all her or his difference.

Just a last thought on how badly we deal with our differences. We can also abandon interest in those who are different. Take the example of those who belong to the "underside" of the world. Today the rich developed world relates to the poor developing world in a manner that spells abandonment. It goes like this: "If you in the developing world cannot deliver the goods and perform the services demanded by us (the rich north), we shall turn away from your predicaments." The fact that these predicaments are often a direct result of histories of economic and political exploitation by those very same northern countries is conveniently forgotten. There is a story in the New Testament that tells of a beaten-up man lying at the roadside. Despite his obvious need, the priest and the Levite pass by, ignoring his plight, minding their own business. They deal with otherness through exclusion and abandonment. It's another excluded person, a Samaritan, who comes to help the already excluded man!

In all this talk about difference there is a danger. If we become too obsessed with our differences we can end up each in our own small defined camps and never have the courage to travel between them, to migrate across borders, to expose ourselves to conversations across our differences. This would be sad. And it would be lonely. It would also stifle any longing for connection. Somewhere across our differences there is a place where we long to make contact. In this place, our differences remain real, but we see that cultures are not pure or fixed, and our identity as hybrids is welcomed.

Our identities are not unbounded, without borders, uncircumscribed. In her wonderful book *Love's Work*, philosopher Gillian Rose writes: "A soul that is unbound is as mad as one with cemented borders." Establishing identity entails acknowledging borders. Why? Let me first explain what I mean by borders. Borders show separation. On the one hand, they protect us; on the other they confine us. They are also an expression of space. Our identities are linked to the space we occupy — in our families, in our communities, in our country. These spaces need borders, not to fix them forever like a place, but rather to contain our struggles for identity. There are strong pulls in the modern world for inclusion. Today, as theologian Miroslav Volf suggests, "'keeping out' is bad and 'taking in' is good." Is this necessarily right? Total inclusion collapses all borders. When this happens, we lose our sense of what criteria to use in deciding between repressive identities and those that are good and affirming. We cannot be all things to all people. Yet, maintaining strict borders can be an act of exclusion and oppression. I am not advocating borders as an act of excluding others from what is considered "my territory". We need to travel to other worlds, those that are different from our own. I am merely pointing out that borders have their own ambiguities. On the one hand, I see borders as a healthy and necessary strategy to make space for the nurture and growth of what is the unique self of every person. On the other hand, if borders serve to exclude me from real conversation and the possibility of change, they are not healthy. But you can no doubt imagine a situation where "the other" wants me to be something that I know is foreign to myself. That is when borders are necessary. Otherwise, we will react violently to incursions made on ourselves or retreat into exclusion. I had problems establishing my own identity. I think that it would have been easier for me if cultural differences had not been a source of conflict in my family. There were no clear borders, only battle lines.

For my entire professional life I have worked in a male world. This has taught me the importance of borders. On the one hand, I have needed to preserve my own voice in a male-dominated discipline. On the other hand, I have learnt a great deal from some of my male colleagues and would not want to maintain the kind of borders that exclude conversation. When I think of you and the cultural mixes from which you have come, I hope that you will struggle critically and thoughtfully with the questions of your different identities, recognising their pitfalls and growing strong as you do so, and that you will draw your borders with firm but kindly hands.

Finally, history and identity merge around the following question: How do we belong, as a white yet hybrid minority, in a country that is overwhelmingly black? As I write, the term "Africanisation" is being debated. It is a contentious term. Some black women ask whether Africanisation is not disguising the reinforcement of patriarchal traditional customs. Some white women ask whether the term is not exclusionary of their histories and their voices. Some women from traditional coloured communities ask whether the themes of Africanisation can embrace their experience of "in-betweenness". There are different understandings of what Africanisation means.

As whites, we cannot allow ourselves to be excluded by a racially determined view of what it means to be an African. I also reject the description "European". When I am in Europe, I feel a foreigner. I am not European. When I come home, I know that this is where I belong. So when I hear the term "Africanisation" I understand it as an inclusive term, a political choice to be critically patriotic to Africa. It spells out commitment to the freedom and dignity of all peoples in our country. It is also more. We live surrounded by great poverty and need. Africanisation means that we must do what we can about the want in our midst, acknowledging our responsibilities to each other as people who live and work, love and die in this place. I wonder whether this term will still be used when you are grown up.

So as I colour in my landscape with sky, sun, bush, food, and people with different identities, I also mark the blight: our racist scars, the ailing bodies of those with AIDS, small children with stomachs bloated by hunger, and women who are too often exhausted and abused. Around the edges I sketch in a few borders to remind myself how necessary they are. I want to pass my sketch on to you so that when you draw your own landscapes you can remind yourselves about what was important to me.

I cannot conclude this letter without telling you something about my own faith because I know that my efforts to live my faith cannot be separated from my identity as someone who calls herself a Christian. Neither can my faith be something I live apart from my love for you both and the place in which we live. "What does she mean by faith?" you may be wondering.

Long before I became associated with any church, I longed for the Holy One without even having words for what or who God is. This yearning, which still persists (albeit in an altered way), has shown me that in essence faith is about a naked desire for God. It is a passion, like being in love and longing for the Loved One. It is not only a longing for the Holy to find a home in me but it is also a longing for a world in which holiness will be at home. What does it "look" like? I found what it "looked" like in the person of Jesus. When I read the stories of his life for the first time as an adult, I found what I had been looking for — a relationship that promised unconditional love, mercy, and hope.

Finding, however, is only the beginning. The life of faith has never been dull and never been easy. In the Gospel of Mark (9:14-29) there is a story about a father who brings his child to Jesus, because he is having convulsions. The father pleads with Jesus: ". . . have pity on us and help us." Jesus says to him: "If you are able! — All things can be done for the one who believes." And then the father cries out: "I believe; help my unbelief!" I am like that man. I believe, yet at the same time I cry out: "Purge my faith of feebleness!" I remind myself that this is, after all, a story of hope and healing. I live with paradox and ambiguity. The psalms tell me that God is present even in the depths of Sheol (Ps. 139:7-12), yet Jesus experiences total abandonment on the cross. The psalms speak of God's presence as well as God's absence, God's loving care as well as God's hiddenness. I speak to and about God, while longing to know more about who God really is. I long for wholeness, yet I persist in brokenness. I try hard to hold the ambiguities together while knowing that it is precisely in the contradictions of life that opportunities live. I am relieved when reminded that we are all people of paradox. So what is it I hope for? Is it for help in my unbelief? Yes, but it is more. The prophet Micah (6:8) asks: ". . . what does the Lord require of you but to do justice, and to love kindness and to walk humbly with your God?" That is what I long for with my entire being while knowing how often I fail. Yes, I live in faith, but not without questions. I believe that as I cry for help, my unbelief will dissipate.

Although I have tried, I must admit that these matters of faith cannot be explained easily. What I do know without any doubt is that they have to be lived. It is in the living that we find the courage to risk, discern, struggle, and hope. If, for instance, I value justice and honesty and demand that my human dignity be affirmed and upheld, then I have to live in such a way that I treat others honestly, fairly, and respectfully. I do not find this plain sailing. The closer we get to the heart of things, the more real the cry: "I believe, help my unbelief!" Why? Because it is a cry for increased trust in the One in whom we place our faith. It is admitting the terrifying tension between the certainty of the love and grace of God, and the gnawing questions about the enormity of human suffering. In the end all I can say is: "I don't know, but I believe."

Having spoken these words, I wait expectantly, grasping the possible, refusing to disengage; like Jacob, I wrestle and will not let go "unless you bless me." Amidst the waiting and the wrestling, there is one thing I *do* know. Beyond the words and thoughts, the tensions and paradoxes, beyond my capacity to reason and to question, there is truth, truth that is the heartbeat of all being. It is the truth of the One who is the Breath inside the breath. There I know Loving Presence. In that I rest.

Now, near the end of this letter, I must tell you about the beginning. I have started every letter in this book with a quotation from the book of the prophet Joel. He describes how the southern kingdom of Judah is devastated by armies of locusts, how the people are called to lament this catastrophe, to repent and to appeal to God for compassion and help. I don't like locusts; in fact I find them creepy. My aversion to these creatures makes them the embodiment of what is nasty. For me they are the symbols of bad times in our country. Fortunately, Joel's story does not end with the locust plague. God answers the people's cries and restores the years that the locusts have eaten.

The quotation at the beginning of this letter promises that God's Spirit will be poured out on the people and that they will prophesy. What does this mean? I think Joel is reassuring the people of God's presence in their midst. "God is with you," he says, "all of you." Then Joel explains what is meant by "all flesh": sons and daughters, old and young, male and female slaves. I am struck by two things immediately. First, in receiving new life there is no difference between men and women! How refreshingly non-sexist this is. Second, those who are less powerful — the old, the young, and the slaves — all receive new life. The outsiders, those who are tired and those who have not yet had their day, are included! God's Spirit is poured out on "all flesh" in its difference, frailty, and need. It is not bound to places or rituals of worship. The Spirit is for all, everywhere. Every person who receives the Spirit can prophesy. This simply means that they can enable others to see God at work in the world — in a million different ways, in a myriad of different cultures and places. God's Spirit is God's breath breathing new life where there is death and decay. Such are the dreams and the visions of the sons and daughters, of the old, the young, the slaves.

I have written to you about identity and difference. I can think of no other event in the scriptures that is more vivid and compelling about identity and difference than Joel's prophecy as it is fulfilled at Pentecost. Pentecost is the Greek name for the Jewish Feast of Weeks, which takes place fifty days after Passover. It is also the word for an event recorded in the Acts of the Apostles. The apostles were gathered in a house to celebrate this feast when God's Spirit came upon them like a violent wind and in tongues of fire that appeared on each of them. They began to speak in foreign languages, which attracted the attention of foreign Jews who were amazed to hear their native languages spoken by Galileans. This miraculous story is not primarily about wind or fire or different languages. The miracle is that people who ordinarily could not communicate with one another — Parthians, Medes, Elamites, people from places as far flung as Libya, Egypt, and Mesopotamia — could suddenly understand one another. No wonder they were confused and even frightened! Can you imagine how you would feel if you heard Eskimos suddenly speaking Afrikaans? The miracle of Pentecost is that people who ordinarily would not understand one another, can now do so with total understanding. All of them, whether Jews, Cretans, or Arabs, do not suddenly stop being who they are. Their different identities are clear and are preserved, but their understanding is common and universal. So you see, the passage from Joel is for you. It upholds our differences while promising universal understanding and community. It also affirms my belief that God's Spirit is alive and well and at work in the world. It is there for you so that you can dream dreams and see visions, especially at times when locusts invade your worlds.

Looking back on what I have written, I have one question left. What is my hope for you both? I hope that you will both forge your own identities in dialogue with your inherited traditions, sifting out what is life-giving from what is moribund. At the same time I hope that you will be open to dialogue within our family and with others in your different places, so that your tastes, desires, and aspirations will be healing and wholesome. You will have to work out what it means to be white in South Africa. I hope that this will truly challenge you to live creatively with difference. And lastly, I hope that you will both be hungry for God, that you will struggle with the vocabulary of faith, that you will never give in to cynicism, and that your journeys will take you to the new Jerusalem.

Blessings and my love,
Granny Denise

NOTES

Rachel Coleman and Jo Ackermann were both born in 1998. Today Rachel lives with her mother Lise in Cape Town and her father Roger lives in England. Jo is in Windhoek, Namibia, with her parents Lourens and Liesa and her half-brother Seth.

Several Afrikaans words appear in this letter. *Oupa* means grandfather. *Broeders* refers to members of the *Afrikaner Broederbond,* a secret society whose membership was confined to white male supporters of the Nationalist Party and whose prime object was to advance their concept of what it meant to be an Afrikaner and the interests of their own members in every conceivable area of the state, church, and society. The *Groot Gariep* literally means the "Great Orange River" in Khoisan. It has been used as a metaphor to describe the emerging identity of South African people of mixed racial descent or by those who are descendants of the Khoisan in preference to the commonly used expression "the rainbow nation". *Fynbos,* literally "fine bush," describes the unique vegetation of the Western Cape. *Snoek* is the local name for a popular small-scaled fish, the *Thyrsites atun,* while *melktert* is literally a milk tart, also a well-known local dish. Another expression that needs explanation is the description "coloured". During the apartheid days this term was used to describe the people of mixed racial origins, a term they rejected during the liberation struggle, in favour of being called "black". I use it here as it has historical facticity in regard to the issue discussed. Today, racially based descriptions of people are the subject of much debate, particularly on issues of difference and identity. Many coloured people are reclaiming the description "coloured" as culturally descriptive of their particular history.

I am aware of the debates on theorizing cultural hybridity. Originally the term "hybridity" had negative connotations, being synonymous with half-breed, cross-breed, or half-blood — all terms redolent with racist undertones. Today in contemporary cultural studies the term is understood in at least three different ways. The first denotes the creation of something new out of the mixing of two or more distinct phenomena. The second suggests that the differences that make up the hybrid retain their original character but admits that this changes somewhat as the differences are woven together. The third questions the existence of pure difference and regards hybridity as necessary to all cultural formation. For a succinct discussion of hybridity see Susan Stanford Friedman, *Mappings: Feminism and the Cultural Geographies of Encounter* (Princeton: Princeton University Press, 1998), pp. 82-104.

On the complexities of the concept "identity" in the South African context, *identiteit in eie kring* (literally "identity in your own circle") as well as *soewereiniteit in eie kring* (sovereignty in your own circle) were used as the battle cry of those theologians who sought to justify apartheid scripturally and did so by a peculiar application of the theological theories of the Dutch theologian Abraham Kuyper. The idea of "separate development" came from this understanding of separate spheres of sovereignty and was ultimately applied in the creation of "homelands" in different parts of South Africa for indigenous people, each with their own structures of governance but fiscally dependent on the central government. People were forced to move to these "homeland" areas. Families were torn apart, unemployment was rife among the poor, and corruption was endemic among those who, as puppets of the apartheid state, governed these areas.

Today a great deal is written about identity, culture, and borders. In sifting through some of this vast body of material, I found the following works helpful in my efforts to apply these categories to my circumstances:

Terry Eagleton, *The Idea of Culture* (Oxford: Blackwell, 2000).

Henry S. Giroux, ed., *Postmodernism, Feminism and Cultural Politics: Redrawing Educational Boundaries* (Albany: State University of New York Press, 1991).

David T. Goldberg, ed., *Multiculturalism: A Critical Reader* (Oxford: Blackwell, 1994) and in particular, the article by Peter Caws, "Identity: Cultural, Transcultural and Multicultural."

Paul Lakeland, *Postmodernity: Christian Identity in a Fragmented Age* (Minneapolis: Fortress Press, 1997).

Linda A. Moody, *Women Encounter God: Theology Across Boundaries of Difference* (Maryknoll, N.Y.: Orbis Books, 1996).

Charles Taylor, "The Politics of Recognition," in Amy Gutman, ed., *Multiculturalism: Examining the Politics of Recognition* (Princeton: Princeton University Press, 1994); also *Sources of the Self: The Making of the Modern Identity* (Cambridge, Mass.: Harvard University Press, 1989).

Other works referred to in this letter are:

Ariel Dorfman, *Heading South, Looking North: A Bilingual Journey* (London: Hodder and Stoughton, 1998).

Václav Havel, address to Harvard University, Cambridge, Mass., 1995.

Antjie Krog, *Country of My Skull* (Johannesburg: Random House, 1998).

To My Granddaughters

Gillian Rose, *Love's Work: A Reckoning with Life* (New York: Schocken Books, 1996).

Edward M. Said, *Culture and Imperialism* (New York: Alfred A. Knopf, 1993), and *Out of Place: A Memoir* (New York: Alfred A. Knopf, 1999).

Donald W. Shriver, *An Ethic for Enemies: Forgiveness in Politics* (New York: Oxford University Press, 1995).

Desmond Tutu, *No Future without Forgiveness* (New York: Doubleday, 1999).

Miroslav Volf, *Exclusion and Embrace: A Theological Exploration of Identity, Otherness, and Reconciliation* (Nashville: Abingdon, 1996).

Michael Welker, *God the Spirit*, trans. J. F. Hoffmeyer (Minneapolis: Fortress Press, 1994).

CHAPTER 2

To My Mother

on Being a Theologian
and Not a Dominee

But the Lord is a refuge for his people,
a stronghold for the people of Israel.
So you shall know that I, the Lord your God,
dwell in Zion, my holy mountain.
And Jerusalem shall be holy,
and strangers shall never again pass through it.

JOEL 3:16B-17

Dear Mom,

There is so much I wish we had spoken about. I never told you how, in your words, I "became religious." Probably because I have never felt "religious" and probably because you expressed distaste at the "blood and gore" of Christianity. I should not have been deterred. My earliest attempts at finding out about Christianity failed because I was put off. I remember going to Sunday school with a *tiekie* for collection. I was about eight and proud of my ability to handle change. My *tiekie* went into the collection plate and I took out tuppence change. The teacher spoke sharply to me in front of the class. I never went back.

When I started to study theology you were perplexed. "Are you going to become a *dominee?*" you asked me somewhat anxiously. Later, in a letter, you questioned me again: "What *is* theology?" I replied with Anselm's well-known dictum: "Theology is faith seeking understanding." You appeared to lose interest and I did not explain any further. After your funeral I had to sort through your possessions and clear up your room in the apartment in the Strand. I was surprised to find a bible on your bedside table. I opened it and a scrap of paper fell out. On it in your handwriting were the words "Theology is faith seeking understanding". If only I had known that you cared enough to want to remember my answer to your question.

I owe you a more thoughtful explanation about what I mean by theology. I need to tell you how I stumbled into theology and how, as a woman, I found my own voice as a theologian. I must admit that I am still sorting this out for myself. To find my way, I am sketching a landscape on which my faith journey is marked with all its vicissitudes. Picturing you sitting in your wing-backed chair listening to me helps me to mark the connections between theology, feminism, ideology, the bible, the church, and the way we speak about God. I wish this were a straightforward task. Instead it is confusing, even muddled, as I try to discern what is life-giving from what is stifling, even noxious. I heard theologian Stacey Johnson once speak about the promise and the promiscuity of religious faith. He was right. Religious faith can be pernicious. It can also express the highest values. If you could see my landscape, you would find markers of approval and some of alarm and dissent.

Before I start filling in the landscape, a word about "being religious". "Being religious" seems too rarefied a state for my liking. I prefer just to say that I have faith. Doing theology requires faith, whereas studying religion does not. I did not suddenly one day "become religious". What I did was to start reading the bible every week together with a group of women. But I am pre-empting my story. I think I have always believed in a Creator. Butterflies from pupas, living shells, a black eagle in flight, the Milky Way, my skin renewing and protecting my body; all these seemed the work of a Creator God. Other than a subliminal sense of awe and wonder, I did not at first see any personal connection between myself and the Author of creation.

At Northlands School for Girls in Buenos Aires, my close friend Saidie was a Christian Scientist. She told me to think of myself as good — an appealing thought. With prayer and belief in my wholeness, everything would be all right. Soon I realized that I could not fly on prayer alone. Having to complete my last two years of high school in one year made me sick. My hair fell out, and the prospect of baldness dampened my interest in the

Christian Science way. I saw a doctor and moved on to dabble briefly in Roman Catholicism, more I think as an act of rebellion against my father Stewie's Huguenot fears about *die Roomse gevaar* (the Roman danger) than out of any genuine conviction. I did not know what I was looking for. I read about Buddhism, but at fifteen it felt too remote. For the next seven years my interest in religion cooled. I had enough on my plate; studying, dating, and trying to grow up.

When Laurie and I decided to get married, we realized it would have to be in the magistrate's office. Neither of us belonged to a church. Laurie was agnostic but agreed with me that it did not "feel" right. I decided to give the church a serious try. I made a date to see Gustav Bam, a young minister in the Dutch Reformed Church who had been at university with us. (Another of life's ironies: Thirty-five years later I succeeded him in the chair of practical theology at the University of the Western Cape!) We agreed to meet weekly and he would coach me in the Christian faith. I liked what I learnt about being a Christian and I could agree with most of it, except the Jesus part. Jesus was a good man, a nifty prophet, but divine? No, this was more than I could believe.

One evening, about a month before the wedding date, I made my decision. I could not confess to belief in Jesus as God. I borrowed Aunt Iris's Mini Minor to keep my appointment with Gustav Bam to tell him that my acceptance into the church was off. When I left her house, I did not believe that Jesus was God. Fifteen minutes later, I arrived knowing that he was. I wish I could say more. I suppose this would be called a conversion experience. I had no words to describe what happened then. I haven't any now. I only remember that when Gustav opened the door I was in tears. He said little but he understood. I simply told him that my acceptance into the church could go ahead. It was as simple as that.

That was only the beginning. Being married, moving from Cape Town and resettling in Pretoria, overwhelmed me. My fragile faith wilted. Church was boring and I knew no Christians. We worked hard, ate lots of spaghetti, and used upturned boxes and your old trunk to sit on in our flat. I was baffled by Pretoria and by what was expected of me as the wife of a struggling young advocate. Those early years are a muddle of miscarriages and no money. I did not think about Jesus except as a pleasant distant memory. Then I landed up at a women's bible study group. Here I found out just how much questioning is in my genes. "What about the charnel houses of the world, God?" "Why all the suffering?" "Why the contradictions, why the gaps in the bible?" "Where are the women?" Final answers I did not find. Instead, this continuous questioning, testing, and delving raised new questions. Slowly, through the incessant questions, the God of the scriptures began to take on shape. No longer merely a mysterious creating Being, this was a God who made promises, was both angry and merciful, just and loving, a God whose presence inspired awe, a God who clearly wanted to relate to human beings. I began to discover that these ancient stories were really modern. I came face to face with Jesus again in the gospels. I liked what I saw and heard. Still, a further "leap of faith" sounded to me like plunging off a skyscraper, a kind of intellectual suicide. I stalled and played for time, caught between my serious doubts and the memories of my earlier commitment. Two years later, I capitulated. My own life was in disarray; my search for truth had reached an impasse. No philosophy, no psychology, no amount of relying on my own considerable survival skills had stilled the yearning for that something more that could alter my often numbing sense of non-being. So, half grudgingly, half despairingly, I said one day: "If you are what this book tells me you are, and if you care about me as a person, please show me." I heard no trumpets or angelic choirs. There was no burning bush. Hardly a techni-coloured religious experience! Instead it has been a tough and often frustrating, but never boring journey of discovery. It has brought small epiphanies, great perplexities, and rare moments of joy. Looking back, I still wonder at the graciousness of God in the face of my half-hearted overtures, my paltry offerings, and my plain contrariness.

With a *chutzpah* that now astonishes me, my friend Elfriede and I began to write bible study guides. Neither of us had any biblical training but we thought we knew what groups of women all over South Africa wanted. I mention this because it led to my study of theology. After a few years in the bible study guide business (yes, we formed and ran a not-for-profit company!) I decided that I needed to become theologically literate. A diploma in theology at the local university would do. Soon I was talked into doing an undergraduate degree. The die was cast. Theology gripped me. I finally found in my middle years what I had been looking for — the seeds of a profession about which I have no regrets.

To revert to your question about theology. Today I find Anselm's description too rational. Yes, theology is about understanding faith, but it is more. Letty Russell tells of hearing "Krister Stendahl quote a rabbinic saying that theology is worrying about what God is worrying about when God gets up in the morning." She understands this to mean that God is worrying about the mending of creation, "trying to straighten up the mess so that all of groaning creation can be set free." Theology is sustained reflection about what we worry about, what we *believe* and what we *do* about what we believe. "Doing" puts theologians in the thick of things. So our enterprise is not clear-cut; it is often messy because we deal with a maze of beliefs and actions. We seek words about God and about all things and all actions in relation to God. Not all theologians may agree with me that theology speaks about our beliefs *and* our actions. My concern about what we do in the life of faith makes me what is called a practical theologian.

German theologian Dorothee Sölle says that all true theology starts with pain. It is concerned with the very stuff of life, our questions, our experiences of alienation, our search for meaning. Theology demands an engagement of the mind and the heart. Dismay at the incongruity between my beliefs and my actions drives me to find more consistency and integrity between my understanding of my faith and how I live my life. I remember theologian Jürgen Moltmann's address to the American Academy of Religion in Chicago in 1994, which started with the following words: "It is simple, but true, to say that theology has only one, single problem: *God*. We are theologians for the sake of God. God is our dignity. God is our agony. God is our hope." He continued:

> For me theology springs from *divine passion:* that is the open wound of God in one's life and in the tormented men, women, and children of this world. . . . But for me theology also springs from God's *love for life,* the love for life which we experience in the presence of the life-giving Spirit, and which enables us to move beyond our resignation, and begin to love life here and now. These are also Christ's two experiences of God, and because of that they are the foundation of Christian theology too: God's delight and God's pain.

All people (not just the academy or the churches) who engage with God's pain and God's delight are doing theology. Theology is, as Moltmann pointed out, public by nature.

If I could talk to you today, I would explain that my experience of sexism and my struggles with racism are just as vital for my interest in theology as my desire to know more about my faith, its history, and its teachings. All levels of experience should be taken seriously because each one opens a window on the world. Over the years I have learnt that theology is not only about the veracity of dogmas, the accuracy of scriptural interpretation or church history, or even about correct liturgical practices, as interesting as these pursuits may be. It is more personal than that. Nietzsche's comment on philosophy could just as well apply to theology. He says: "Gradually I have come to realize what every great philosophy up to now has been: the personal confession of its originator, a type of involuntary and unaware memoir. . . ". You see, theology starts with our experiences, and no theology is done outside of human experience. Human stories, both ancient and modern, are its lifeblood. Doing theology should not be a disembodied, "higher plane" activity. It comes out of our particular life situations. Reflecting on his faith, physicist John Polkinghorne writes:

> Many theologians are instinctively top-down thinkers. I do not deny
> a role for such ambitious intellectual effort. I am merely wary of it
> and wish to temper its grand generality with the questionings that
> arise from the consideration of particularity.

I agree with him. Being a theologian is, in short, to reflect on the daily struggle to live and act as a person of faith. I am a bottom-up thinker. The scarab I wear on a chain around my neck reminds me that my theology is like the work of the dung beetle. Collect the dung, roll it into shape, push and prod it endlessly, often in no discernible direction, but stick to the task. There is an awful lot of dung in the world. My thinking owes everything to conversations within my different communities and to the stuff of life itself. Theology has been an adventure. I have explored different paths and often arrived at dead ends. What has kept me going is an almost insatiable longing to know, while being confronted daily with just how little I actually do and can know.

Clearly my understanding of theology is coloured by what I understand by faith. Faith is not about churchgoing, an activity that has little point in itself. Faith is not about reading the scriptures daily, or about praying with regularity. All these actions have no merit in themselves unless they are impelled by the naked desire to know God more intimately. Having faith means wanting to know more about God's creative, life-giving, and life-sustaining power and desiring to understand more about God's being and God's will, while at the same time realising how fleeting and inadequate all knowledge of God is. I remember how repelled I was when I first encountered the phrase "the fear of God." Now I understand that to fear God includes being self-critical about one's words concerning God. I have heard it said that faith is not knowledge. I disagree. Faith *is* about knowing. Scientific knowledge, for example, works in defined areas, requires proof of a particular nature, and trusts in the certainty of progress. On the one hand, faith shares some of this trust in progress, otherwise academic theology would be impossible. On the other hand, as my friend, German theologian Michael Welker, puts it, faith is more impressed "by a child in a manger and a man put to death on a cross in the name of Jewish and Roman law than by highly developed scientific forms of gaining knowledge." Faith is validated by the faithfulness of the God in whom we trust. It lives in a triangle of longing, hope, and reality. Longing for God is hunger for the Holy One as well as longing for a world drenched with holiness. Longing is not something we cultivate. I can only guess its origins. Is it not a perpetual hunger deep inside us nurtured by the Spirit that makes us want to touch the mystery of Being? Hope is not religious optimism. It is tough-minded perseverance in dire times because we believe in God's promises and know that faith without hope is simply not possible. Reality focuses our hope. Clear-sightedly we see the hunger, pain, and suffering around us. We also note the courage and care and dare to hope that the hungry will be filled with "good things." Being involved with theology means drawing on our faith, our imagination, our experience, and our longing to know more about God and translating this into words and actions.

"Theology" is a broad term and it is not limited to one single enterprise. I wonder now what you would make of theology with all its tags: reformed theology, liberation theology, feminist theology, African women's theology, womanist theology, *mujerista* theology, and so on? Different contexts and experiences give rise to different theologies. I call mine a *feminist theology of praxis*. I want to unpack this concept bit by bit and see how its pieces fit into my faith landscape.

"Feminist," I hear you say. "What on earth do you mean?" (You often said "What on earth . . . ", never "What in heaven . . ."!) How could you have known about feminism — it was foreign to your circles and removed from your interests. Yet you lived with an unrepentant patriarch who, ironically (but perhaps not unsurprisingly), ended up having a feminist daughter! Before going further, let me explain a few terms.

"Patriarchy" quite literally means "rule by the father". Today we use the word "patriarchy" when we refer to an ideology and a social system that support the dominance of men over women. In patriarchy, men are privileged beings and male experience of reality is made the norm for all persons, including women and children. "Sexism" is based on the conviction that men are superior to women simply because they are men. I do not want to confuse you, but I have to use the words "patriarchy" and "sexism" in describing my theology. These tedious but necessary explanations lead me to the word "feminist".

Calling oneself a feminist in South Africa today elicits a variety of responses. For some it raises the spectre of militant, insensitive, demanding women who eschew marriage and motherhood for a form of gender apartheid. It is amazing how this picture of feminism has persisted. I encountered it this very year in my teaching. For certain black women, feminism justifies the label "decadent, bourgeois, European import". Among a growing number of younger women who now reap the benefits of the struggles of early feminists, feminism is seen as an outmoded ideology that has served its day. After all, say this new breed of women, our rights are now enshrined in the constitution, thirty percent of our parliamentarians are women, and there are more women in places of economic and social power than ever before. Yes, in some respects gains have been made; in others, women still have far to go before equity is the norm. After this explanation I suspect you might say "You are being otherwise again!" In a sense you are right. Calling oneself a feminist does put one on the margins; it makes one "other".

I understand feminism as a movement to end sexist oppression, a cause that surely brooks no opposition. This is no fad or fashion trying to be controversial for no good reason. Philosopher Mary Midgley points out that feminism stands for a steady, systematic correction of an ancient and very damaging bias. It is sad that the word causes so much resistance. It is also sad that feminism, as a political and social movement, has not been an unqualified success. It made mistakes in its early days because it began among white middle-class women, some of whom were blind or insensitive to the fact that their interests were not the same as those of women who struggled to survive and who belonged to cultures, races, and classes different from their own. Early feminism got off to a bumpy start. The dream of a common language among women was not only false, it was also riddled with imperialist assumptions.

Despite having been in existence for over a century, feminism has not succeeded in uniting all women to end gender oppression. Why is this so? We women are different from one another. We have different views, and our experiences of being women in different places diverge. We do not agree on how we understand sexism and how we should deal with it. Some feminists contend that women are essentially different from men, not just biologically but in every aspect of our beings and often advocate a separatist stance for women. Other feminists argue that history, culture, and society shape our identities as women in diverse ways. They in turn advocate analysing and understanding what happens socially in order to devise strategies for change. Yet other women, who would not dream of calling themselves feminists, want to break through sexist barriers and advance themselves in male-dominated structures, but choose to do so by way of a "soft entry". They will lobby for women's rightful place, hoping to influence and civilise male dominance, rather than challenge it head on. They do not like the more radical language and the critical analysis of feminists. There are also black women who prefer not to use the description "feminist" because it is seen as too western, even when their lifestyles and their choices are those of independent and self-assertive women. Then there are women of all races who identify with the feminist cause with ease. I tell you this to illustrate that women are different. Background, race, and upbringing all play a role in how we identify ourselves and how we embrace our causes.

Another reason why women who want equality for themselves are not united in the feminist movement is because women do not share the same view of history. Some women in the feminist movement have promoted a romantic version of history in which all men are bad and all women are innocent victims. Women, according to this view, are treated appallingly (I agree). They cannot be held responsible for any of the shameful happenings in human history (I disagree) and are, in fact, always the innocent victims (I disagree again). Angela West in her provocative book *Deadly Inno-*

cence points out that Nazi women were unswervingly loyal to their leader. You and I know only too well how many white South African women supported apartheid policies uncritically and had no qualms about benefiting from the cheap labour of their domestic helpers who were separated from their children and families. Sadly, women are no more immune than men to the seductions of power, to the abuse of privilege, or to the distortions of racism. Therefore, any version of feminism that sees women only as innocent victims is painfully lacking in critical political and social awareness.

Despite these varied reactions and reservations, I persist in calling myself a feminist. I know of no other term that describes so well the total and active commitment to the infinite value of women's lives in every sphere of life. I am too old to want to be apologetic for a way of understanding life that has taught me much. At the same time, I must admit to an unease with labels. I don't like being boxed into categories, whatever they may be. But I am politically and personally committed to the cause of justice for women. Feminism is a comprehensive ideology which is rooted in women's experience of sexist oppression and discrimination, is critical of patriarchy, and embraces an alternative vision for humankind and the earth. At its best, feminism is an egalitarian movement, alive to the oppression of women wherever it occurs and always concerned with *any* kind of discrimination, because it seeks justice. That there are many different feminisms is a testimony to the coming of age of feminist thought. It remains for each woman calling herself a feminist to unravel what this means in the political, social, and religious circumstances in which she finds herself. "Feminism" is therefore an umbrella term for active political involvement with women's liberation in a great diversity of circumstances, often in very specific ways.

I wonder what you make of the idea of feminism? When you felt that Stewie was acting the patriarch, expecting you to shoulder all the household chores, I can remember you complaining to me. But I cannot remember more than complaints. I never heard you say: "This will not do." You knew the anger that many women feel at male assumptions about their roles. Thinking about this anger rationally and critically and then finding ways of acting on it to change matters is what feminism is about.

Initially, my *feminist theology* drew on the impulses of the feminist movement and on early liberation theology. Liberation theology has its roots in Latin America. It has spawned liberation theologies in other parts of the world, including black theology in South Africa. In a nutshell, liberation theologies are theologies that are done from the standpoint of those who are victims: the poor, the oppressed, and the needy. The founding cause of early liberation theology remains close to my heart. Over the years this kind of theology has become rooted in different places, is more communal, more prophetic, and more interested in social action. This is not surprising. The world has changed. The Soviet Union has broken up, the end of modernity is trumpeted, global market capitalism is the economic order of the day, but the poor are still poor. It is true that those on the margins of our societies are not the only reality in our world. However, theology that is not accountable to their suffering is in danger of losing its moorings. It forgets that God has a particular concern for those that are the least and who have the least. Jesus taught us this. He did not stand aside from the suffering of the outcasts of his time. I read liberation theology before I knew about feminist theology. What I found made political and theological sense to me as a white South African.

Then, within the course of a few weeks, I read Mary Daly's *The Church and the Second Sex* and Letty Russell's *Human Liberation from a Feminist Perspective.* Truth erupted. I was bowled over. I went on to read Rosemary Ruether, Beverly Harrison, Carter Heyward, and more. As my reading progressed, I knew where I wanted to go. I wanted, from my place, to "do" feminist theology that had women's experience of oppression and women's desire for justice and liberation at its core.

"How exactly do you 'do' theology?" you ask. Apart from reading every book on feminist theology I could find, I began to apply what I was reading to being a South African. Experience had taught me that the blunt opinion of Henry Higgins of *My Fair Lady* fame — "Women are irrational, that's all there is to that" — was a common sentiment. In the early 1980s, filled with much apprehension, I read my first theological paper to a virtually all-male group of theologians in Pretoria. It was about women's ordination, a hot topic at the time. The walls did not come tumbling down and I felt encouraged to press on. I learned that to "do" feminist theology means to be critical, constructive, and collaborative. I saw how the leading feminist theologians tackled at least three tasks.

First, they were critical of male dominance in Christian tradition and practises. The absence of women's voices, derogatory attitudes towards women, practises and structures that excluded women, and doctrines and teachings that upheld patriarchy had to be analysed and exposed. It is rather strange that throughout the ages, male theologians did not deem it necessary to object to women being called "... a sick she-ass ... a hideous tapeworm ... the advance post of hell" (John Damascene), "... the Devil's doorway" (Tertullian), or "... a misbegotten male" (Aquinas). One wonders what their mothers felt about their sentiments! Things were terribly wrong and needed to be subjected to critical scrutiny. Second, feminist theologians delved into the past to attempt to recover women's history which had been hidden, ignored, or devalued. This was the work of recovery. Women had not only been victims in the Christian tradition. Despite the inherent sexism of the Christian church, women did and do play significant roles in it and in its theological reflection. These discoveries then raised the question: What difference would women's theology make to theology today? The third task for feminist theologians was therefore the work of reconstruction. New insights and materials were used to construct contemporary theology. When women "do" theology, we aim to reshape the church's teachings about revelation, God, Jesus Christ, the Holy Spirit, and creation; what it means to be a human being; what sin, grace, and salvation offer; and what and how the church should be.

Today, feminist theologians make use of a body of work generally known as feminist theory. How we use feminist theory and where we place our emphases differ and have given rise to debate, sharp differences of opinion, and new challenges. My work has been challenged continuously by my membership in the Circle of Concerned African Women Theologians on our continent. I will not bore you with the ins and outs of our discussions. What I call a *feminist theology of praxis* commits me to emphasizing that individuals live in particular social and historical settings. These settings have many layers: family, friends, work, church, club, political party, bird-watching society, and so on. We play different roles in different settings, some more multilayered than others. Our identities are complex, multiple, and fluid. At a certain stage of life I was a mother to young children. Now I am a grandmother. I move from the classroom to the kitchen, from the library to the mountain. The theological challenge is to hold the continuities, dissonances, and differences that make up the often untidy and tangled experience of living in conversation with the Christian faith.

To sum up: I feel both proud and slightly uneasy when I look at the future of feminist theologies. I am proud of the gains we have made. I find the work of a number of younger feminist theologians in different parts of the world inspiring as they extend boundaries and confront the challenges of feminist theory and different cultural contexts. Our agenda is ambitious, our scholarship prodigious. I am uneasy when some of the younger generation of feminist theologians, particularly in North America and Europe, tend to lose sight of the lifeblood of feminist theologies — an uncompromising embracing of moral and political involvement. I wonder whether they have not sold out uncritically to postmodern theory at the cost of practice and whether they will become sufficiently self-critical of their own cultural dominance to be open to the voices and experiences of women who live in circumstances very different from their own. In the words of one of my favourite feminist theologians, Beverly Harrison,

> Feminist work envisages no formalized "fixed" starting point and
> no final resting place. Such a perspective makes the need for ongo-
> ing reformation not a ponderous platitude but a continuing source
> of theological energy and excitement.

Thankfully, feminist theologians of different races, cultures, ethnic groups, and denominations are infected with energy and excitement and are producing a rich variety of feminist theologies in many different parts of the world today. When all is said and done, I believe that, at best, feminist theologies are innovative, open, scholarly, challenging, and infusing all theology with new perspectives. Again in Harrison's words ". . . [we] do best when we live toward freedom, refusing to settle for anything less." I like to think of feminist theologies as a fulfilment of Joel's prophecy. Not only the sons but also the daughters will prophesy as God's Spirit is poured out. This is cause for celebration.

I started off this part of my letter to you by labelling what I do as a feminist theology of *praxis*. I hear you say, "What on earth do you mean by 'praxis'? Don't you mean 'practise'?" No, I mean "praxis," a word I use because it is the only one that says exactly what I mean. It is not to be confused with mere action. Praxis describes the inseparable relationship between reflecting and acting, between what I think and believe and what I do to achieve the goals of my beliefs. Praxis is not the opposite of theory. It is opposed to separating theory and practise. For liberation theologians, praxis always has an historical and social character. Any theology, including mine, which is praxis-based is theology in the making because the goals of liberation and justice are expressed in the very act of doing theology. Structuring theology on the basis of what we do has a long history. Let me give you an example. The early Christians did not have carefully worked-out doctrines or theological theories about what they believed. They acted out their faith by preaching, teaching, praying, baptizing, and breaking bread. When they started to reflect on what they were doing they began, over time, to develop a comprehensive system of belief. This in turn fed back into what Christians did and still do today. So this continuous movement from action to reflection and back to action is one in which actions and thinking about these actions cannot be separated. This is praxis.

Why do I speak of a feminist theology of praxis? I want to make sure that the theology I do will not lose this critical relationship between acting and reflecting, between thinking and doing. I am very chary of armchair theologies that deal only with theories and are divorced from the reality of living one's faith. My own struggle to make my actions consonant with my beliefs reminds me continuously how easy it is to separate them, to play mind games, to stay in the realm of ideas, unchallenged by the dirt on one's hands. A feminist theology of praxis is interested in women's diverse circumstances, in what we do for the liberating and healing of ourselves and our communities and what we think about our circumstances and our actions in terms of our faith. The aim of such a theology is healing and liberating praxis. Ambitious? Yes. Utopian? Perhaps. But why not? I can't imagine life without something bigger than myself to reach out to.

I want to tell you about my concern for the future of theology in South Africa (and elsewhere). How has it come about that a discipline that was one of the founding subjects of universities in the western world and was once called the "queen of sciences" is now endangered? I can understand, on the one hand, the reaction against theology faculties in South Africa (four of them) that over many years trained ministers exclusively for the white Dutch Reformed churches on taxpayers' money! To make matters worse, these faculties spawned and nurtured apartheid theology. On the other hand, creative, ecumenical, and liberating theologies were and are taught in South Africa. That is why the demise of my faculty at the University of the Western Cape has filled me with anger and sadness. It should not have happened. Its closure was never justified on either academic or economic grounds. The destruction of an exciting and viable enterprise was caused by a failure of vision and a lack of understanding (on the part of management) of theology's role in the community we had served for over thirty years.

Sadly, theology is also under threat worldwide. Universities decide what sort of learning is appropriate in an academic setting. When this process of sorting out takes place, a hierarchy of importance among the disciplines develops. Today that hierarchy places the physical sciences, mathematics, economics, and business management at the top, with theology at the bottom — although the humanities do not fare much better. Does society really need theologians, philosophers, literary theorists, and the like? Who will employ them? What jobs can they create? What food or consumer goods do they produce? Who needs theology? As someone said, do they bake bread? Let the churches take care of their own educational needs, the present thinking goes. Theologians, on feeling the heat, react in different ways. Some resort to a mixture of religion, philosophy, and ethics that is determinedly non-aligned and often openly anti-confessional. Others struggle to be genuinely ecumenical. Still others retreat to the safety of their denominational seminaries.

Regrettably, theologians themselves are not without blame. So much of our scholarly and intellectual work has little relevance for communities of faith, and it is not surprising that these communities themselves take little interest in it. As John Cobb remarked, "Scholars write for one another and for students to whom they can assign their works." The failure to speak theological words into the moment has been costly. What is the moment? It is a time when the scandal of famine claims millions of children's lives every year, when squalid camps are home to millions of refugees, when HIV/AIDS (a dreadful scourge that you will not have known about, but which has already killed many millions) is ravaging the African continent, when women and children are abused and raped every minute of every day, and when human greed is threatening the very future of our planet. We grapple with evil and suffering while we seek hope. In these circumstances the navel gazing and in-house games of certain bourgeois theologies are irrelevant, even reprehensible.

At the same time as our leaders call for the moral and ethical renewal of our country so that it can become truly civil, faculties of religion and theology that teach about values, morals, and ethics in a religious context are being put out of business. Yet students still turn up at the doors of theology departments because they want to learn how to think about God. The ability of a well-grounded academic theology to respond to these needs is rapidly being eroded. The danger is that when theological education is left to the churches alone, it can barely escape becoming narrowly denominational, even fundamentalist. We cannot afford this kind of theology in South Africa. We need theology that is aware of our different cultural and ethnic groups with their own codes of behaviour and ways of thinking. Only the proper academic setting can produce this kind of theology.

"Experience" is a word I used frequently. By now you would be justified in wondering whose experience I am talking about. It is certainly my own. Otherwise, it isn't authentic. Yet my experience is not something private. "'Experience' was never 'in' a private arena," Harrison comments. My experience is limited, yes, but it is shaped and tested by my relationships and is made up of different perspectives. We do not live alone on islands! This kind of experience, tested and revised by being in conversation with others, is the starting point for my theology. I would not do feminist theology if I had not experienced sexism and had not been able to think it through with other women! The trap that tempts us all is to assume, even for a split second, that my experiences are the norm for others. Women's experiences are as diverse as are women: poor and privileged, old and young, married and single, belonging to different races, cultures, and religions. Does this mean that theology is simply a cacophony of experiences? I don't think so. I agree with African American theologian Shawn Copeland that it is more helpful to think of experiences in terms of patterns. Some of our experiences are biological, others psychological, some are artistic, and others practical. Some are mystical and others are intellectual. Although my experiences are solely mine, experiences can overlap. Writing from experience means being aware of the different patterns of experience and how they connect to one another. One has to be up front about what one considers important and why, as well as discerning about what is good and what is not. My experience of being a white South African woman is the starting point from which I write. But I am also, among other things, a wife, a mother, a grandmother, a friend, a teacher, a lover of the mountains, a back sufferer, and a cashew nut addict. Some of my experiences are more telling, more formative for my thinking than others.

As I said, there are traps to negotiate. Those of us who start our theology from experience walk a tightrope between claiming the authority of experience while at the same time acknowledging that it is relative to history and circumstance. Our personal experiences are shaped by our backgrounds and our prejudices. We cannot only depend on our perceptions and experiences when we seek to understand and act politically. Our experiences are tested by interacting with the experiences of those who oppose us and of those who are foreign to us. Those members of our family who supported apartheid were bolstered in their convictions by like-minded people in their communities. They refused to hear the dissident voices among themselves, such as that of a Beyers Naudé, and refused to give credence to the worldwide condemnation of apartheid.

Another less common trap is to appeal in an individualistic way to my religious experience in isolation from my religious communities. I claim that *my* religious experience is so unique that you, a poor ordinary mortal, cannot possibly understand it. In order to nurture it I need to retreat from community into a "holy" place. Sadly, such a retreat inevitably leads to political and social apathy and even to further fragmentation of communities of faith.

The traps aside, the appeal to experience as a source of knowledge in the hands of those who feel oppressed and discriminated against can become a useful tool in opposing authoritarian powers. Take the issue of women's ordination. When women started to agitate for ordination in their churches, they argued, among other things, that they had *experienced* the "call" to ministry. Their experience of a "call" is authoritative for them and, as such, is difficult to counter. If, however, experience has no authority in these matters, it is also invalid for men to lay claims to "calling". The strength of this appeal to experience lies in the fact that it is shared by others. Many women in many different churches experience the call to be ordained. Thoko Mpumlwana's is charmingly blunt: "I don't believe God is so sexist that she only calls men." Happily your fears were not realized, Mom. I never experienced the "call" to become a *dominee!* If being "called" to a task or a profession means working in a field that feels right, that you enjoy, that is accompanied by sense of service in obedience to something outside oneself, then I have been "called" to be a theologian.

Clearly, experience is a powerful source of knowledge. It is the fire in which we test what we know and what we do. You know that. When

Grandpa Fichat died, you had to abandon further education and go out to work to support your mother. Times were tough and this experience taught you to value education and influenced the way you dealt with money for the rest of your life. Our thinking and acting are born of experience. Experiences of pain and of joy shape our views and our values, past and present. Experience is never "pure" or unmediated; it is always impinged on by the communities and the circumstances in which we live. This I learnt growing up white in South Africa.

Feminist theologians like stories. They tell of experiences. "[T]hrough experience we meet endless otherness," says Harrison. Telling stories breaks the silence that blankets women's lives and opens us to the endless possibility of the other. Stories are a source of self-knowledge. Each woman has her own story to tell. We also hear others' stories. Telling my story and learning yours changes our stories. Our stories evoke memories and can cause us to relive pain or joy. They are as diverse as we are, filled with the contradictions of our lives and the colour and smell of our different contexts. Some of our stories can perpetuate oppressive patterns of behaviour. Others can call for change. Experience related through stories is central to doing feminist theology. Not all stories have happy endings. Mostly they have no endings. They are simply ongoing tales in which grit, doubt, and hope are part of life. If you had heard the stories told to the Truth and Reconciliation Commission you would know what I mean.

Appealing to experience means acknowledging the fact that experiences are often ambiguous, certainly limited, and often contradictory. Any claims to truth are therefore partial. I do not know how else to start doing theology other than by reflecting on my experiences in conversation with others. Just a thought — Do you think men can be feminists, even if they have not "experienced" gender discrimination? They certainly can have sympathy for the feminist cause and even stand in solidarity with women who struggle against sexism. A friend once remarked impishly: "Some of my best friends are feminist-inclined men!"

I did not grow up with the bible. I do not blame you for this. Although I often wish that its texts were engraved in my memory from the beginning, I am grateful that you did not pretend an interest. Discovering the biblical stories for myself as an adult has kept them fresh and enthralling. When I was a child, you were often exasperated on finding me reading when you felt I should be doing something more "useful"! I wonder whether you were ever aware of the worlds I lived in — from cowboys on the range to the antics of the Greek gods, from romance with the Scarlet Pimpernel and the heroes of the French Foreign Legion to the enchantment of Rider Haggard's mysterious *She*. Reading the bible seemed unutterably dull by comparison. It was the book of the church, and the church was a very alienating place. Thankfully, the much-quoted aphorism that education is wasted on the young is only partly true because, despite my priorities having had little to do with studying during my first stint at a university, shadows of the great works in English literature clung to the recesses of my consciousness. I do remember noting at the time how Shakespeare, T. S. Eliot, and Milton, in particular, assumed that I, as the reader, had a knowledge of the bible. I'll read it one day, I thought.

"One day" only happened in my thirties. I come back to my bible study group. Curious as to why a dear friend, who in no sense appeared "religious," went to a weekly bible study group, I went with her one day. What I saw was puzzling yet interesting. I found a group of women who were so different from one another that I could not understand what kept them coming back week after week. Was it the unexpectedly gripping story they were reading? Contrary to the stereotype of the "meek and mild" shepherd walking ahead of a flock of dumb-looking sheep, this story was about a vital, active iconoclast whose life was astonishingly congruent with his teachings. I liked the way he related to people, especially those in need. The title of Albert Nolan's enduring work, *Jesus before Christianity*, describes my experience. This Jesus was a real person, not a figure caught up in doctrine and ritual. He was a fully human person living in difficult times in a way that I found compelling.

I tried to find false notes in his life and teachings. I had a million questions. My participation in the bible study group was punctuated with "Yes, but . . ." What kept me going was the fact that the other women did not pretend to be experts; they too were willing to explore and to question and, most of all, they were patient enough to put up with my misgivings and doubts. The rest, as the saying goes, is history. This introduction to the bible showed me that these ancient scriptures actually had something to say to my life. I found that they had the power to challenge me and, eventually, to turn my life upside down. The political and social implications of these discoveries were also riveting. Jesus' followers were a ragtag group of people. He seemed to prefer their company to the powerful and learned in his society. He was concerned about their miseries, sicknesses, and needs. What was this saying about my white world of comfort and privilege?

My tale of discovery does not end here. My excitement became tempered with caution, followed by dismay. Did you know that apartheid was legitimated by biblical texts? Did you know that other texts are used to support men's dominant role in the church and to present women as inferior to men? Reading the bible as a woman was unsettling, equivocal, and often simply embarrassing. As my feminist consciousness grew, I began to find passages in the scriptures offensive because they were frankly sexist and supported a patriarchal order. I found that this book, so extraordinary in many ways, was actually written largely, if not exclusively, by men, about men, and for men. What authority could it have in my life? I was caught in a bind. On the one hand the bible had changed my life. On the other, I could not cope with its sexism, or for that matter with the texts that condoned slavery. Scoffing at these motley anomalies in scripture or attempting to ignore them was not a satisfactory way out of my dilemma. Even recent attempts to substitute inclusive language in those texts that refer to humanity only as men, cannot sidestep the fact that the bible has its origins in a patriarchal world. You may well ask: "If that is the way you feel, why continue to read the bible?" You may even be wondering how I can be both a feminist and a Christian. Sadly, a number of women have not found this possible. The source document of the Christian faith with its all-male God and Saviour is simply too patriarchal for them, and consequently they have left the church. Many more have, however, stayed. As one of them, I ask: How can I hold on to this book with its sexist, violent, contradictory, and often alien texts?

The study of theology has helped me, over the years, to deal with this dilemma. First, I learnt that the church's official acceptance of the bible only took place over many centuries. This long and complicated history of deciding on which writings to include and which to exclude shows that there was no litmus test, such as divine inspiration, to establish which texts were to be part of the church's canon or not. What happened was that texts were established as part of the canon by believing communities who read these ancient texts and found that they rhymed with their faith. Who made the decisions in these communities and on what basis? Quite simply, the biblical canon was established by men, from male writings that were about men's experiences, interests, and theology. In other words, male experience set the standard for the experience of all Christians. Small wonder that women to this day have to dig deep into the bible to find their own voices.

Second, I saw that we all read texts through our own lenses. What I am talking about is interpretation, a process we all use when we try to understand any phenomenon. This was a liberating discovery. I understood that when a person reads a text, the text is interpreted and given meaning. Texts do not have only one "right" meaning waiting to be discovered by the clever reader. I have seen this in my book club, when the same book means different things to different, equally insightful members. Even if the writer wants to convey a particular "meaning", she or he cannot control what the reader finds in the text. When I, or you, or anyone else reads a text, the way in which we interpret it is influenced by our experiences and our needs. Picture it as a conversation. The reader and the text address each other and meaning emerges. Feminist biblical scholars, like Elisabeth Schüssler Fiorenza in her groundbreaking work *In Memory of Her*, read the scriptures through feminist lenses. By delving into the silences surrounding the lives of women in the bible and by uncovering clues about women's lives in ancient times behind its stories, she has opened new ways of reading the bible for women. Feminist theologian Rosemary Radford Ruether has a different approach. She describes two different strands in biblical thought. The one reflects the dominant thought of the day while the other is a kind of counter-voice, a prophetic and liberating strand that questions and even assails the dominant voice. Women can take heart and identify with this dissident voice. Despite the accounts of powerful kings, the corrupting effects of their wealth and authority, there are "other" voices, those of the prophets calling the people to be obedient to God and to act justly and lovingly towards one another. The early pioneering work in biblical scholarship has been picked up by a growing band of feminist biblical scholars, opening up new ways of reading the bible. There are still moments of rupture and there are still unanswered questions. But for me the bible has begun to take on new and interesting dimensions. I cannot let go of the alienating texts as easily as I did before — I shake them, turn them upside down, yell at them, and tag them on the sketch of my landscape as recalcitrant and present.

Third, I remind myself that the bible is a collection of stories, poems, historical narratives, and theological insights written down in times that in some respects were very different from my own but in others startlingly the same. Just as I write from out of my time, so these ancient writers wrote from out of theirs. The eternal fascination of the scriptures is actually quite straightforward. The attempts of people to live creatively and lovingly with God are not limited to any particular time in history. Our struggles are no different from those of the ancient writers of the bible. The people of Israel describe the human condition as it is. They suffer, doubt, do awful things, and cry out that the good will triumph. They experience God as distant yet present, exacting yet merciful, just yet full of grace and love. So do I. The bible is a book of countless layers of meaning. Hans Schürmann describes the bible as a "remarkably pluralistic library with traditions spanning more than fifteen hundred years." Not only is the bible a "pluralistic library" but it is the book of faith for roughly one third of humanity, who themselves live in dazzlingly pluralistic realities. There are a thousand different voices in the scriptures. It is the collective and cultural memory of people struggling to live in relationship with God. It is, in Michael Welker's words, our "canonic memory". By memory I do not understand that it has one great theme that we remember. As a feminist theologian I am naturally suspicious of the idea of "one great story". The "great story" has always been exclusively male. The biblical traditions and cultural contexts are complex and challenge readers of the texts to balance coherence and complexity.

Lastly, generation upon generation of people, throughout the ages, have known the power of the bible to inspire faith. In South Africa it is read by candlelight in shacks in informal settlements, in modest churches in townships and suburbs, in cathedrals and homes, in all-white reformed communities, and in all-black indigenous churches. All over the world people read these ancient texts as food for their lives of faith. To ignore this fact as a Christian and as a theologian is dangerous and patronising. There is no Christian theology without the bible. They belong together. The bible is theology's source document. It gives rise to reflection which, whether simple or sophisticated, constitutes doing theology. Of course there are many different ways of dealing with the relationship between theology and the bible. That is why we have a plethora of theologies and many different interpretations of its texts. When all is said and done and despite the often turgid maleness of the texts, I still find in the emotional honesty of the psalms, in the earthy stories of the Hebrew scriptures in which human frailties are not glossed over, and in the accounts of the life, teachings, and actions of Jesus, the stuff that nurtures my fragile faith, feeds my meditations, and challenges my practices in my communities. While I struggle to make sense of these difficulties, I still find that the scriptures can rock the established order, surprise me with their power to dislodge my deeply held views, and make my heart sing in response to their prophetic vision. Can this be God's Spirit at work? The freshness of the biblical stories and the excitement of discovering new connections has not paled. Did you discover some of this excitement when reading the bible I found at your bedside?

I can no longer avoid talking to you about the church. You hardly ever went to church. I remember your caustic comment about Stewie, who became a churchgoer in his last years: "He is trying to assure his ticket to heaven!" You were not going to "buy" your way in. Yet you had me baptised an Anglican, the church to which you nominally belonged. I am grateful for that. I wonder what you would have made of your own funeral service — conducted in a sterile Dutch Reformed Church by a man who barely knew your name. I hated it.

Dorothy Day, the Catholic social activist, a saint if ever there was one, said that the church "is often a scandal to me". She believed that one must live in a state of permanent dissatisfaction with the church. I am not surprised that Nietzsche found the church "precisely that against which Jesus preached — and against which he taught his disciples to fight." I take this seriously. When I set out to mark the church on my faith landscape, the crosses I scatter over the landscape are made of gold, wood, tin, pipe cleaners, palm leaves, and nails — broken, polished, rusty, large and small. Outside some churches there are signs like: "Welcome, no women clergy here"; "Yuppies, young and old, welcome"; "Whites only"; "Communion for members only". Some churches are identified as Catholic, Anglican, Reformed, Pentecostal, and so on. Others have no signs: those in homes, under trees, on the grass verges of roads in our cities, in barns on farms, and in ghettos. All are the church.

Let me tell you a story. In May 1993 I spent some time in Chambone, a small village five hundred kilometres north of Maputo in Mozambique. Since the early 1970s civil war had raged through this country. Then, in October 1992, a peace accord had been brokered between the two contending movements. After six months of relative calm people were beginning to emerge out of the bush, trying to pick up their lives again. Bishop Dinis Sengulane had sought the help of the Institute for Christian Spirituality in reestablishing their rural faith communities. One hot morning we were sitting under a spreading wild fig tree. It was my turn to speak. "What *is* the church?" I asked. Alicia, a woman of indeterminate age with worn hands and feet, drew herself up and replied: "*We* are the church. When they locked our churches, we held church under the trees and we baptized our children in the river. When the commissar tried to stop this, we took them to the sea at night. We just kept on being church. Tell them, *we* are the church."

As I write to you about the church, I keep this story before me. It helps me to stay on track. Sadly, the scandal of the Christian church is its fractious, fragmented nature, its proclivity for power games and the violence of its exclusiveness. No wonder Mercy Amba Oduyoye writes: "I believe that the experience of women in the church in Africa contradicts the Christian claim to promote the worth (equal value) of every person." To begin with, we confess that we are one body ("I believe in *one,* holy, catholic, and apostolic church" we all say), but we are not. We are a divided body of people, being "church" in a million different ways. Don't misunderstand me. I am not pleading for everyone to belong to the same church. The long and complicated history of divisions within Christianity is a given. The fact that our world is pluralistic is not a curse! But when our differences become cause for unbridgeable chasms between people who call themselves Christian, we need to question what we mean by "church". We disagree so unnecessarily. If I believe passionately that only adults should be baptized (which I do not) and do so on grounds of what I read in the bible (which is perfectly possible), I ought to remain open to the fact that the bible can also be used to support infant baptism. If only we Christians were less arrogant and judgmental about our certainties and more open about our differences, our place in a world of pluralities would be more realistic and authentic.

Power games are usually about exclusion. Women know this. We have a long history of being excluded from positions of authority in the church. At times I have been unable to stomach the extent of male dominance and have sought church elsewhere. For years I found a house church warm and welcoming. I have enjoyed women's liturgical groups that discard the alienating male symbols in worship and institute those that affirm women's humanity. But I still belong to my church. My membership is one of radical, critical fidelity. When I try to unravel why, despite my experiences of sexism, power mongering, bad teaching, and indifferent liturgical leadership, I am still a member of my church, I come up with seven reasons. Let me tell you about them. Doing so might just convince me more about the "fidelity" bit.

First, I found out that I need to be a member of a community that is not self-selected. Why? I cannot deny that the bible study group, house church, and women's groups have all played an indispensable role in nurturing my faith. Compared to the church they were and are cozy places. But snugness is not enough. I need the challenge of being a part of a community of such difference that I am shaken out of my ghetto. After all, that is how the world is, permeated with difference. In my letter to Rachel and Jo I have tried to explain why living well with difference is important. I wonder whether you agree? In your years abroad you experienced different places and people, in an official sort of way. The wife of an ambassador meets other diplomats and the local hierarchy. I know you did not enjoy those years. Was it because of the demands of the role you were given, or was it that you shied away from difference?

In the Anglican Church in Southern Africa, I meet people who are poor and needy, conservative and radical, sexist and feminist, straight and gay. I do not choose who goes with me to the altar rail for communion. I am a member of a body with great differences, but which has one common feature — its members profess faith in Jesus Christ. I have needed this, as well as the kinder climes of my small chosen groups, to crack my self-protecting beliefs and assumptions about myself and my place in my world. And to nurture my faith.

Second, I have memories that keep me in the church. I don't like saying this, but there was no uniform resistance to apartheid by the churches. Racist people, complacent people, frightened people also sat in the pews. Fortunately, there were individuals who resisted. In retrospect, I am sure

47

you were alarmed at my membership in the Christian Institute, particularly when it was banned, and you probably did not approve of my work with the South African Council of Churches or the Institute for Contextual Theology. How can I explain the solidarity, the excitement, the sense of purpose we had in those organizations? They helped me to channel my anger and my guilt. The memories of those times keep me loyal to the church.

Third, I have discovered over the years that the sacraments of baptism and communion are important to me. As I said, I am grateful that you had me baptised. My baptism made me a member of a community, long before I knew what that meant. The tenuous thread of belonging to the Christian community survived years of ignorance and avoidance. Rachel's baptism reminded me poignantly of the promises I made when my children were baptised. How little I understood then and on how many counts I have failed to honour those promises! Thankfully, God's promises are not trifling. That I know. Baptism is *the* sacrament of equality. It's a great leveller in which we are no longer Jew or Greek, slave or free, male or female, for we are all one in Christ Jesus (Gal. 3:28). I like that.

To outsiders, the Christian rite of communion is at best mystifying and at worst cannibalistic mumbo-jumbo. When I first became part of the church I felt little for the celebration of communion other than a vague sense of guilt because one was told to make things right with God, otherwise one could "eat and drink condemnation" on oneself. Later when I learnt about the different views of Catholic and Protestants about what happens at communion, I was filled with dismay at how unimportant such debates are in relation to this rite, so central to Christian worship. Over the years I began to discover what was really communal about communion. Sharing the wine and the bread with a *bergie* seeking warmth in the cathedral, with street children who wander in looking for money to spend on bread or glue to sniff to dull their pain, with women and men across all racial and class divides, with the Nationalist politician whose ideology I despised, with the church council member whose sexist attitudes undermine vestry meetings, and the cleric who believes that only men may consecrate the meal — all of this is an immediate and concrete experience that at this meal all are unconditionally accepted as equally precious bearers of the image of God. Only self-exclusion keeps us away from the table. We give thanks and we remember what God has accomplished for us through Jesus

Christ. The bread and the wine, the gifts of creation, also remind us with gratitude of how God provides for our daily needs and how abundant creation can be. God is intent on reconciling us to Godself, to ourselves, to one another, and to the whole world. That is why we remember Jesus' death. When we eat the bread and drink the wine we take part in the renewing of creation begun on the cross.

My favourite story about the healing potential of communion comes from the theologian of mission, Inez Daneel. Before taking part in the communion, members of the Zimbabwean Association of African Earth-keeping Churches confess their ecological sins: tree-felling without planting in return, overgrazing, river bank cultivation that causes soil erosion, ". . . taking the good earth for granted, exploiting it without nurturing it or reverencing it in return." Can you picture their communion table with its bread, wine, and a number of tree-seedlings, the songs, the dancing, and the line of communicants approaching the table each with a seedling in hand who, after receiving the sacrament, go out and plant the little tree so that the earth can be re-covered? These people do not treat the earth contemptuously as "the other". Their kind of communion sets about redeeming our innate relatedness to creation. It saves us from our ecological sins.

Fourth, like many other Christians, I struggle with prayer. You may wonder why talking or listening to God should be a problem at all. Talking to God is simple. Hearing God is another matter. Hearing God? Yes, we can hear if we trouble to take time out and tap into a rich vein in the church's age-old traditions of spiritual direction, times of quiet, retreats, and contemplation — demanding, often disappointing, yet profoundly vital aspects of being a Christian. This I learnt from Francis Cull to whom I have also written a letter in this book.

Fifth, I cannot do theology outside the church. I believe that theology should feed the church. It should be in a critical, even permanently dissatisfied, yet continuous and caring conversation with the church. Once theology loses its moorings, it gives up on the church. Who are we in fact talking to? A small band of like-minded scholars, an academic elite? I have seen friends and colleagues drift away from the church. I understand why. They are no longer comfortable in the church (who is?). Yet, they continue to write and teach Christian theology. Students find this confusing and end up feeling as uncomfortable as do their teachers. Being comfortable is not the aim. Being a comrade in an often bloody battle to find God's will for the world and the church — this is what theology should be doing.

Sixth, the church is, at its best, a tool in the hands of God for making good the promise of healing creation. Called the Body of Christ by Paul in his first letter to the Corinthians, it is equipped for God's purposes by at least one gift being given to every baptised member to be used for the common good. All the gifts, like all the members, are of equal value; all are indispensable. The foot is not greater than the eye, nor the hand than the ear. The gift to heal is not greater than the gift to utter wisdom. All the members of the Body are interrelated and interdependent. "If one member suffers, all suffer together with it; if one member is honoured, all rejoice together with it." I like this picture of the church. What is clear is that the church as the Body of Christ is to be a place where God's promises find flesh, as every single member acts on her or his gift. Most churches have ignored this. All churches have until recently denied women's gifts. The (male) pastor or priest is supposed to have all the gifts while those in the pews are passive recipients of clerical riches. I know that I, like all the baptised, have a gift to be used for the good of the body, so I am not quitting. I stay on, troubled and troublesome, trying to be accountable to the church for my task in making the Body more Christlike.

Lastly, as I have just said, I am sufficiently contrariwise not to want to give up on an institution which, though often scandalous and even reprobate, has a remarkable history and an indispensable role to perform today. I am not prepared to back off and hand the church over to the patriarchs. I have no idea to what extent the church's survival is due to God's grace. What I do know is that judgment on the church is surely stayed because there are caring people who are faithful to this one Body. I want to be part of this struggling band.

I can't end here. I must say something about the use of language in worship. Many years ago, I was jolted into a raw awareness about the use of language in church. In a collect I was asked to pray "that I might grow to my full manhood". Such errant nonsense! Sadly, not much has changed since then. In my church, humanity is still described in exclusively male terms in our hymns and in many of our prayers. I can no longer sing "Rise up, O men of God." Nor do I want to. I am tired of the mental gymnastics required to find myself included as a woman in the language of worship. I simply shut out many of the prayers and the hymns, relieved when they

are over, yet always uncomfortable and a bit angry; all this despite my love
for the rhythm of the liturgy.

This is not all. Can a feminist be comfortable in a religion that gives
God the title of "Father" above all other names? Can the title "Father" in
fact be eradicated from our tradition in order to accommodate the sensibil-
ities of women? I know of no other issue raised by feminists that generates
as much antagonism and incomprehension as does the question of God-
language. It is feminist theologians' most knotty problem. I need to qualify
this last statement. Oduyoye points out that this is not a problem for all
women. "The disinterest of African women in the grammar of sexism, is
caused not only by their own languages with inclusive pronouns but also
because the maleness or femaleness of God is literally immaterial to
them." It is, however, a problem for me. I experience sexist language for
God as reinforcing the maleness of God and this despite the fact that on
both sides of the God-language debate all agree on one fundamental point.
God is not a gendered being, and certainly not a male being. What we cannot agree on is how to speak about God. I do not find the solution in simply substituting inclusive language or adding female images of God from
our biblical traditions, like Mother or Sophia. A sprinkling of metaphors
for God does not deal with the fact that in the Jewish and Christian traditions, God is consistently spoken of as male. Jesus in fact taught his disciples to pray "Our Father". This has uncomfortable consequences for
women. I personally have no quarrel with "Father" as *one* of our images for
God. I too need a Father who will give me bread not stone, a fish and not a
serpent. But when "Father" becomes *the* dominant image of our worship,
used at least twenty-one times in a service, it is not only limiting but also
dangerous. Why? Christian sculpture and painting often represent God as
an old (white) man with a beard, in situations of earthly power. This com-
municates that God is similar to male authority figures. Rosemary Ruether
puts it baldly: "When the word *Father* is taken literally to mean that God is
male and not female, represented by males and not females, then this word
becomes idolatrous." I am afraid that this does happen. It is carried over
into the modern tendency in my church to address male priests as "father".
This is dangerous in view of our exclusive use of this term for God. The
situation has become so ludicrous that I have heard women priests addressed as "father"!

To make matters worse, the church has a long tradition of believing that woman, unlike man, is not fully made in the image of God. No doubt the church fathers found Paul's views convincing when he wrote: "For man ought not to have his head veiled, since he is the image and reflection of God; but woman is the reflection of man" (1 Cor. 11:7). Once God is viewed as exclusively male, females are simply not in the running as complete human beings. What feminist theologians reject is patriarchal ideology — not just the fact that it subjects women, but that it lends divine justification for doing so. This is much broader than objecting to the maleness of the language of worship and of the bible itself. We know that exchanging mother for father will not solve the problem because it still comes from male-orientated structures and ways of thinking.

There is no real consensus among feminist theologians on how to resolve the problem of God-talk. As I have already mentioned, some feminists reject Christianity altogether as too irredeemably male. Others advocate inclusive language in the liturgy and omit calling God "Father" because it is a source of pain. Still others live with the "Father" in the liturgy while using non-gendered terms for God in their private devotions. However women respond, feminist theological thought on God-talk is seriously challenging core metaphors and ideologies of male power and dominance in Christianity. I am hopeful that the depth and complexity of the Christian religion will enable it to be resilient and responsive in the face of these challenges. In the meantime, I continue to explore my own experience of the person of God in conversation with the biblical sources, hoping always to understand more about the accessible mystery that is God. *Si comprehendis non est Deus,* said Augustine (If you comprehend what you are saying, you are not talking about God). Ultimately, our language cannot fully embrace the mystery that is God. It always remains a seeking, testing, tasting, and speaking that is tentative, open, and vulnerable, for speak we must.

You did not hide the fact that you did not share my faith convictions. To this day I am not sure what you believed. I know you valued telling the truth and being honest in your dealings. You were naturally suspicious and often critical. I wonder what made you so? You, like me, had your own ideology. We often disagreed, but neither of us thought that our disagreements were caused by ideological differences. We simply found each other different, even difficult. Today I see more clearly how our thinking was shaped by the influences of our different times and how it was ideologically driven. We did not agree about politics, and we had different versions of what the future should look like. Forty years of white Nationalist rule was our common reality. Most nationalisms are embraced uncritically. Ours certainly was. Tom Nairn justly warns that "[a]ll nationalism is both healthy and morbid. Both progress and regress are inscribed in its genetic code from the start". Some traditions are worth holding on to, others are not. The problem is how to decide. I think that this is where you and I had many disagreements. Neither of us was prepared to concede that our traditions and our ideologies could be interpreted in a multitude of ways. We disagreed on our utopias and were quite dogmatic in doing so. I know that Stewie thought that I was forsaking my traditions. He was right. I did reject the parts that had become nationalistic. Now, despite all those years of being force-fed French Huguenot history, my resentment has abated. I am rediscovering my history.

The very word "ideology" can trip one up. Often it means "everything that I am not"! Sometimes it is a convenient term to pit one set of ideas against another in a battle that has no winners. At its most neutral, as philosopher Johann Degenaar reminded me, ideology is an action-oriented set of beliefs. Understood this way, Christianity itself is an ideology. Unexamined ideologies are the problem. They become traps that snare our thinking and rob our minds of the freedom to roam unfettered into unknown and often unpopular territories. I now need to mark the snares and traps of ideology on my landscape of faith with bright red triangles. They are there to remind me never to stop examining my own beliefs and questioning my assumptions. Have I, in my writings and striving for the liberation of women, examined my ideology vigorously enough to know its face? I have been critical of hierarchies and dualistic thinking, while at the same time holding on to a hierarchy of beliefs and admitting being at home with paradox and ambiguity. Some of the old hierarchical ideologies with which I grew up are easier to identify than others. Whiteness is superior to blackness, maleness to femaleness. They have to be unlearned, layer by layer. Examining ideologies honestly welcomes nuances. Not all whites are bad, neither are all blacks good. Some men understand, others don't — that's the way it is. The way to deal with an old ideology is not to embrace a new one uncritically. All ideologies have snares. One such snare is hatred for the "enemy." As Susan Griffin points out, "When a movement for liberation inspires itself chiefly by a hatred for an enemy rather than from this vision of possibility, it begins to defeat itself. Its very motions cease to be healing."

What Griffin calls "the way of all ideology" is an inner war waged within onself. Our new ideologies are probably born out of genuine feeling. But we all have a history of past experiences, of old beliefs and ideas. The old will always impinge on the new. The oppressive theories of the past steal unnoticed into my thoughts. The poor are poor because they are lazy, a woman's place is really in the home. The genuine feelings that inspire change are at war against the old beliefs lurking at deep levels in my being. "It is mind over body. Safety over risk. The predictable over the surprise. Control over emotion," writes Griffin. My battle is to recover the original desire for justice, freedom, healing. If, on the one hand, I allow impulses born only of feeling to be transformed into a set ideology, I lose the original quality of truth that comes from my whole being, both feeling *and* thought. If, on the other, the ideologue in me censors my feelings, not allowing them to live long enough to be explored and understood, the most dangerous brand of ignorance may be the result: ignorance of myself. Censoring my feelings, silencing my doubts, denying my anger because I feel guilty about them, blinds me to the snares of my new ideology. My feelings become enemies, and in order to deal with them I project them onto others. This is the danger of unexamined ideologies. To get out of these snares, I have to own my feelings and know that efforts to understand myself are never-ending, as is the search for my own healing. And I mark these traps on my landscape with danger signs.

As I come to the end of this letter, I can imagine you asking: "What is the purpose in all that you are trying to do?" So much that is done in the name of Christian faith and praxis is stifling and oppressive. Instead of being good news, it is either a yawn or off-putting. The teaching and the life of Jesus are in fact the best news I know of. They promise healing, freedom, food for life, and hope for the day. What I am passionate about is being healed and free. I don't mean my healing or my freedom alone. I mean both in the broadest possible sense. They go together. I know that our crying need as South Africans is to "bind up the wounds" at every level and for all in different ways. Then healing means liberation, justice, forgiveness, and hopefully reconciliation. Healing has to do with bread, a roof over people's heads, jobs, education, health care — all that is needed to live with dignity. I think that what theologians have to say should be measured by whether it contributes to human healing and freedom.

Does this sound like a pipe dream? No more so than the prayer Christians have uttered for two thousand years — "May your Kingdom come". Another religious phantasy? When approximately one third of the human race pray "may your Kingdom come", what are we in fact hoping for? When I place healing at the centre of my theology I am, in fact, speaking "reign of God" language. To explain, let me begin with the pharisees. They asked Jesus when the reign of God was coming. Jesus replied:

> The kingdom of God is not coming with things that can be observed; nor will they say, "Look, here it is" or "there it is!" For, in fact, the kingdom of God is among you. (Luke 17:20-21)

How is it among us? It is among us as an emerging reality, an "already not yet" paradox that has begun and will continue to transform the world. It is both present and future, to be perceived both internally and externally. It is difficult to define and pin down because it is not conspicuous and is easily dismissed. We fail to see divine power in all its creativeness at work around us. In his parables, Jesus likened it to a mustard seed or to leaven. The language of the parables, those enigmatic teachings of Jesus, shows us how difficult it is to recognise and to understand the inconspicuousness of the reign of God. We take for granted that yeast makes bread rise. We do not stop to think about yeast leavening the loaf when we bite into a fresh warm crust.

How do we know the reign of God is present? Simply by being aware of daily acts of mercy and self-giving, when people are genuinely able to put love of neighbour above self-interest, when we attempt to live in mutual interdependence with one another. I shudder at what the world would be like if the reign of God was only a future reality. Yet our attempts at living like citizens of the reign of God are limited. So the idea of the reign of God at the same time remains in the future. It is, as I have said, an emerging ideal anchored in present reality to be fulfilled in the future. That is why Christians pray "may your Kingdom come". We are saying that we are willing to live in such a way that the world will be renewed, a place in which God will reign.

What would the reign of God look like? It is beyond my imagining, but I do hope for the renewal of creation. I would like to sit down at the feast that the "Lord of hosts will make for all people" (Isa. 25:6), and I hope to see a time when "the wolf and lamb shall feed together" (Isa. 65:25). I dream of the flourishing of justice, love, freedom, equality, wholeness, peace, and righteousness. When, in Joel's words,

> So you shall know that I, the Lord your God,
> dwell in Zion, my holy mountain.
> And Jerusalem shall be holy,
> and strangers shall never again pass through it.

The trick is that when we take part in making things new, our healing begins. To hope for a world that is whole means I commit myself to struggle against conspicuous evil and for the values of the reign of God. That's all. And it's enough. There is nothing cosy or safe in the work of healing.

This search for healing is not without self-interest. I have fears about the future. Can we rise above the wounding of the past and the iniquities of the present in South Africa? What future will my children and my grandchildren have? I know that their future is inextricably bound up with the future of all other children, those in shacks, those homeless on the streets, those alienated from their roots by the bad times. I am thrown back on my resources. What does my faith require of me? To be vigilant about justice, to love boundlessly, never to cease hoping, and to be actively involved in the work of healing. I find this daunting. I tremble with self-doubt. I struggle with my own faintheartedness and the desire to opt out. Could this struggle be my own search for a deepened sense of what it means to be a human being. And in the struggle, the insistent longing eggs me on, never resting on what is, but reaching out for what must be.

It has taken me many words to answer your question: What is theology? It is a question that, on the one hand, merits far more than I have written. On the other hand, the essence of theology is not complicated. At heart it speaks words about God. My friends who do not share my faith may well sniff and mutter: "Pure speculation!" No more speculative than theories about the cosmos, scientific guesses, or the belief that love exists, is my reply.

My friend and colleague Dirkie Smit put the following question to a postgraduate student of his: "Did God make us human in order to make us Christian; or did he make us Christian in order to be human?" Surely we are meant to be wonderfully human first, for then we shall know the God who dwells on Zion. When all is said and done, that is what it is all about. If theology helps us along the way, it is doing the right thing.

I am glad we could have this conversation. I wish I knew that you were also.

With my love,
Denise

NOTES

My mother Violet Ruth Fichat was born in 1903 in a small hamlet called Port Alfred. Her father was a magistrate, which meant that the family moved about considerably. She married my father Stephanus Francois du Toit in 1932 and, after living in Cape Town for many years, she lived abroad in Sweden, Argentina, Portugal, Italy, and France from 1946 to 1960 as the wife of a diplomat. She died in 1984. In this letter my father is referred to as *Stewie* (pronounced Stevie), the name I gave him as a child.

Three Afrikaans words need translation. A *tiekie* was a thrupenny coin that is no longer in use, a *dominee* is a minister in the reformed tradition, and a *bergie* is the term usually used to describe a homeless person living on the slopes of Table Mountain in Cape Town.

In certain orthodox theological circles, "experience" as a central category for doing theology is derided. Early on in my theological studies I read the German philosopher and theologian Friedrich Schleiermacher. I remember being delighted at finding that this male theologian who wrote a century and half ago supported the authority of experience and that he related experience to communities in specific historical contexts. In Schleiermacher I found firm ground for a theology that draws on experience and context. See his *On Reli-*

gion: Speeches to Its Cultured Despisers (New York: Cambridge University Press, 1988).

The expression "pluralistic library" comes from Hans Schürmann and was used by Michael Welker in a paper given at the Center for Theological Inquiry, Princeton, February 2000.

Feminist theologies are written in Asia, Europe, Latin America, North America, Africa, and Australasia. African women's theology, i.e., theology born in Africa, is distinct from *womanist* theology, which is theology done by African American women. *Mujerista* theology is theology done by Hispanic women who live in the United States of America.

It is simply impossible to mention all the works that I have found interesting over the last twenty-five years. There are, however, certain early publications by feminist theologians that I return to over and over again. I have learnt much from these works and would like to pay tribute to them by mentioning them with pleasure, for they helped to shape the future of feminist theologies: Anne E. Carr, *Transforming Grace: Christian Tradition and Women's Experience* (San Francisco: Harper & Row, 1988); Carol P. Christ and Judith Plaskow, eds., *Womanspirit Rising: A Feminist Reader in Religion* (San Francisco: Harper & Row, 1979); Mary Daly, *The Church and the Second Sex* (Boston: Beacon Press, 1968) and *Beyond God the Father: Toward a Philosophy of Women's Liberation* (Boston: Beacon Press, 1973); Denise Dijk, Fokkelien van Dijk-Hemmes, and Catharina J. M. Halkes, eds., *Feministisch-theologische Teksten* (Delft: Meinema, 1985); Elisabeth Schüssler Fiorenza, *Bread not Stone: The Challenge of Feminist Biblical Interpretation* (Boston: Beacon Press, 1984) and *In Memory of Her: A Feminist Theological Reconstruction of Christian Origins* (New York: Crossroad, 1983); Mary Grey, *Redeeming the Dream: Feminism, Redemption and the Christian Tradition* (London: SPCK, 1989); Catharina J. M. Halkes, *Met Miriam is het Begonnen* (Kampen: Kok, 1980) and *Zoekend naar wat Verloren Ging: Enkele Aanzetten voor een Feministische Theologie* (Baarn: Ten Have, 1984); Daphne Hampson, *Theology and Feminism* (Oxford: Blackwell, 1990); Beverly Wildung Harrison, *Making the Connections: Essays in Feminist Social Ethics* (Boston: Beacon Press, 1985); Carter I. Heyward, *The Redemption of God: A Theology of Mutual Relation* (Lanham, Md.: University Press of America, 1982); Catherine Keller, *From a Broken Web: Separation, Sexism and Self* (Boston: Beacon Press, 1986); Sallie McFague, *Metaphorical Theology: Models of God in Religious Language* (London: SCM Press, 1982); Elisabeth Moltmann-Wendel, *A Land Flowing with Milk and Honey: Perspectives on Feminist Theology*, trans. J. Bowden (New York: Crossroad, 1986); Nelle Morton, *The Journey Is Home* (Boston: Beacon Press, 1985); Mercy Amba Oduyoye, *Hearing and Knowing: Theological Reflections on Christianity in Africa* (Maryknoll, N.Y.: Orbis Books, 1986); Rosemary Radford Ruether, *Women-Church: Theology and Practice of Feminist Liturgical Communities* (San Francisco: Harper & Row, 1985), *Sexism and God-Talk: Toward a Feminist Theology* (Boston: Beacon Press, 1983), and *New Woman New Earth: Sexist Ideologies and Human Liberation* (New York: Seabury Press, 1975); Dorothee Sölle, *The Strength of the Weak: Toward a Christian Feminist Identity* (Philadelphia: Westminster Press, 1984); Elsa Tamez, ed., *Through Her Eyes: Women's Theology from Latin America* (Maryknoll, N.Y.: Orbis Books, 1989); Susan Thistlethwaite, *Sex, Race and God: Christian Feminism in Black and White* (New York: Crossroad, 1989); Phyllis Trible, *God and the Rhetoric of Sexuality* (Philadelphia: Fortress Press, 1978) and *Texts of Terror: Literary-Feminist Readings of Biblical Narratives* (Philadelphia: Fortress Press, 1984); Letty M. Russell, *Becoming Human* (Philadelphia: Westminster Press, 1982) and *Feminist Interpretation of the Bible* (Philadelphia: Westminster Press, 1989); Sharon D. Welch, *Communities of Resistance and Solidarity: A Feminist Theology of Liberation* (Maryknoll, N.Y.: Orbis Books, 1985).

I do want to include certain recent works by feminist theologians that are important for anyone with an interest in women doing theology in a variety of contexts. This list (and the previous one) is offered to students as a reading guide. My choices are eclectic and reflect my own interests: Denise M. Ackermann and Riet Bons-Storm, eds., *Liberating Practices: Feminist Practical Theologies in Context* (Leuven: Peeters, 1998); María Pilar Aquino, *Our Cry for Life: Feminist Theology from Latin America* (Maryknoll, N.Y.: Orbis Books, 1993); Riet Bons-Storm, *The Incredible Woman: Listening to Women's Silences in Pastoral Care and Counseling* (Nashville: Abingdon Press, 1996); Riet Bons-Storm et al., eds., *Feminist Perspectives in Pastoral Theology* (Leuven: Peeters, 1998); Lisa Sowle Cahill, *Sex, Gender and Christian Ethics* (Cambridge: Cambridge University Press, 1996); Rebecca S. Chopp, *The Power to Speak: Feminism, Language, God* (New York: Crossroad, 1989); Rebecca S. Chopp and Sheila G. Davaney, eds., *Horizons in Feminist Theology: Identity, Tradition, and Norms* (Minneapolis: Fortress Press, 1997); Ada María Isasi Díaz, *En la Lucha: Elaborating a Mujerista Theology. A Hispanic Women's Liberation Theology* (Minneapolis: Fortress Press, 1993); Teresa Elwes, ed., *Women's Voices: Essays in Contemporary Feminist Theology* (London: Marshall Pickering, 1992); J. Cheryl Exum, *Fragmented Women: Feminist (Sub)versions of Biblical Narratives* (Valley Forge, Pa.: Trinity Press, 1993); Virginia Fabella and Mercy Amba Oduyoye, eds., *With Passion and Compassion: Third World Women Doing Theology* (Maryknoll, N.Y.: Orbis Books, 1988); Margaret A. Farley, *Personal Commitments: Beginning, Keeping, Changing*

(San Francisco: Harper & Row, 1986); Margaret A. Farley and Serene Jones, eds., *Liberating Eschatology: Essays in Honor of Letty M. Russell* (Louisville: Westminster/John Knox Press, 1999); Mary McClintock Fulkerson, *Changing the Subject: Women's Discourses and Feminist Theology* (Minneapolis: Fortress Press, 1994); Daphne Hampson, ed., *Swallowing a Fishbone: Feminist Theologians Debate Christianity* (London: SPCK, 1996); Linda Hogan, *From Women's Experience to Feminist Theology* (Sheffield: Sheffield Academic Press, 1995); Lisa Isherwood and Dorothea McEwan, *Introducing Feminist Theology* (Sheffield: Sheffield Academic Press, 1993); Elizabeth A. Johnson, *She Who Is: The Mystery of God in Feminist Theological Discourse* (New York: Crossroad, 1994) and *Friends of God and Prophets: A Feminist Theological Reading of the Communion of the Saints* (New York: Continuum, 1998); Serene Jones, *Feminist Theory and Christian Theology: Cartographies of Grace* (Minneapolis: Fortress Press, 2000); Joan Martin, *More Than Toil: A Christian Work Ethic of Enslaved Women* (Louisville: Westminster/John Knox Press, 2000); Catherine Mowry LaCugna, ed., *Freeing Theology: The Essentials of Theology in Feminist Perspective* (San Francisco: Harper & Row, 1993); Judith Plaskow, *Standing Again at Sinai: Judaism from a Feminist Perspective* (San Francisco: Harper & Row, 1990); Kwok Pui-Lan, *Introducing Asian Feminist Theology* (Cleveland: Pilgrim Press, 2000); Letty M. Russell, *Household of Freedom: Authority in Feminist Theology* (Philadelphia: Westminster Press, 1987) and *Church in the Round: Feminist Interpretation of the Church* (Louisville: Westminster/John Knox Press, 1993); Dorothee Sölle, *Thinking about God: An Introduction to Theology* (Valley Forge, Pa.: Trinity Press, 1990); Emile M. Townes, ed., *A Troubling in My Soul: Womanist Perspectives on Evil and Suffering* (Maryknoll, N.Y.: Orbis Books, 1993); Dolores S. Williams, *Sisters in the Wilderness: The Challenge of Womanist God-Talk* (Maryknoll, N.Y.: Orbis Books, 1993); Sharon D. Welch, *A Feminist Ethic of Risk* (Minneapolis: Fortress Press, 1990).

An indispensable reference work for the study of feminist theologies is the *Dictionary of Feminist Theologies,* ed. J. Shannon Clarkson and Letty M. Russell (Louisville: Westminster/John Knox Press, 1996).

Feminist theologians show an increasing interest in ecology as seen in the following works: Catharina J. M. Halkes, *New Creation: Christian Feminism and the Renewal of the Earth* (London: SPCK, 1989); Sallie McFague, *Models of God: Theology for an Ecological, Nuclear Age* (Philadelphia: Fortress Press, 1987), *The Body of God: An Ecological Theology* (Minneapolis: Fortress Press, 1993), and *Life Abundant: Rethinking Theology and Economy for a Planet in Peril* (Minneapolis: Fortress Press, 2001); Rosemary Radford Ruether, *God and Gaia: An Ecofeminist*

Theology of Earth Healing (San Francisco: Harper & Row, 1989) and her edited work *Women Healing Earth: Third World Women on Ecology, Feminism, and Religion* (Maryknoll, N.Y.: Orbis Books, 1996).

After years of struggle African women's voices are now being heard, and the first among them is Mercy Amba Oduyoye. In addition to the works mentioned previously, see her *Daughters of Anowa: African Women and Patriarchy* (Maryknoll, N.Y.: Orbis Books, 1995). The work of the Circle of Concerned African Women Theologians, which was formed in 1989 in Ghana and now has chapters all over eastern, western, and southern Africa, has been responsible for encouraging African women to write and be published. Here I think of works such as *Talitha Qumi!* ed. Mercy A. Oduyoye and Musimibi Kanyoro (Accra: Sam Woode, 2001); *Divine Empowerment of Women in Africa's Complex Realities,* ed. Elizabeth Amoah (Accra: Sam Woode, 2001); *Will to Arise: Women, Tradition and the Church in Africa,* ed. Mercy A. Oduyoye and Musimbi Kanyoro (Maryknoll, N.Y.: Orbis Books, 1992); *Groaning in Faith: African Women in the Household of God,* ed. Musimbi Kanyoro and J. Nyambura (Nairobi: Acton Publishers, 1996); *Claiming Our Footprints* by the Cape Town chapter of the Circle, ed. Eliza Getman, Hantie Kotze, Judy Tobler, and Denise M. Ackermann (Stellenbosch: EFSA, 2001). Notable too is *In Search of a Round Table: Gender, Theology and Church Leadership,* ed. Musimbi Kanyoro (Geneva: WCC, 1997), and the work of Christina Landman, *The Piety of Afrikaner Women* (Pretoria: Unisa, 1994). For the work of African women biblical scholars, refer to *Semeia* 78 (1997) entitled *Reading the Bible as Women: Perspective from Africa, Asia and Latin America,* ed. Phyllis Bird, in particular the articles by Musa Dube, Madipoane Masenya, Dora Rudo Mbuwayesango, and Elna Mouton. Two other recent works are *Other Ways of Reading: African Women and the Bible,* ed. Musa W. Dube (Atlanta: Society of Biblical Literature, 2001), and *Reading a New Testament Document Ethically,* by Elna Mouton (Atlanta: Society of Biblical Literature, 2002). An interesting South African journal, *Agenda,* devoted a special edition to "African Feminisms." See no. 50 (2001).

The Christian Institute, launched by Rev. Beyers Naudé in 1963 as a multiracial, ecumenical body, did much to promote the cause of Black Consciousness and Black Theology during the 1970s. "In June 1968, the Institute, in cooperation with the South African Council of Churches (SACC), issued 'A Message to the People of South Africa,' essentially a white initiative rooted in the rejection of apartheid on the basis of the 'good news that in Christ, God had broken down the walls of division between God and man, and therefore also between man and man [sic].'" See Peter Walshe, "Christianity and the Anti-

Apartheid Struggle: The Prophetic Voice within Divided Churches," in Richard Elphick and Rodney Davenport, eds., *Christianity in South Africa: A Political, Social and Cultural History* (Claremont: David Philip, 1997).

Works referred to in this letter are:

Linell E. Cady, "Identity, Feminist Theory and Theology," in R. S. Chopp and S. G. Davaney, eds., *Horizons in Feminist Theology: Identity, Tradition, and Norms* (Minneapolis: Fortress Press, 1997).

Rebecca Chopp, *The Power to Speak: Feminism, Language, God* (New York: Crossroad, 1989).

Yves Congar, *Lay People and the Church,* trans. D. Attwater (Westminster, Md.: Newman Press, 1965).

M. Shawn Copeland, "Journeying to the Household of God: The Eschatological Implications of Method in the Theology of Letty Mandeville Russell," in M. A. Farley and S. Jones, eds., *Liberating Eschatology: Essays in Honor of Letty M. Russell* (Louisville: Westminster/John Knox Press, 1999).

M. L. Daneel, "African Independent Churches Face the Challenge of Environmental Ethics," *Missionalia* 21 (1993): 311-32.

Mary Daly, *The Church and the Second Sex,* with the Feminist Postchristian Introduction and New Archaic Afterwords by the author (Boston: Beacon Press, 1968).

Elisabeth Schüssler Fiorenza, *In Memory of Her: A Feminist Theological Reconstruction of Christian Origins* (New York: Crossroad, 1983).

Paul Germond and Steve de Gruchy, eds., *Aliens in the Household of God: Homosexuality and Christian Faith in South Africa* (Cape Town: David Philip, 1997).

Susan Griffin, *Made from This Earth: An Anthology of Writings* (San Francisco: Harper & Row, 1982).

Beverly Wildung Harrison, "Feminist Thea(o)logies at the Millennium: 'Messy' Continued Resistance or Surrender to Post-Modern Academic Culture?," in Farley and Jones, *Liberating Eschatology.*

Janet R. Jakobsen, *Working Alliances and the Politics of Difference* (Bloomington: Indiana University Press, 1998).

Marié Henry Keane, "Women in the Theological Anthropology of the Early Fathers," *Journal of Theology for Southern Africa* 62 (1988).

Mary Midgley, *Philosophy and the 'Body'* (Oxford: Oxford University Press, 1997).

Jürgen Moltmann's 1994 address referred to is published in *Theology and the Future of the Modern World* (Pittsburgh: ATS, 1995).

Friedrich Nietzsche, *Beyond Good and Evil,* trans. M. Cowan (Chicago: Gateway, 1955).

Friedrich Nietzsche, *The Will to Power,* trans. W. Kaufmann and R. J. Hollingdale (New York: Random House, 1967).

Albert Nolan, *Jesus before Christianity* (Maryknoll, N.Y.: Orbis Books, 1993).

Mercy Amba Oduyoye, *Daughters of Anowa: African Women and Patriarchy* (Maryknoll, N.Y.: Orbis Books, 1995).

Karl Rahner, *The Shape of the Church to Come,* trans. E. Quinn (New York: Seabury Press, 1974).

Rosemary Radford Ruether, *Sexism and God-Talk* (Boston: Beacon Press, 1983).

Letty Russell, *Human Liberation in a Feminist Perspective — A Theology* (Philadelphia: Westminster, 1974).

Letty Russell, *Household of Freedom: Authority in Feminist Theology* (Philadelphia: Westminster, 1987).

Edward Schillebeeckx, *Church: The Human Story of God,* trans. J. Bowden (New York: Crossroad, 1990).

Dorothee Sölle, *Thinking about God: An Introduction to Theology* (Valley Forge, Pa.: Trinity Press, 1990).

Angela West, *Deadly Innocence: Feminist Theology and the Mythology of Sin* (New York: Cassell, 1995).

CHAPTER 3

To Elfriede

on Locusts and Bodies

Tell your children of it,
and let your children tell their children,
and their children another generation.

What the cutting locust left,
the swarming locust has eaten.
What the swarming locust left,
the hopping locust has eaten,
and what the hopping locust left,
the destroying locust has eaten.

JOEL 1:3-4

Dear Elf,

Years ago we drove through the semidesert of the Karoo on a hot summer's day and came upon swarms of locusts. I remember the darkened sky, the clicking noise of their wings, and the swirling brown patterns of their flight. We stopped the car and waited for them to move away. When they did, they left the small grey bushes of the Karoo stripped of their leaves. It was an eerie sight. With my own eyes I saw what the prophet Joel described; the cutting, swarming, hopping, and destroying locusts had eaten all that lay in their path. A month later on our way home from the sea, we drove through the same area in the middle of a rainstorm. There were pools of water along the roadside, coots on the farm dams. The air smelled of wet earth. As we slowed down to cross over a cattle grid, I saw a ewe suckling her late summer lamb, her back turned to the driving rain as she nibbled a grey bush. The *veld* was recovering.

You and I have lived through the locust years of apartheid. Now we are grandmothers with creaking joints, well into the last cycles of our lives. We are both hybrids, half Afrikaners, speaking both languages and all that means. For thirty-five years we have shared joy and sorrow. We know what keeps us going. Do you remember our bible study years, how we argued, often agreed, and had a lot of fun? You have been such good company along the way. Now we live in changing times, when old habits are hard to break and hope is still fragile. As I write to you, poverty and unemployment are increasing, education and health care services are buckling under the strain of trying to meet the needs of our people, more corruption is being unearthed, and beneath all, the terrible spectre of HIV/AIDS silently stalks the lives of millions. In the midst of these realities, war is being waged against the bodies of women and children. Between us we have seven daughters and nine granddaughters. We know what it is to fear for them as females.

I have been sketching an imaginary landscape on which I mark what has been harmful and what has been healing over the decades we have shared. The locust years honed us and made us aware of how prone we are to self-deception. We were forced to acknowledge our share in their swarming destruction. We saw how rotten a state could be as we clung to our hopes. We are left with the stuff of a lifetime on our hands. Yet we cannot breathe easily and move on. New swarms of locusts are hovering over the land. The "bleak immensity" of AIDS is our new calamitous reality. The new growth of the *veld* on my landscape is pitted with open graves and ailing, abandoned bodies. Bodies become my theme. That's why I am writing to you. I want to think about how our bodies tell our stories through the locust years and in a present that, in John Chrysostom's words, is being "grazed thin by death."

You and I know that everything starts with our bodies. Feminists say "our bodies, ourselves." What we mean is plain. Human beings do not live disembodied lives. The fact that we can see, hear, touch, smell, and feel is the source of what we know. All reality and all knowledge are mediated through our bodies. Making love, giving birth, dancing, eating, wrestling with depression or arthritic joints — these are not only bodily realities. They shape our experience of ourselves, what we know and what we yearn for. Nietzsche understood this. "Essential: to start from the *body*," he said, "and employ it as a guide. It is the much richer phenomenon, which allows of clearer observation." Not unexpectedly, he continued to say that belief in the body is better established than belief in the spirit. Strange that such a clever thinker falls into the trap of separating body and spirit! But more about that later. We learn in the body. It is not for naught that we speak of "bodies of knowledge" or "the body politic". The power to love begins with our bodies, as much as the power to injure. Sallie McFague, in her book *The Body of God,* points out that we do not *have* bodies, we *are* our bodies, "body and soul." She explains: "whatever we say about that part of ourselves we call brain, mind, or spirit, it evolved from and is continuous with our bodies."

Bodily matters have historically been considered inferior to those of the mind, rather as though our minds were floating somewhere outside our skulls. We failed to see the body as a source of knowledge. Fortunately now, as German feminist theologian Elisabeth Moltmann-Wendel points out, "the body has emerged from the shadow of the head . . . the head, which for centuries was the crown of human beings, is only a part of the person." We now also understand that our bodies are both the private and the political terrain on which the oppressions of race, gender, and class are played out. Our bodies are not prenatural or ahistorical!

Body talk is open to misunderstanding. Take the idea of "body consciousness". This perfectly valid notion is nowadays understood as either a commodity or a joke. The cosmetic industry and all unnecessary plastic surgery turn bodies into commodities on which excessive time and money are devoted to making them leaner, younger looking, and more appealing according to the dictates of current fashion. Girls, more than boys, are taught that their bodies are not their selves, but are rather commodities to be decked out to display consumer products. This has been women's burden for ages. Body talk, as I understand it, is not primarily concerned with what bodies look like. Bodies are who we are, the most powerfully tangible aspect of our shared humanity.

I know that "our bodies, ourselves" can be experienced negatively. You know that too. If the body has been a source of pain, one prefers not to be identified with it. One tends not to trust it. Besides that, we women do not want to be defined solely in terms of our female bodies in such a way that our anatomy is our destiny. I think this is a misunderstanding of "our bodies, ourselves". Our bodies are more than skin, bone, and flesh. Our bodies encompass the totality of our human experience, our thoughts, our emotions, our needs and memories, our ability to imagine and to dream, our experiences of pain, pleasure, power, and difference, as well as our beliefs and our hopes. Our bodies are, in fact, the intricate tracery of all that is ourselves, the good and the bad.

Why am I telling you all this? Over the years you and I have watched our own bodies slowly rust, and we have been apprehensive about what can happen to them. You have had to learn to listen to your body, to hear it in new ways. I have learnt the hard way that I *am* my body. For years I took my body for granted. Tempted to think that I was in control, I ignored pain, pushing my body until it simply refused to match my illusion. As you know, the walls came tumbling down. I am left with what is euphemistically called a "compromised" immune system, soft tissue that screams, aching joints, and at times, a tiredness that warns me not to thwart the signals demanding rest. My body is speaking a new language — one I am having to learn to trust. Bodies are not fools. Bodies react to dangers and neglect. Bodies know when to put up defences and to take the illusion of control out of our hands. Bodies are personal and private, political and public, bone, flesh, blood, and spirit. Bodies are our reality.

As I pore over my landscape, I am conscious of our shared years. Your wisdom and our joint struggles to live the life of faith in our country makes writing this letter to you fitting. I want to make sense of our common story, of how bodies were debased by apartheid and how women's bodies are hurting today as HIV / AIDS claims its victims. It is also more. As white, ageing, "hybrid" women we have, in Joel's words, to "tell your children of it and let your children tell their children" while we still can. What follows is my attempt to "tell it" as I strive to understand our common history and find hope for life.

Isn't it a startling irony to discover that the architects of apartheid understood "our bodies, ourselves" so well? We were all defined by our bodies with sickening precision. White bodies to the right, black bodies to the left. No black bodies on this bench, no black bodies in this bed, no white bodies in shacks, no white bodies collecting their own refuse, no black bodies in this ambulance, no white bodies carrying water and fuel. Our bodies defined our entire existence — our political, social, cultural, and in some cases, religious realities. We were stigmatised, classified, and also privileged by the colour of our bodies. For a time we took all of this for granted. Born into a racist culture and fed by tales of the concentration camps and the defeat of the Boers, our bodies, we were told, had to survive as a minority race in South Africa. So our white bodies, like most, not only survived, but benefited as we basked in the privileges of separateness. Some whites did put their "bodies on the line", opposing apartheid. Imprisonment, torture, and even death followed for some; for others, banning, house arrest, conscientious objection, and for yet others, loss of jobs and alienation from families, friends, and communities. Flashes of memory revive feelings of guilt, anger, powerlessness, and some pride: Molly Blackburn in the townships of Port Elizabeth; Beyers Naudé, a solitary white face at funerals; a firm but defiant Denis Hurley; Sheena Duncan, tenacious and resilient; Black Sash women holding placards; Donald Woods with Steve Biko.

For the vast majority of black people, their bodies were the battlefields over which the armies of locusts moved. Of all the testimonies emerging from the Truth and Reconciliation Commission, one haunts me incessantly. Do you remember the moment when Joyce Mthimkulu held up scraps of her son Siphiwo's hair to show the effects of a poison forced into him by his police interrogators? Crying softly, she said: "I don't want to cry, I know this is my day. If I do cry, it is not due to the pain, but to the hatred. For fourteen years we have (lived) with the pain. The Boers are liars." And later: "I will never forget the Boers." Siphiwo was poisoned with Thallium. He left Livingstone Hospital on 14 April 1982 and was never seen again. Both of us are part "Boer," those whom Joyce Mthimkulu cannot forget. Our whiteness protected our bodies; her son's black body was destroyed and hers left with pain and hatred.

What about women's bodies? For generations our bodies were assigned by patriarchy to traditional places. When we were young, most white women stayed at home minding the hearth, and most black women left their homes to mind ours. The gross stupidity of those times — a so-called Christian state that kept man and wife apart in the interest of white supremacy, that wrenched hundreds of thousands of mothers from their children and took them to prison because they did not have their pass-books on their bodies. The locust years showed us just how vulnerable bodies are to the machinations of political power.

All women's bodies are vulnerable to sexual abuse. I have another indelible memory. "Elsie", a student of mine, dropped out of a university. She was deeply depressed. One day she told me her story. Five young men had gang-raped her in her last year of school. "They shoved me in the car. They put a jacket over my head. They drove around for a long time. They laughed at me. They told me what they were going to do. I wanted to die. They raped me. Many times. . . . My mother took me to the police station. I tried to tell them. The one policeman said: *'Dis maar weer 'n rape'* (It's only another rape). Our minister said it would be better if I said nothing. He did not speak to me again. I'm scared I have AIDS." This story is one small echo in the cacophony of abuse in South Africa. It is an abuse that knows no barriers of race or class, even if the bodies of poor women walking home at night down ill-lit streets are more vulnerable than ours as women of privilege behind our security systems.

These stories do more than anger me. Rage and sadness compete in me. I want to shout: "Stop! — no more of this," while knowing that my protest is futile. Much has been written about the abuses of apartheid and about sexual violence. Telling these stories risks being repetitive. I do not care. We dare not forget these painful memories. Do you think one can "unlearn" memories of abuse? Do you think that Joyce Mthimkulu or "Elsie" can ever forget? I do not think so. Body memories cannot be erased. For the body remembers long and well. A phrase from Michel Foucault sticks in my mind. He talked about "the stigmata of past experiences". Our wounds are our memories. Joyce Mthimkulu's story and the stories of other victims are "embodied" memories. They are stories remembered in the body and they are stories of bodies. Hearing these memories into speech, to paraphrase Nelle Morton's memorable phrase, ruptures the silences of wilful ignorance. Victims now become witnesses for those who disappeared or were killed but live on in their hearts, just as women who have the courage to speak of rape break the years of silence about sexual abuse. More than being witnesses, they become agents for change. History is rewritten as justice is sought.

Memory is complex. It is much more than simple retention. Remembering something entails forgetting something else. We remember what matters to us. Our memories of pain and evil are a vital shield against future wrongs. Forgetting past wrongs only pleases those who have inflicted them. We must remember in order to redeem. Otherwise there will be no justice. But here's another thought about memory. If the past is always with us, its wounds remain present wounds. Is it possible to undo these past wounds so as to heal our wounded selves? If healing and redemption of the past are what we want, is Miroslav Volf right when he argues that "only those who are willing ultimately to forget will be able to remember rightly"? I suspect that the right kind of forgetting is possible when the lens of faith turns our gaze to God's intent to heal us. The ultimate hope according to Volf is that we will progress through mourning, injury, loss, and suffering to "non-remembering" in God's arms. The promise is that all things will be made new, every tear will be wiped away, "mourning and crying and pain will be no more, for the first things have passed away" (Rev. 21:4). I have no idea whether this means that we will one day be "perfectly forgetful". I do know that the power of memory must not be denied. Volf says: "Erase memory and you wash away the blood from the perpetrator's hands. . . ". Christians have compelling reasons for honouring memory. After all, when we celebrate communion we do so "in remembrance of me." We remember Jesus Christ crucified. There is, as Volf reminds us, no Christian faith without *that* memory. We just need to bear in mind that memory can be redeemed.

Often, on listening to the testimonies of victims given before the Truth and Reconciliation Commission, I was confounded by the matter-of-fact way in which experiences of unspeakable pain were articulated. Then I understood that, unlike grief, intense physical pain is difficult, even impossible, to describe. As Elaine Scarry points out in her fine study *The Body in Pain*, physical pain "does not simply resist language, but actively destroys it, bringing about an immediate reversion to a state anterior to language, to the sounds and cries a human being makes before language is learned." Such a place has no vocabulary. Torture, she writes, aspires to the totality of pain spilling over the entirety of the victim. Those "Boers" knew that the victim's pain became the perpetrator's power. I ask myself, "How could they?" Were they psychopaths, were they insane, were they products of brutalising childhoods? Such questions have a familiar ring. They have been asked countless times. They also relegate the perpetrators to the sphere of the abnormal, an answer that is too easy. There is a more intractable question: How could seemingly ordinary South African men have done such monstrous things to fellow South Africans? Does the answer lie in human beings' propensity for depravity, particularly in circumstances where reprehensible ideologies create fertile soil on which human iniquity can flourish? Or is this answer another diversion, a trick to blame it on "the system"? Yes, the apartheid system was iniquitous. It gave power as malign dominance into the hands of a minority and justified doing so in the interests of everything from Christian values to resistance to communism.

Perhaps these torturers saw themselves as spearheading the war against the "total onslaught" of atheistic communism on behalf of western Christian values. We watched our sons and sons-in-law drafted into the army as "foot soldiers" for apartheid. We saw how the maintenance of compulsory military service for young white males required ideological indoctrination and justification, an assault on their humanity. Fresh from school, our sons learnt the litany of the "total onslaught" and were sent off to defend us and our borders against the forces of evil. Those that resisted faced harassment, prosecution, imprisonment, and even exile. No doubt Siphiwo's torturers and their like did their service in the army. Did indoctrination coupled with the ideals of Afrikaner nationalism turn them into torturers? In some respects war and torture are alike. Both are intent on inflicting injury. The scale of injury in war is of course vast, while torture is usually inflicted on comparably few people. While torture can never be justified, there is a certain moral ambiguity about war. Soldiers cannot be equated with torturers except when they too torture. No doubt some soldiers did learn to torture in the army. But the explanation for men becoming torturers does not lie simply in the fact that these torturers were once soldiers. No, men torturing defenceless fellow citizens are in a category of their own. It is the horror of personal intimacy associated with torture that is usually lacking in general acts of war.

Willed amorality is ultimately a question of choice. Not all "Boers" were torturers, not all men are rapists, and not all oppressed people resort to violence. Deliberate injury to bodies is a matter for which we have personal moral and ethical responsibility. The utter cynicism of those men who gave Siphiwo Mthimkulu electric shocks and then drank liquor and held a *braai* around him is no different from those German guards at Auschwitz who planted beautiful gardens on the slopes of the crematoria and forced prisoners to play Bach and Mozart while other prisoners were being tortured and killed. The malevolent abuse of power is willed amorality.

What about the five young men who gang-raped "Elsie"? What about fathers and relatives who abuse babies and young children leaving memories of such trauma that the ability to trust is destroyed forever in the lives of these victims, let alone permanently scarring their bodies? What is happening here? I wish I really knew. I can only name it as depravity. It is an evil that feeds on assumptions that children and women's bodies are at the service of men. Ultimately it is about the heinous abuse of power.

According to Scarry, "Power is cautious. It covers itself, it bases itself in another's pain and prevents all recognition that there is 'another' by looped circles that ensure its own solipsism." Such solipsism is not unique to the torturers of apartheid or the rapists. Hannah Arendt, in *Eichmann in Jerusalem,* explains how torturers do not deal with their consciences but, in order to cope with the instinctive pity that human beings normally feel in the presence of physical suffering, force pity away from the victims onto themselves. "So instead of saying: What horrible things I did to people!, the murderers would be able to say: What horrible things I had to watch in the pursuance of my duties, how heavily the task weighed upon my shoulders!" The torturer first inflicts pain, then objectifies it, and then denies the pain, for, as Scarry points out, if the torturer allows "the reality of the other's suffering to enter his own consciousness, [it] would immediately compel him to stop the torture." The victim's pain becomes the torturer's self-blinding power. Arendt continues, "It is not merely that his power makes him blind, nor that his power is accompanied by blindness, nor even that his power requires blindness; it is, instead, quite simply that his blindness, his willed amorality, *is* his power, or a large part of it." The torturer's ability to distance himself from the bodies of those being tortured leads to the destruction of the tortured body. This distancing mechanism probably has its origins in the torturer being inured to his own body. His lack of feeling for other (non) bodies comes from his own body being a disconnected body, a solipsistic body. No wonder death usually follows torture.

Scarry has helped me peer into this heart of darkness. Does all this help you? I am obsessed with trying to understand. I need to let it rest. You and I are people of the locust years. They have defined our stories. Had we lived in other times in other places, I would probably not be writing to you about bodies and power in this way. By now it is clear that power is at the centre of the story about bodies. Marking bodies on my landscape of faith is simple, but power defies easy illustration and shows up the limits of my sketching. However, let me try.

Mention the word "power" and people experience a kaleidoscope of images of varying kinds and intensity. I suspect that initially most people conjure up pictures that evoke negative feelings. I see Russian tanks sweeping into Budapest, Casspirs in townships, mob violence, multinational juggernauts, a raised arm. I also have other images of power. Waves crashing against a cliff, volcanoes spewing rock and lava, a lion bringing down a zebra, and then the power of a humorous or kind remark, the love of a small child, enduring friendships. What are your images? I have touched on power over bodies as well as the power in bodies. Is there simply just good power and bad power, power-over and power-to? I don't think so.

Power is actually a neutral word. Power is simply the ability to accomplish the ends I desire. It is qualified only through the way it is used. The power to control or eliminate disease is good. Power that seeks to control and dominate our bodies or our inner lives is bad and is rightly to be feared. As parents we made decisions for our children, exercising power over them. Such power is not necessarily bad power. The tendency to link power to gender is questionable. Apartheid gave us white women power as dominance over black men and women. We are just as capable of exploiting power as men are. Power is the ability to make things happen. Our experience of power, our sense of how it feels, who has it and where it comes from, has everything to do with the way we experience reality. Power does not expect favours; it expects results. Power is a means to action and is experienced in diverse ways, as power-over, power-to, power-for, power-with, as related to knowledge, love, difference, and embodiment. There is power to influence, power to include or exclude, economic, social, political, and religious power. Life is saturated with power. Hannah Arendt says that ". . . power, like action, is boundless; it has no physical limitation in human nature. . . . Its only limitation is the existence of other people." Power is ubiquitous. It cannot be limited to the political, and it is not only external to us human beings. Power is also internal; its attraction is insidious. Unfortunately, the abuse of power is perennial.

Living through the last forty years showed us that power, whether power for life or power for control and dominance, whether vested in bodies or in military, economic, or political structures, whether exercised by men or by women, is simply integral to being human. Clearly, no person or group of people is either totally powerful or completely powerless. Power constantly shifts as circumstances change. Power is present in the very fabric of our lives, and it has both visible and invisible aspects. The power of the most ruthless dictator is not limitless, for even the most downtrodden person always has some measure of power in her or his life.

My ideal of power, true power, is the reciprocal energy that engages us with one another and with God in such a way that power becomes synonymous with the vitality of living fully and freely. So you see, power has many faces. Do you think the past decades have sharpened our ability to distinguish power that is life-giving from power that controls and even destroys? I hope so.

I have said that power is not limited to politics. It will not surprise you that I cannot ignore the particular mix of power and politics in South Africa, so just a further thought on power in relation to naming. Naming can redefine reality. This is something our leaders knew. You were branded a "terrorist" if you opposed apartheid. If you were black you needed "separate development", often in some barren place called a "homeland". The "bureau for civil co-operation" operated death squads. There were the tragicomic contortions. Do you remember when, for a brief time, black people were called "plurals"? Sadly, the naming game continues. The HIV virus is renamed a "syndrome" by South African politicians intent on muddying the waters in the futile debates around this issue, and the recent patently flawed election in Zimbabwe is termed "legitimate" to avoid having either to condemn it or to pronounce it "free and fair". Reality is named in the interests of those with the power to name.

During the Truth and Reconciliation Commission's hearings, some of the victims of apartheid took the power given to them to name their reality. They did so with the authority born of suffering. As testimony followed on testimony, the agony of the victims was laid bare and perpetrators were called to account. There is power in naming your demons.

Naming them means knowing their faces, recalling their power to hurt and to diminish, flushing them out into the open. So the baseness of power as dominance is played out on the body. As Foucault points out: "The body is also directly involved in a political field; power relations have an immediate hold upon it; they invest it, mark it, train it, torture it, force it to carry out tasks, to perform ceremonies, emit signs." Siphiwo's vital, young body was destroyed by men abusing the power given to them by an illegitimate state. "Elsie's" body was abused and denigrated by callous, depraved men.

Abusive power does not have the last word. The tears, the voices, the bodily presence of women and men telling their stories before the Truth and Reconciliation Commission were a power for a new just order. Courageous people did not shrink from bearing their private pain in public by telling about the loss of a child, a spouse, a lover, a friend. The shroud of propaganda so carefully constructed to obscure the past was shredded. We glimpsed the promise of a future where people will no longer be tortured and dispossessed. Body memories become a site of power for life.

A few last thoughts on power. Sally Purvis in her book *The Power of the Cross* makes a useful distinction between four dimensions of power: interpersonal, institutional, cultural, and theological. These dimensions are interrelated. By now you may be wondering: more theory on power? I defend myself by saying that I find her distinctions useful as I sketch the markers on my landscape. I can't mark power *per se,* but I can mark the variety of terrain on which it operates. This helps me to navigate my way between power as dominance and power as life.

It is not difficult to imagine abuses of power in the *interpersonal* sphere. Think of battered women, abused children, or just plain harassment or endless criticism. There is another side to this coin. Benign power, the power of love and life, is also found in the interpersonal dimension of power: the power of love between parent and child, between lovers and friends. Purvis says: "We either love one another into being or we fail to do so." We have a choice. Either diminish ourselves and others through domination and control, or affirm through loving. We see the face of *institutional* power in school, in the state, and in the church, for example. Life without institutions is unthinkable. The problem is that legitimate authority too easily becomes authoritarian. Those who have power in institutions forget that it is given in order to serve those whose lives it touches. Politicians have short memories about who pays their salaries; clergy forget that the church only exists by the grace of the gathered people of faith.

Nowadays we hear and see a great deal about *cultural* power. I have heard gender discrimination, appalling social practices, sexual violence, and "gay bashing" all being justified on cultural grounds. Culture is not an innocent concept. Dominant cultures trample on differences between people. Yet true power in cultures can mean hospitality, open conversations, intriguing valued customs and artistic expressions.

Finally, *theological* power also has two sides. Take women in the academy. The very fact that I can write about issues such as bodies, power, and difference is an exercise in power. I have had the luxury of a job that has enabled me to think about such matters. But I am uneasy. Can I trust my insights given the fact that I have been shortsighted before? Do I recognize the limits of my understanding? When does academic writing become another power ploy? Rowan Williams writes provocatively about theological integrity. He says speech that lacks integrity is speech that conceals its purposes. Concealment is a strategy for the retention of power. "Having integrity, then, is being able to speak in a way which allows answers." Williams suggests that religious and theological integrity is possible as and when our speech or our writing about God "declines the attempt to take God's point of view." If this is so, can theology make claims about the moral universe and about living a moral life? Williams' answer is that theology should show what is involved "in bringing the complexity of the human world to judgment before God; not by seeking to articulate or to complete that judgment." I wonder about theological integrity. Have I desisted from pressures to use the power of the academy to control, and am I really willing to be open, self-critical, and vulnerable in my writing? As I write the word "vulnerable" I know that it is one that some feminist theologians fight shy of. They argue that women cannot afford vulnerability. It has been our lot for too long. While I understand their fear, I have found that I cannot do theology that lets go of vulnerability. Vulnerability is just too deeply part of my faith. But more about that later.

Relating power to God raises intriguing questions. What level of power do we ascribe to God? How do we tackle the nature of God's power as women of faith? What can one say theologically about God's power? These are unnerving questions and they deserve more than my brief answers. To begin with, I do not understand God's power as dominating. I do not find theologies that glorify an imperious, authoritarian God attractive or true. The very hiddenness of God simply does not accord with the picture of a God who dominates creation. Theologically speaking, I see the power of God in the power of life, throbbing in glorious profusion in the midst of suffering and death. I see the power of God in the "foolishness" of the cross. Take the Christian community in Corinth. They knew the power of the Roman Empire only too well. Yet Paul writes to them: "For the message of the cross is foolishness to those who are perishing, but to us who are saved it is the power of God." This is about a different kind of power. "Has God not made foolish the wisdom of the world? For since in the wisdom of God, the world did not know God through wisdom, God decided through the foolishness of our proclamation, to save those who believe," Paul explains. Instead of direct confrontation with the military and political power of the Roman Empire, there is a man on a cross — the very opposite of dominant power. Everything is inverted — no dominance, no control, only defeat and death. To find power for life in the cross seems foolish. Yet the power of the cross is the resurrection. That is why Paul can say: "For God's foolishness is wiser than human wisdom, and God's weakness is stronger than human strength" (1 Cor. 1:18-25).

As locust survivors we have experienced power in different guises. Sometimes naked and obvious, at other times hidden and shifting, power is the hardest thing to depict on my landscape of faith. The victims of abusive power are clearly seen. The destructive power of swarms of locusts is also not difficult to mark. It is more difficult to pinpoint the pervasive presence of power that seeks to control how we think, behave, and relate to one another, just as difficult as it is to mark the power of Joyce Mthimkulu's words, the power to survive the destructiveness of others' inhumanity and the power of ordinary people to change their lives. So, on my landscape of faith, I make power that is life-giving purple, and power that destroys the colour of old blood.

Pages ago I was critical of Nietzsche's separation of body and spirit. I react instinctively to this kind of thinking because the well-known split between body and soul (or mind) lies at the heart of a distorted view of women's nature and has had pernicious consequences for women. Dualism is the belief that there are two distinct mutually exclusive parts to the human being: mind and body, each living within its own separate sphere. Western philosophy has a long history of separating the mind from the body. This thinking crept into early Christianity. Later, it was further entrenched and complicated by Descartes who, with his well-known dictum "I think therefore I am," coupled the mind-body split to the foundation of knowledge itself. It is almost as though the mind exists outside the body on some free-floating pedestal! The catch for women lies in the fact that for ages we have been identified only with the body, that is, with the less rational and the more physical, earthy, and emotional qualities. In contrast, men are seen as the active possessors of reason and of spiritual and cultural values that make them fit for leadership in all spheres. In other words, men are by nature the possessors of "superior" characteristics that equip them for leadership in the human community. As power and gender difference form an unholy alliance, men's power to dominate women is made legitimate.

To a feminist theologian the splitting of our bodies from our spirits, minds, or emotions simply does not make sense. I don't know where the spirit resides other than in my body. What happens in my belly is not unconnected to my brain. I am not advocating that one collapse different aspects of the human person into an amorphous jelly, or saying that my longing to be held is exactly the same as my ability to explain an isosceles triangle. What I do reject is a hierarchy that gives more importance and therefore more power to certain qualities of being human over others, and does so in terms of gender. Although dualism is less fashionable these days, it is still a tenacious barnacle on the thinking of the Christian church, and it is not easy to dislodge.

All theological reflection starts with the body. To think that theology is an activity separate from the concreteness of the human body and concerned solely with some abstract realm of the spirit is nonsensical. Sadly, traditional Christian theology has either ignored, denied, or denigrated the human body. Etty Hillesum in *An Interrupted Life* comments wryly: "It is difficult to be on equally good terms with God and your body." For centuries, denial of the body by means of ascetic practices was held up as a holy grail to the truly faithful. When mediaeval Christians thought about evil, they cottoned on to the "flesh" and more particularly to the "fallen flesh." Sadly, shame in regard to the "lowly nature of the body" has permeated Christian thought.

It is ironic that the Christian tradition which has been so wary of the body is in fact a faith that is incarnational. The Christian belief that "the Word became flesh and lived among us" is a statement of faith that God became "embodied" as one of us. John writes, "What we have seen with our eyes, what we have looked at and touched with our hands . . . we declare to you" (1 John 1:1-3). Incarnation is about meeting God in the body. Isn't this a scandalous claim? It is shocking yet unique to believe that in the person of Jesus, God came bodily into this world. It is also a powerful claim. As you know, it is one I struggled with for years: Jesus, a human person born in a stable (an image of poverty), who dies on a cross (a symbol of criminality), is God in the world? The person who is depicted in the gospel stories as having outbursts of anger, who groans, sighs, and weeps, who sleeps, eats, prays; a vital, compassionate human being with a vision, yet one who knows doubt and despair, is God in the world? Powerful and preposterous! And there is more. According to the gospel accounts, the man Jesus healed people, exorcised those who were possessed, stilled raging storms, walked on water, raised the dead, fed the thousands, and, most incredible of all, was resurrected three days after being crucified. "Touch me and see; for a ghost does not have flesh and bones as you see I have," says Jesus Christ (Luke 24:39). These stories are rejected by many who find them unbelievable. I did too. Now I know that a resurrected person with a body like ours is God in this world. I also know that despite this deeply held incarnational belief, Christians still struggle to meet God in the body. This is why when Paul says ". . . your body is a temple of the Holy Spirit. . . . Glorify God in your body" (1 Cor. 6:19-20), it unsettles us.

The Christian idea of salvation has no meaning outside the well-being of the body. Salvation is concerned with the whole person. So when we speak of the Word who became flesh, we are hungering for healing, wholeness, and life eternal. It is the very tangible bodily quality of the Jesus story that draws us into "the Word made flesh". Understanding and the body come together in faith. That is what it means to "live and move and have our being in God." God is closer to us than we are to ourselves, to *all* ourselves, said Augustine. Our bodily experience is the fundamental realm of the experience of God. So, as the Word became flesh, the church of the Word becomes the Body of Christ. We Christians can be properly fleshy!

There are many different ways of describing the church. I opt for the church as the Body of Christ. I like this description's organic feel. I enjoy the fact that as members of the one Body we are *all* indispensable for its proper functioning. It makes us all equally valuable for God's purposes. There is only one warning — that we use our gifts for the good of the Body in a loving way. When we do so the reward is greater knowledge of God and greater communion with one another. In the Body of Christ I see something of how God is at work in the world. Despite our dawdling, our sloth, and our truancy, we are here to be God's hands in making things new. This requires being in tune with one another. Here lies the rub. Intuitively, we know that being in communion with one another is not cosy or straightforward. There is a further caution. "If one member suffers, all suffer together; if one member is honoured, all rejoice together" (1 Cor. 12:26). We want to avoid the suffering bit. Today there is no escape. The Body of Christ is riddled with a new and virulent disease. We are the church with AIDS.

The statistics are a nightmare. They smack of the apocalyptic. Over thirty-six million people are infected worldwide. Forty percent of South Africans who died in 2000 died of AIDS-related diseases. Ten million South Africans will have succumbed to AIDS by 2010, and we will have over two million orphans to care for. Five thousand infected babies are born every month. One in every nine South Africans is living with HIV. These bare facts paint a picture of a situation beyond repair. They banish hope. Can it be so hideous, so implacable? But when one of my favourite science writers, Stephen Jay Gould, declares that the AIDS pandemic may rank with nuclear weaponry "as the greatest danger of our era" and that it may kill as much as a quarter of the human race, I have to settle for the apocalyptic. Before me are images of twelve-year-olds trying to keep younger siblings alive because both parents are dead, large-eyed babies filling hospital wards, women abandoned, even killed, by their partners, bodies piling up as undertakers grow rich and clergy struggle to find words at incessant funerals, the youth defiant and fearful as a deadly swathe is being cut across our people, killing those in their most productive years. On my landscape, the Body of Christ is grievously ill. The crosses I have dotted all over my sketch turn the colour of khaki as infection seeps into the Body. As the Body musters its defences to fight off the invading affliction, touches of luminous blue appear on the edges of the khaki. What might this mean?

I see these touches of blue as modest but significant clues on how the Body of Christ can act to encourage hope rather than despair. Life without hope is numb, unadulterated fatalism or unmitigated gloom as we anticipate that what we hope for will never be fulfilled. Neither despair nor fatalism is a companion to the life of faith. Søren Kierkegaard said that hope is a "passion for the possible". I remember philosopher Johan Degenaar, years ago, defining hope as "creative expectation". Both understandings imply that we have to be actively and passionately involved in trying to bring about that for which we hope. This implies hands-on "doing". Hope is not an armchair activity. Hope has very little currency if it is just a "pie in the sky when we die by and by", a trick masquerading as optimism covered with a religious veneer. True Christian hope is tougher, more realistic; it is essential to the life of faith and actively involved in life. Yet it often seems as though hope has "emigrated from the church". Perhaps this is so because it is too often understood as referring only to the future. Or perhaps it is seen as simply unrealistic. Undoubtedly the present and the future, our experience and our hope, seem to stand in contradiction to one another. There is always conflict between hope and experience. Paul recognises this when he writes, "For in hope we were saved. Now hope that is seen is not hope. For who hopes for what is seen? But if we hope for what we do not see, we wait for it with patience" (Rom. 8:24, 25). For Paul, hope is enigmatic and requires the ability to wait patiently while never letting go of what we hope for.

I mentioned that Christian hope is tough. Hoping against hope is not easy. No theologian in recent times has had a greater impact on Christian thinking about hope than Jürgen Moltmann. According to him, Christian hope quite simply means that there will be a new creation of all things. This is not a narrow hope — one that offers comfort to Christians and lets the rest of humanity take care of themselves. It is hope for *all* of creation, for Israel, for the peoples of the world, for this earth and all that is in it. That is what the bible means when it says, "See, I am making all things new" (Rev. 21:5). Nothing can ever be very good for some unless there is the promise that all things will be made new for everyone. My good is contingent on yours and *vice versa*. Hope is for all. It is a passion for the possible in every possible sense. But no matter how wide or how profound our hope, it still remains contradictory. Calvin understood the conflicting nature of Christian hope when he wrote:

To us is given the promise of eternal life — but to us, the dead. A blessed resurrection is proclaimed to us — meantime we are surrounded by decay. We are called righteous — and yet sin lives in us. We hear of ineffable blessedness — but meantime we are here oppressed by infinite misery. We are promised abundance of all good things — yet we are rich only in hunger and thirst.

Then Calvin asks: But what would become of us if we did not take our stand on hope? Indeed! It is in these contradictions and conflicts, comments Moltmann, that hope must prove its power. We hope even when it seems foolish to do so because we dare not abandon hope. Quite simply, life without hope is a wasteland of non-fulfilment. Faith promises a different reality because hope is the inseparable companion of faith. Faith is the foundation on which it rests. We hope because we have the expectation of those things that have been promised by God. Once again hope is linked to Christ. Fundamentally "Christian hope is resurrection hope," writes Moltmann. Yes. Our hope is centred on the promise of the resurrection. Without knowledge of what Christ means and has done, hope is truly just an airy fairy utopia. To believe that Christ was raised from the dead is not just a consoling thought about how God has triumphed over humiliation, suffering, and death. It is in fact a contradiction of suffering and death, a divine protest *against* suffering. And it does not only deal with the future. Hope is sterile if it does not transform our thoughts and our actions here and now. Hope opens a future outlook that embraces all of life, everything we do and know, and that includes sickness and death.

So disaster, disease, and death do not have the last word. Despite death and dying challenging our language of hope, Moltmann can say "in the end is the beginning." When Dietrich Bonhoeffer took leave of a fellow prisoner in the Flossenbürg concentration camp, he said: "This is the end for me — for me the beginning of life." T. S. Eliot echoes this in his poem "Little Gidding":

What we call the beginning is often the end
And to make an end is to make a beginning.
The end is where we start from.

These expressions affirm that the locusts will not have the final victory. Despite their destruction, God promises hope: "I will repay you for the years that the swarming locust has eaten." And later, "You shall eat plenty and be satisfied." And still later, "I will pour out my spirit on all flesh" (Joel 2:25, 26, 28).

Our present reality is the devastation of HIV/AIDS. If hope offers us a new way of thinking about our experiences and the imperative to act upon our hopes, what is there for the Body of Christ to do in the present crisis? How can hope be nurtured in the shadows of graveyards all over our landscape?

A good place to start is with the truth. The nature of the HIV/AIDS crisis has to be understood without prevarication, obfuscation, or qualification. It is our virus, it is in our Body, and we must know all we can about what it means to live with and alongside it. Hope cannot take root in unreality or untruths. However, there is more to this pandemic than facts about a virus. Teresa Okure, an African theologian, startled her hearers at a theological symposium on AIDS held in Pretoria in 1998, by saying that there are two other viruses more dangerous than the HIV virus because they are carriers enabling this virus to spread so rapidly.

The first virus is the one that makes people regard women as inferior to men. This is the virus that causes men to abuse women. It is the virus that is responsible for the shocking fact that in many countries in Africa the condition that carries the highest risk of HIV infection is that of being a married woman, says Okure. Now, there is a decisive link between traditional Christian views of the body and the present crisis. When the dominant religious tradition in our country (bolstered by cultures that are male centred) has a long and sad history of treating women as second-class citizens, we cannot be surprised that women are victims in a particular way in this pandemic. HIV/AIDS thrives on disordered gender relations. I know that the virus is no respecter of class, race, or gender, but it does have its greatest impact on the most vulnerable members of our society: poor women and children. If you have little or no education and live in a patriarchal relationship, you have little or no power to negotiate what happens to your body. Once infected, you run the risk of being beaten, thrown out, or even killed, ironically by partners who themselves are the cause of your infection. This is happening daily. So dis-empowered women therefore choose the path of concealment. Your children have to eat and you need a roof over your heads. You end up dying quietly, often before your children, who then join the growing bands of orphans. If, instead of a long history of discrimination against women, the Body of Christ were to treat women and men equally, recognising women's gifts and our calling, according us dignity and justice, it would not be party to bolstering male-dominated structures and relationships that presently constitute death traps.

According to Okure, the second virus that enables HIV/AIDS to spread at devastating speed is found mostly in the developed world. It is the virus of global economic injustice that causes terrible poverty in many parts of the developing world. Capitalist market economies are thrust on societies that are not geared for them and structural adjustment programmes imposed that are designed to meet the requirements of the developed world rather than those whose need is the greatest. *Of course the HIV virus causes AIDS.* But it does not act in a vacuum. That is another truth to be told. HIV/AIDS is a pandemic that thrives in situations of poverty, unemployment, and the uprooting of people. It is no coincidence that HIV/AIDS is at the moment prevalent in the poorer southern half of the world. Imagine the struggles of millions of people who have no access to clean water, basic health care, primary education, nutrition, or sanitation, all of which grievously affect their physical well-being and make them vulnerable to disease. Life is simply about survival. To those who live in the relative "safety" of the developed world there is also no escape. In time, the effects of this virus will emigrate. Nothing so grave is regional, local, or limited. A problem of this magnitude is destined to become global.

I want to add a third virus to Okure's list — the virus of denial. I have no trouble understanding people who, suspecting that they may be infected with HIV, refuse to be tested because the prospect of disease and death is simply too overwhelming. Sadly, this kind of denial does not help to change patterns of behaviour, and the virus's progress becomes more rampant. Neither do I blame people who are HIV positive for remaining silent about their status. Who wants to add the burden of stigma to an already fraught situation? Can we forget Gugu Dlamini, who was stoned to death in 1998 for revealing her status? More pernicious than individual denial is the denial of the South African state that its citizens are trapped in a pandemic. As the world watched in dismay and people died daily, president Thabo Mbeki and his cabinet continued to debate "scientific questions" in regard to HIV/ AIDS, opinions that were greatly informed by dissident views on the subject, while refusing virtually free treatment to pregnant women that would have greatly reduced the number of infected babies born. The government still continues to drag its heels despite the Constitutional Court's order in 2002 to make such treatment available to pregnant women. Documents on HIV/AIDS distributed in the ruling party bear all the hallmarks of scientific twaddle and deeply anti-white, anti-western sentiments that run contrary to the African National Congress's long tradition of non-racialism. One of South Africa's most eminent scientists and president of the Medical Research Council, Professor Malegapuru William Makgoba, recently delivered a stinging rebuke to the South African government.

> When the government is provided with answers — the best scientific opinion in the world that is available — they simply refuse [to accept them] and this behaviour is the *sine qua non* characteristic of a refusenik or denialist. Government has rather enjoyed dabbling with scientifically unproven ideas that it uses as the basis of debate. In order for any government to make a policy decision it is duty bound to seek the expertise of the professionals . . . so that they can make informed decisions in the best interests of the public. Whenever they have been given this kind of information they have simply refused it.

There is another way. Speak the truth, lend both hands to those who suffer, and draw on the rich resources of the Christian tradition for courage and guidance. Take the creeds. Week after week we Christians piously repeat them. We claim that we are "one, holy, catholic, and apostolic" church. But what does this actually mean in the midst of this HIV/AIDS crisis? If we are truly *one,* we are the church with HIV/AIDS. People living with HIV/AIDS are found in every sector of society and every church denomination. We are all related; what affects one member of the Body of Christ affects us all. We are all living with HIV/AIDS. There are no "us" and "them." We dare not forget that inclusion, not exclusion, is the way of grace. If we are *holy,* we are not living some superhuman mode of existence. Marjorie Suchocki writes about the marks of the church and says that "Holiness does not require a transcendence of our human condition, but a full utilization of our condition toward the concrete reality of love." Holiness is not withdrawal from the smell of crisis, but engagement, often risky, in situations where God is present. If we are *catholic,* we are in solidarity because we are connected, in communion, with those who are suffering and who experience fear of rejection, poverty, and death. If we are *apostolic,* we stand in continuity with the church in its infancy and we strive to live, as Ignatius of Antioch put it, "in the manner of the apostles." This means that we are true to the heart of our teaching, that we are zealous for the Word, and that we continuously examine the ideals of the early church and measure ourselves against them. This is nothing new. It is simply a call to put the words of the creed into practice.

Having told the truth and said it "as it is" takes me to my next thought on where we can find clues for hope. I believe we should make space in the Body of Christ for storytelling. We really can't survive without stories. When people who live with the virus tell their stories, they name and claim their identities. Instead of others labelling you or speaking on your behalf, you name *your* experience of *your* reality. Telling our stories also helps us to make sense of what is happening. I cannot begin to imagine what the last thirty years would have been like if we had not been able to tell our stories to one another, over and over again! Retelling what has happened has shown that I only begin to make sense once I hear my own voice.

I have heard stories that speak of triumph, of resistance, and of hope. Imagine a kaleidoscope with thousands of different-coloured fragments. As it moves, it forms patterns. The myriads of stories of suffering and joy make up the big story of AIDS, in which each fragment is unique. My life has been changed by knowing the stories of people living with the HIV virus. Hearing and telling stories challenges stigmas and prejudices. The question of a stigma is particularly relevant to persons suffering from HIV/AIDS. Once you are infected, you simply become "an HIV positive", a statistic whose identity is now defined by your status. Stigmas can paralyse us. They deny the active, meaningful, and contributing lives of many HIV-positive people. Through telling and hearing stories, we discover connections and then, hopefully, we begin to care in new ways because the shared story of our faith is our sounding board. It shows not only Jesus' care and concern for the suffering but confronts us with a person whose life makes sense and gives hope even when he suffers death on a cross.

My third thought is about ethics and morals. Today we hear a great deal of talk, and very necessary talk, about abstinence, prevention, and medication in the face of the present crisis. The Catholics say abstinence is the only answer. The Anglicans say yes, but use condoms if you must. Where is the debate that begins by recognising that the Body of Christ is a community of sexual human beings and then goes on to think about what a moral community of sexual beings would look like? All this talk of fidelity and abstinence in sexual relations is not heard or understood unless it is part of the larger debate on what makes a moral community.

What does a moral community look like? Heaven? Partly, yes. Anne Lamott says that heaven is like having new glasses. Thinking ethically is like trying on new glasses to see in new ways, often from what William Schweiker calls the "human edge of thinking". I have a mental picture of balancing on that edge with a few handholds to keep me steady as I try to think about moral issues. The first handhold that steadies me is the Christian tradition's teaching that people have inviolable worth. No action is morally justifiable if it denies or diminishes the inherent worth of a person. The second is that moral thinking aims to make this world a better place. Moral community is fostered when everyone's actions are for the common good. Responsibility and grace go hand in hand — we do our bit and trust that God will fill in the gaps. A third handhold is simply the reality that we live in a world of great diversity, that we have different social roles, different religions and cultures. Moral thinking for the common good is alive to the fact that the common good is the good of *all* human beings in *all* our diversity. A moral community is not discriminating or exclusive; it respects the dignity of all people. It is hospitable and shares its resources.

The difficult part is how we get there. Gripping onto my handholds, I ask myself: What would Jesus do in these circumstances? He would certainly take the side of those on the margins of the community, those who are sick, displaced, and alienated. His concern for us in the midst of the most serious crisis for humanity in modern times would not end with the tip of a condom. He would, I imagine, teach about relationships that are caring and responsible, committed and sustaining. And then, within this loving community with its eyes clearly on the values that make for human wholeness, he might talk about our sexuality and how we use it. The nature of the person who is at the heart of our faith holds out the possibility of the moral life. The deceptively short answer to the question of what we ought to do is simply to love more and to pursue justice unendingly. Loving more is a tall order — no more prejudices, no stereotyping, no judging, no mean-spiritedness. Justice for all means challenging the excesses of greed for power and possessions that exploit the poor and deny them the means to live with dignity and hope. I know with a sinking feeling that this means examining my own lifestyle daily to see how it accords with my beliefs. Small wonder we recoil instinctively from such demands.

Sadly, I have seen members of the Body of Christ tempted to stand aloof from this shattering crisis because they are "moral" while those who are infected are paying the price for being "immoral." I am reminded of a story told by Bruce Birch and Larry Rasmussen in their book *Bible and Ethics in the Christian Life,* about Dom Helder Camara meditating in the middle hours of the night on the attitudes of the rich towards the poor and then writing the following poem:

> I pray incessantly
> for the conversion
> of the prodigal son's brother.
> Ever in my ear
> rings the dread warning
> "this one [the prodigal] has awoken
> from his life of sin."
> When will the other [the brother]
> awaken
> from his virtue?

As I go on searching for clues on where to find hope, I come up against the question: What can I say to a member of the Body of Christ who is dying of AIDS when many Christians believe that death is a punishment for sin? Where is hope in the midst of disease and death? I want to begin by saying: "God is a lover of life." Death is not a punishment for sin. Yes, death can be caused by sin. We kill one another. We are destroying our environment. But death is not God's ultimate judgment on us. That's how I want to start the conversation. I continue to believe that God loves life so much that it continues into eternity. I cling to the promise of the resurrection of the body. Not that I know what this really means. Talk about the resurrection of the body is, not surprisingly, camouflaged in conjecture. I cannot know or understand the details except that resurrection talk is clearly body talk. But I can hope. Why? Because God has made the dead live. I don't only mean the biblical characters like Lazarus or Talitha. I believe that in the unique power of Jesus' death and resurrection there is life in eternity for us. I don't see death as the end, or resurrection only as "life after death". Life, death, and resurrection all belong together. They make up the whole of life. When John writes "We know that we have passed out of death into life, because we love the brothers and sisters" (1 John 3:14), he means that love is passionate about life, that we must say a hearty "Yes" to life, life that ends in death. Resurrection does not mean a deferred life — something we put off until after we die. In Moltmann's words, "I shall live *wholly* here, and die *wholly,* and rise *wholly* there." It is all a package. Eternal life is all of me, all of everyone, all of creation, all healed, reconciled, and completed. Nothing will be lost.

Another question keeps popping up, probably because of the unfortunate tendency among some Christians to see AIDS as a punishment for sin. Susan Sontag in her interesting book *AIDS and Its Metaphors* says that "Plagues are invariably regarded as judgments on society. . . ." We are very quick to link any sexually transmitted disease with sin as if there are no innocent victims. This has happened for ages. Christian thinkers like Paul, the old church fathers, and Augustine saw death as punishment for "the wages of sin." James (1:15) writes that "sin brings forth death". I wonder whether the fear that this language breeds does the trick? Despite those terrifying mediaeval pictures of judgment that drove women and men to seek comfort and salvation in the arms of the church, people do not seem to have stopped sinning because of a fear of death. Fear just seeps into places where we did not previously know it. Fear of sexuality, fear of bodily fluids, fear of the communion cup, or as Susan Sontag comments, "fear of contaminated blood, whether Christ's or your neighbor's." Not surprisingly, Nietzsche commented acerbically on what he called the "holy lie" — the invention of a God who punishes and rewards by holding out the afterlife as some sort of "great punishment machine".

To be fair, not all Christian traditions see death as a judgment on sin. Some hold that death is simply the natural end to our finite lives. And so we find ourselves on a theological merry-go-round. Angels are deemed immortal but according to Peter (2 Pet. 2:4), they sinned! Animals, birds, fish, and the trees don't sin, yet they die. Through human beings death has been brought into nonhuman creation. We know that death has been with us from the beginning. God's first commandment to human beings was "be fruitful and multiply." We were mortal right from the start. Death is certainly not a punishment for contracting AIDS. Imagine God punishing defenceless, infected women and children with death! Yet death can certainly be a result of sin. We are a very violent species. The body is implicated in the process of sin. The very context in which we live is affected by sin. Innocents suffer. Everything that is "born" must die. It is part of our condition. The only way to get off the theological merry-go-round is to accept that our responsibility is to live and to die in loving solidarity with that sighing and groaning community of creatures described by Paul as waiting for "the redemption of our bodies" (Rom. 8:23). We all await what Letty Russell calls "the mending of creation" and hope in the face of death for what she describes as "thinking from the other end", looking at life with all its injustice, suffering, and death from the perspective of God's new creation.

So, like Moltmann, I would say to the person dying of AIDS, "You are not going to be annihilated, death is not your end. Every life remains before God forever." In case you think I am looking at death through rose-tinted glasses, let me say that I think the more we love, the more death can be frightening and mysterious. I have and I will experience the death of those I love with profound grief and mourning. What about the babies and the children dying of AIDS, the young people cut off before they have had time to live and grow? I know that all our lives are unfinished, but there is something really awful about the death of the young. After all, we were promised life. If I am so sure that I will be truly myself, transformed and made whole, but still me, after death, what does this mean for the young who have not had the chance to "become"? I really don't know. It worries me. It would be comforting to think that the Spirit of eternal life will make a special space for those whose earthly lives have been cut short. Whatever there is, I can only trust in God's love and faithfulness. I haven't any smart answers.

In the face of suffering and death, I dare not forget to pray "May your reign come on earth as it is in heaven, sooner rather than later." As pictures of emaciated sick children, weary old people, poisoned rivers, and war-weary landscapes crowd out hope, this is the only prayer I know. But I know that having faith means having to persist: "Your reign will come. Come Lord Jesus, come." I hang on to the hope that one day I will hear my name together with the countless names of all of creation being called to a place where peace reigns, where love and justice hold hands forever. God's reign as revealed in Jesus' life and ministry — and which we anticipate coming in its fullness, sooner rather than later — is the power of the future pressing in on the present. This gives me hope — the "already, not yet" taste of God's reign is pregnant with wild, unpredictable, yet sustaining hope.

HIV/AIDS is our kairos; it is a time when the ordinary rhythm of life is suspended. It is make-or-break time for those of us who have faith. Will it be a time of doom and no hope, or will we find a new unveiling of God's presence and love for us here and now?

My last thought is about holy communion. Hope, bodies, life, and death all come together in our celebration of the Supper or what I am used to calling the Eucharist. How does a sip of wine and a piece of bread relate to the themes in this letter? Let me begin with why I find comfort in the Eucharist. Most if not all Christians agree that the Eucharist is extraordinarily significant for the vitality and renewal of the church. It is the "source and summit of the Christian life", writes Michael Welker, a symbolic meal at which the gathered community celebrate what Jesus Christ has done for us. Yet its origins do not lie in success or triumph but in human betrayal. The Eucharist was instituted on the night that Jesus Christ was betrayed and handed over to "the powers of this world". Our successes do not take us to the table. This I find comforting and full of hope.

The Body of Christ has AIDS. Thankfully, we do not have to have a disease-free body to come to the table. The Eucharist is the bodily practise of grace. The bodies of those who are sick, who suffer and even despair, partake bodily of the feast. Together we eat the bread and drink the wine and give thanks for the gifts of creation. Bodies are absolutely central to the Eucharist, our bodies and the body of Christ. Participating in this rite unites our bodies in a mysteriously wonderful way. "The bread that we break, is it not a sharing in the body of Christ? Because there is one bread, we who are many are one body, for we all partake of the one bread" (1 Cor. 10:16, 17). I don't need to get into theological knots trying to understand the strange but wonderful oneness of bread and body. I simply have to eat the bread and drink from the cup. "The Supper," writes Welker, "centers on a complex, sensuous process in which the risen and exalted Christ becomes present. The Supper gives Christians a form in which they can perceive the risen and exalted Christ with all their senses." However this perception of Christ is experienced, one thing is clear — differences between sick and healthy bodies disappear as we are all drawn into the one body of the risen Christ. The abused bodies of women and children and the bodies of people living with HIV/AIDS are received together with the bodies of the healthy into the crucified and resurrected body of Jesus Christ whom we remember and celebrate in the Eucharist.

How can I be so sure that there is hope in the Eucharist when the AIDS virus lurks deep inside the Body of Christ? Robert Jenson uses a wonderful phrase when discussing God's incarnation in Christ. "God is *'in, with, and through'* Christ — he is above all, *deep in the flesh* [my italics]. . . ." As deep as the virus is inside the Body, so "God deep in the flesh" is there, hidden but present, no abstract deity but a God who meets us in Jesus Christ. When we eat the bread and drink the wine we are taken into Christ's body, where God deep in the flesh holds out the promise of new life.

Truly the Eucharist is a bodily event that has the power to comfort the afflicted and liberate us all. We forget that it has its origins in the events of the Jewish Passover meal, itself a celebration of freedom from bondage and the promise of a new beginning. The Exodus was a political event, in which bodies were liberated from slavery and oppression. We can't let it lose its political edge, because the Eucharist is about the renewal of the covenant: "This is my blood of the new covenant shed for many" (Mark 14:23). The new covenant promises freedom from poverty, oppression, sickness, and suffering. If we believe that we are truly one body as we partake of the one bread, there is no ducking solidarity with those who suffer.

The Eucharist is *the* sacrament of bodiliness and *the* sacrament of equality at which all participants are accepted unconditionally. Only self-exclusion can keep us away. The Eucharist is also the sacrament of repentance. Much has been made of the text in 1 Corinthians 11:27-29, 31-32 about eating the bread and drinking the wine in an unworthy manner, particularly in the reformed tradition in our country. We are unworthy to eat and drink if we do not discern the Body of Christ in those present, says Paul. It is a pity that the sacrament of reconciliation becomes what Welker calls "an anxiety-producing means of moral gatekeeping", when people set themselves up as arbiters about who is worthy and who is not. Of course we should all meditate on the meaning of the Eucharist. We should not take it frivolously. But isn't it a sad irony that some Christians exclude the "unworthy"? God's unconditional acceptance of us is apparently not good enough!

I must confess that as I take the cup and sip the wine, I "drop" the bodies of those who are in my heart into the reddish liquid with a short plea to

God to touch them with grace. I cannot rest with the possibility that those I love may exclude themselves from the touch of God. I have come to the end of my search for hope. Is this sufficient to tell our children and for them to tell their children? Of course not. As new swarms of locusts invade their worlds after we have gone, I can only trust that they will find cause for hope in their encounters with the Holy One.

I look forward to your thoughts when you have read this letter. You are wiser than I am.

With my love,
Denise

NOTES

Elfriede Bremer, born Rein in 1924, has been my closest friend for thirty-five years, first in Pretoria and now in Cape Town. For decades she ran bible study groups at her home, and together we wrote bible study guides for group study. She has five daughters, fifteen grandchildren, and the kind of wisdom that comes from the willingness to look inside even when it is painful.

Words in this letter that need explanation are: *Karoo,* the vast inland semi-arid plateau lying in the centre of South Africa; *braai,* which means barbecue; and *veld,* which has gained international acceptance as a term describing grassland with scattered shrubs and trees. *Casspirs* were armoured police vehicles used to quell uprisings in the townships during apartheid.

The Truth and Reconciliation Commission was set up in 1996 with the threefold task of investigating human rights abuses during the apartheid era, determining reparations for the victims of gross human rights violations, and granting amnesty to perpetrators of human rights abuses who have made a full and frank disclosure to the Commission of their misdeeds. It was chaired by Archbishop *emeritus* Desmond Tutu.

I have drawn a great deal on Jürgen Moltmann's *Theology of Hope* and his *The Coming of God* in this letter, a fact that I want to acknowledge unreservedly. I have also found Letty Russell's work very useful when wrestling with what is meant by "the end times" and have included some of her work below.

First, books consulted on bodies and theology:

To Elfriede

Jonneke Bekkenkamp and Maaike de Haardt, eds., *Begin with the Body: Corporeality, Religion and Gender* (Leuven: Peeters, 1998).

Caroline Bynum, *Fragmentation and Redemption: Essays on the Human Body in Medieval Religion* (Cambridge, Mass.: MIT Press, 1991).

Sarah Coakley, ed., *Religion and the Body* (Cambridge: Cambridge University Press, 1997).

Paula M. Cooey, *Religious Imagination and the Body: A Feminist Analysis* (New York: Oxford University Press, 1994).

Sallie McFague, *The Body of God: An Ecological Theology* (Minneapolis: Fortress Press, 1993).

Elisabeth Moltmann-Wendel, *I Am My Body: A Theology of Embodiment* (New York: Continuum, 1995).

I have found the following books on hope and related topics in Christian theology helpful and consulted them in writing this letter:

Carl Braaten and Robert Jenson, *The Futurist Option* (New York: Newman Press, 1970).

Frederic Burnham, Charles S. McCoy, and M. Douglas Meeks, eds., *Love: The Foundation of Hope: The Theology of Jürgen Moltmann and Elisabeth Moltmann-Wendel* (San Francisco: Harper & Row, 1988).

Margaret Farley and Serene Jones, eds., *Liberating Eschatology: Essays in Honor of Letty M. Russell* (Louisville: Westminster/John Knox Press, 1999).

Mary Grey, *The Outrageous Pursuit of Hope: Prophetic Dreams for the Twenty-First Century* (London: Darton, Longman and Todd, 2000).

Jürgen Moltmann, *The Coming of God: Christian Eschatology* (Minneapolis: Fortress Press, 1996).

Jürgen Moltmann, *Theology of Hope: On the Grounds and Implications of a Christian Eschatology* (London: SCM, 1967).

Letty Russell, *Growth in Partnership* (Philadelphia: Westminster, 1981).

Gerhard Sauter, *What Dare We Hope? Reconsidering Eschatology* (Harrisburg, Pa.: Trinity Press, 1999).

Michael Welker, *What Happens in Holy Communion?* trans. J. F. Hoffmeyer (Grand Rapids: Eerdmans, 2000).

David Willis and Michael Welker, eds., *Toward the Future of Reformed Theology: Tasks, Topics, Traditions* (Grand Rapids, Eerdmans, 1999).

The HIV/AIDS crisis has spawned a large number of publications. Here are some of the books I have found useful, both from theological and socio-logical perspectives:

C. Baylies and J. Bujra, *Aids, Sexuality and Gender in Africa: The Struggle Continues* (London: Routledge, 2000).

J. Bujra, "Risk and Trust: Unsafe Sex, Gender and AIDS in Tanzania", in P. Caplan, ed., *Risk Revisited* (London: Pluto Press, 2000).

Carole A. Campbell, *Women, Families and HIV/AIDS: A Sociological Perspective on the Epidemic in America* (Cambridge: Cambridge University Press, 1999).

Jack Dominian, *Sexual Integrity: The Answer to AIDS* (London: Darton, Longman and Todd, 1988).

M. Foreman, ed., *AIDS and Men* (London: Panos Publications/Zed Press, 1999).

Tim Trengove Jones, *Who Cares? AIDS Review 2001* (Pretoria: University of Pretoria, 2001).

James F. Keenan, ed., *Catholic Ethicists on HIV/AIDS Prevention* (New York: Continuum, 2000).

Hein Marais, *To the Edge: AIDS Review 2000* (Pretoria: Centre for the Study of AIDS, 2000).

Kenneth R. Overberg, ed., *AIDS, Ethics and Religion; Embracing a World of Suffering* (Maryknoll, N.Y.: Orbis Books, 1994), in particular chapter 9 on Women and AIDS by Carole Campbell.

William A. Rushing, *The Aids Epidemic: Social Dimensions of an Infectious Disease* (Boulder, Colo.: Westview Press, 1995).

Letty Russell, ed., *The Church with AIDS: Renewal in the Midst of Crisis* (Louisville: Westminster/John Knox Press, 1990).

Aylward Shorter and Edwin Onyancha, *The Church and AIDS in Africa: A Case Study: Nairobi City* (Nairobi: Pauline Publications Africa, 1998).

Heather Snidle and David Yeoman, *Christ in Aids: An Educational, Pastoral and Spiritual Approach to HIV/AIDS* (Cardiff: Cardiff Academic Press, 1997).

Susan Sontag, *AIDS and Its Metaphors* (New York: Farrar, Straus & Giroux, 1989).

Emilie M. Townes, *Breaking the Fine Rain of Death: African American Health Issues and a Womanist Ethic of Care* (New York: Continuum, 1998), in particular chapter 6.

WCC, *Facing Aids: The Challenge, the Churches' Response* (Geneva: WCC, 1997).

Alan Whiteside and Clem Sunter, *AIDS: The Challenge for South Africa* (Cape Town: Human and Rousseau, 2000).

Articles abound on the subject of HIV/AIDS. I found the South African periodical *Agenda* extremely helpful, especially nos. 39 and 44; also *Social Science and Medicine*, nos. 34, 41, and 52. The document referred to as "scientific twaddle," issued and distributed by the African National Congress, was written by Castro Hlongwane and titled *Caravans, Cats, Geese, Food and Mouth and Statistics: HIV/AIDS and the Struggle for the Humanisation of the African*.

Others works quoted or consulted are:

Hannah Arendt, *Eichmann in Jerusalem: A Report on the Banality of Evil* (New York: Penguin, 1976).

Bruce L. Birch and Larry L. Rasmussen, *Bible and Ethics in the Christian Life* (Minneapolis: Augsburg, 1989).

Pamela K. Brubaker, *Globalization at What Price? Economic Change and Daily Life* (Cleveland: Pilgrim Press, 2001).

Albert Camus, *The Plague,* trans. S. Gilbert (New York: Knopf, 1948).

Lisa Sowle Cahill, "AIDS, Justice, and the Common Good", in James F. Keenan, ed., *Catholic Ethicists on HIV/AIDS Prevention* (New York: Continuum, 2000).

T. S. Eliot, "Little Gidding" in *Collected Poems 1909-62* (London: Faber and Faber, 1963).

Michel Foucault, *Critique and Power: Recasting the Foucault/Habermas Debate,* ed. M. Kelly (Cambridge, Mass.: MIT Press, 1995).

Etty Hillesum, *An Interrupted Life* (New York: Henry Holt, 1996).

Anne Lamott, *Traveling Mercies: Some Thoughts on Faith* (New York: Anchor Books, 1999).

Friedrich Nietzsche, *The Will to Power,* trans. W. Kaufmann and R. J. Hollingdale (New York: Random House, 1967).

Sally B. Purvis, *The Power of the Cross: Foundations for a Christian Ethic of Community* (Nashville: Abingdon, 1993).

Elaine Scarry, *The Body in Pain: The Making and Unmaking of the World* (New York: Oxford University Press, 1985).

William Schweiker, *Power, Value, and Conviction: Theological Ethics in the Postmodern Age* (Cleveland: Pilgrim Press, 1998).

Marjorie Suchocki, "Holiness and a Renewed Church", in L. M. Russell, ed., *The Church with AIDS: Renewal in the Midst of Crisis* (Louisville: Westminster/John Knox Press, 1990).

Miroslav Volf, *Exclusion and Embrace: A Theological Exploration of Identity, Otherness, and Reconciliation* (Nashville: Abingdon, 1996).

Rowan Williams, *On Christian Theology* (Oxford: Blackwell, 2000).

Finally, the description of AIDS as "a bleak immensity" is borrowed from Wole Soyinka's book *Art, Dialogue and Outrage: Essays on Literature and Culture* (New York: Pantheon Books, 1993). John Chrysostom's phrase "grazed thin by death" is from *de Virginitate* 14.1, quoted by Peter Brown, *The Body and Society: Men, Women and Sexual Renunciation in Early Christianity* (New York: Columbia University Press, 1988).

CHAPTER 4

To My Children

on the Language of Lament

Yet even now, says the Lord,
return to me with all your heart,
with fasting, with weeping, and with mourning;
rend your hearts and not your clothing.

JOEL 2:12, 13A

Dear Lise, Lou, and Tess,

It is the end of September 2001. About three weeks ago, I watched the unimaginable happen. On a small, fuzzy television screen, hastily installed in the secretaries' office at the Center for Theological Inquiry in Princeton where I am writing, I saw a plane approach one of the World Trade Center's towers in New York on a perfect autumn morning, skirt the billowing smoke from the adjacent tower and then plunge into the other shining steel frame in a burst of orange fire. I remember blinking, expecting that when I opened my eyes the image would simply be some cheap trick. It wasn't. The horrors of that day flashed endlessly across television screens; diminutive bodies plunging to their deaths, grey-white figures running, people searching for loved ones. I watched the brave, the grieving, and the fortunate tell their stories. I marvelled at the courage of the police and firemen of New York.

Why do I find myself caught between conflicting reactions? Of course I feel stricken about the loss of life. I am angry at the mass murder of people, and I fear for a future on which more such madness will be let loose. Yet at the same time, I want to shout out — "Every day over thirty-five thousand children die of hunger in this world!" My friends tell me that this fact, for fact it is, cannot be related to what happened in New York and Washington. Those acts of terror were intentional. No one intends children to die. Yes, I agree. What I rail against are our selective reactions to such appalling events. Of course we must grieve the deaths of some three thousand civilians in the United States. Justice must be sought, perpetrators punished, and reparations made. But why are we not grieving for the vast numbers of children dying of starvation every day? Is it because we feel helpless in the face of the enormity of poverty and its consequences?

Yet, ironically, it may probably prove easier to feed the hungry than to "eliminate" terrorism. We may just discover that the two are linked. I don't see the same lust for justice, punishment, and reparation for the suffering poor. I am not surprised, but I cannot deny my feeling that something is grotesquely skewed. The images multiply. The hungry eyes of Afghan children, the bloated bellies of children all over Africa, abandoned babies, the orphans, the sick, the children dying as a result of AIDS, all point to the fact that something is awfully wrong in our world. The suffering of the innocent and most of all the suffering of children raise the problem of evil and suffering in the most unambiguous way. It is the kind of suffering that can drive us mad because it seems so utterly pointless.

This litany of suffering is hardly an auspicious way of starting a letter to you. I am tempted to apologize for it. Instead I ask you to bear with me and hear me out. Sick and hungry children are a public and a political shame, one that is a step removed from my or your personal experience. Suffering in different guises is not, however, foreign to us. It crops up under our own roof. I need to write to you about my own struggles to deal with the question of suffering. This letter is risky. I can picture your reactions as I type: "What's Mom on about now?" Suffering is not an attractive theme. I risk putting you off even before I begin. I myself tend to avoid films or books that are about suffering. Give me a good thriller, or a novel with a happy ending, or a programme about polar bears, eagles, or the Namibian desert rather than human tragedies. I thought about writing this letter to a friend. In the end, I couldn't. You see, my discovery of a language to deal with suffering has been too momentous not to share with you. I simply have to tell you about it. I know something of the pain each of you has had to deal with in your lives and the ways in which you have reacted to your suffering and that of others. So this letter is about the eternal problem of suffering and how I have found a way of carrying on despite its unending nature. I have no guarantees for you, only the hope that this letter will find an echo in each of you.

Not only is writing about suffering risky, it is also difficult. We react differently to suffering, and its causes defy easy answers. Why do the innocent suffer? Can suffering ever be eliminated? Can I live with suffering in such a way that it makes me more and not less human? I know that each of you are finding your own answers to these questions. I go on struggling with them and find that I am compelled to face the reality of suffering for no other reason than that I may be party to perpetuating it. I also know you do not all share my faith convictions. This makes the writing of this letter even more hazardous. I will not pretend that my prayers for you are not at the core of my being. You know this. Here I want to tell you about the most significant shift in my own life of faith. I have found a language for dealing with, although not solving, the problem of suffering.

I think I would have been more chary about writing to you of suffering had it not been for what happened in Chambone, Mozambique, on a visit there in the 1990s with Francis Cull and Sergio Milandri of the then Institute for Christian Spirituality in Cape Town. The civil war had ended, and we were in the countryside some five hundred kilometres north of Maputo, the capital. It was a Sunday morning, warm and sunny. The church, which was really only a roof covering a cemented space with an altar at one end, was crowded with mostly women and children and a few elderly people. We sat up in the altar area, respected guests. On the floor in front of the altar rail were many small children, gazing at us with large dark eyes. As the Eucharistic prayer started, the church grew very still. When the priest said: "This is my body, broken for you," I was seized by a swirling vortex of darkness in the pit of my bowels. Small pieces of white cloth fluttered, trying to escape the murky grey. I tried to open my eyes to blot out the image but could not move my eyelids. I was gripped by a vast sadness. For a brief moment I saw the suffering of the world and began to cry. Nothing could stop my tears, not my embarrassment, not my dribbling nose. I saw that suffering was endless. This fleeting experience compels me to face suffering squarely, for in those moments I saw a reality beyond anything I could have dreamed up.

As I have said, we react differently to suffering. Over the years I have done so in a number of different ways. First, I have known apathy. It is interesting that the Greek word *apatheia* literally means non-suffering. That is precisely the purpose of apathy, to block awareness of suffering to such an extent that one becomes immune to it. Apathy has some unwanted spin-offs. I discovered that if one chooses to be a stranger to suffering, one risks becoming a stranger to one's self. Human relationships simply become too risky because they always involve some pain. Apathy becomes a protective cover. Soon apathy makes one incapable of perceiving suffering. Opting out is then an easy slide into numbness. Secondly, I have reacted with muteness. Suffering and pain can become so overwhelming that one sinks into a kind of silence. This silence can be respectful, even compassionate, but it can also signal withdrawal, not into apathy, but into inactive spectatorship. My most common reaction to suffering is anger. Lou, you have said that your mother walks about in a continuous state of high moral outrage. How trying that must be for you and how politically naïve of me! Trying, because it is tiresome to be with; politically naïve, because anger *per se* is not enough. Moral dudgeon serves a purpose only if it fuels actions to alleviate suffering. Lastly, I know that one can react with atheism to the problem of suffering and conclude that there is no God. (I wonder — without theism, atheism is surely irrelevant?) Conscious atheism can be a stoical stance, a sort of "let's grin and bear it, we're on our own, let's get on with living!" Human beings, after all, are little more than cogs in a giant mechanical wheel of life. There is, however, a banality in assuming that if one's questions about suffering are not dealt with satisfactorily by God, they are answered by deposing God. I find that atheism is a retreat from suffering and a refusal to continue wrestling with the "why" questions. Cogs simply do not question. But the "why" questions return relentlessly. They are, for instance, persistently raised in great literature, from the *Iliad* to the bible, from Shakespeare to Dostöevsky. Dostöevsky's *Brothers Karamazov,* more than any other work I know, best describes two different reactions to extreme suffering in the lives of the brothers Ivan and Alyosha. In the face of the suffering of innocent children, Ivan rails and rebels against the God who causes or allows such suffering. His deep concern drives him to atheism. Alyosha, who says very little, listens to Ivan in agony, for he too is deeply affected. He is not angry at God, but he looks at the sufferers and puts himself beside them — two very different reactions.

But I have never been a proper atheist. I have been so angry that I have wanted to turn my back on God. In the end I have chosen confrontation rather than turning my back. Not surprisingly, this letter is about a kind of confrontation. How familiar are these reactions to you?

I am sure that we human beings have wondered about evil and suffering in the world for as long as we have been able to formulate beliefs and problems. Take the Greeks and their gods; a mischievous bunch who were forever plotting against one another when they were not embroiled in open conflict. The ancient Greeks traced evil to the character of the gods themselves. So do the Hindus, whose god Šiva is both the wise and kindly creator of all as well as the destroyer, the one who eventually brings the cosmos to a cataclysmic end. How one understands "God" and what one means by "evil" naturally determine how one tackles the problem of evil and suffering. To try and explain what I mean when I say "God" is so deeply part of what I believe that it may sound like the tongues of Babel to you. Let me try. For me God creates, God knows, God can do, God is good, God is just, God is love. God desires to be in relationship with all of creation, including me. I am not saying that God is a nice, pleasant deity who is always around, or that God is always comfortable. I am saying that God is worthy of worship. I remember reading somewhere that Dietrich Bonhoeffer said: "God is the Great Beyond in the midst of us." I also told Rachel and Jo that God is the "Breath inside the breath." I don't know what you will make of this. Either one puts God in the equation and wrestles with the question of suffering or one accepts that suffering is just a fact of life and there is therefore little point in railing against it.

You note that I say "evil and suffering". Are they the same? No, but they do overlap. I can't understand evil unless I have a pretty clear idea of what is good. If good is all that enriches and fulfills life, then evil is all that thwarts and impedes what is good and of value. Evil is malevolent brutality, like the chill in Himmler's words: "We will never allow that marvelous weapon — fear — to grow dull, and we will enrich it with new meaning." Structures and systems of oppression and discrimination are also evil. Indifference, indifference to exploitation and injustice, simply not caring and turning one's back on the needs of others, rates high on my list of sins.

Years ago I read Simone Weil, the French Jewish philosopher who became a non-confessional Christian (more ready "to die for the church than to join it"). She never made the slightest distinction between thinking and acting, a fact that led to her premature death at thirty-four. She knew suffering; she was often ill and she immersed herself, quite literally, in the life of workers in France before the Second World War. What she calls "affliction" has three essential dimensions: physical, psychological, and social, and all these dimensions are present in true suffering. Her categories are useful. Suffering can be physical, caused by disease or injury. Often this kind of suffering can be remedied. Take out a rotten tooth and the pain is gone. Suffering can also be mental, experienced as estrangement, meaninglessness, loneliness, guilt. Social suffering is caused by prejudice, degradation, injustice, and ostracism. When we experience all three, we are, in Weil's word, "afflicted." I want to add abandonment or rejection to this list of affliction. I have a vivid picture of you, Lise, as a little girl, slipping past astonished customs and immigration officials at the airport in order to find us on our return home after a trip abroad, one of your ways of dealing with your pain of abandonment.

We are, of course, mostly the cause of suffering and evil in the world. We can't make a volcano erupt or tectonic plates shift, but we are very adept at sowing mayhem. Christians would say that suffering is not unrelated to sin. George Bernard Shaw quipped that the statistics on death were quite impressive: one out of every one person dies. The same could be said of sin! We certainly have a large hand in causing suffering! Does all evil entail suffering? I would think so unless, for instance, a person is in a comatose state and does not experience suffering. Undoubtedly such a person's potential for good is cut short. Conversely, not all suffering is evil. In the end I think that evil is more clear-cut than suffering. We recognise it when we see it with greater certainty. Some suffering can make people more sensitive and concerned for others. As your mother I have found myself in a bind. On the one hand, I cannot bear to see you in pain. I would do anything, and I mean anything, to relieve your times of suffering. On the other, I know that some of the most valuable lessons I have learnt in my life have been through the hard times. At the same time I cannot justify suffering, and I do not will it to happen.

For me, God cannot be God and at the same time be the cause of evil and suffering in the world. The question "Why suffering?" will not, however, go away. If God is all-powerful and good, how can there be evil and suffering in the world? Not only theologians ask this question. Philosopher David Hume wrote:

> Is God willing to prevent evil, but not able? then he is impotent. Is he able, but not willing? then he is malevolent. Is he both able and willing? whence then is evil?

The ancient Hebrew poet (Ps. 13) asks the same question in a different way:

> How long, O Lord? Will you forget me forever?
> How long will you hide your face from me?
> How long must I bear my pain in my soul
>   and have sorrow in my heart all day long?
> How long shall my enemy be exalted over me?

However you ask the question, it is a perennial nut that theologians and philosophers cannot crack. Either one must compromise God's power or God's love. Evil exists because God is not powerful enough to deal with it or God does not care enough to use power to eradicate suffering and evil. Questions multiply and become repetitious. Is God unwilling or unable to prevent radical evil and suffering? If God is unwilling, is God a sadist? If God is unable, is God truly God? You were intrigued by this when you were four years old, Lou. You asked me: "If God is so strong, why does he allow the devil to roam around like a roaring lion?" I had no neat answer then, nor do I have today. Darwin, when struggling to interpret nature, was torn between choosing design and chance. Could an omnipotent God by design have created "a cat to play with mice" or is everything just the result of "brute force"? He concludes, "I am in a thick mud yet I cannot keep out of the question." I am suspicious of the original question and the quest for solutions. Skirting the "thick mud" of a question that cannot be answered does not, however, help. It simply does not go away, and any hope we may have for changing suffering or learning from it disappears.

By the way, questioning the reasons for suffering only seems to have become a challenge to Christian beliefs after the seventeenth century. Before that the existence of evil and suffering did not seem to bother Christians in the same way it does today. Evil and suffering abounded but were not the occasion for scepticism or doubt. The early Christians did not need evil and suffering "explained away". It was simply a fact of life. What was needed was the means to go on in the face of suffering. Suffering was a practical problem. When a fact becomes a question, we are on dangerous ground. Who is asking the question, who gets a say in answering it, and whose interpretation of the problem raised is correct? The real question then is a question of power: Who has the power to ask the question? I am not easy with the idea that the question of evil and suffering is one for philosophers or theologians to "solve". There is no solution anyway. Questions about the Holocaust, Hiroshima, Rwanda, and AIDS belong in the mouths of victims and those who identify with their suffering.

Admitting the intractability of the question of suffering does not, as I have said, make it go away. What we cannot solve, we then try to explain. This becomes a battleground of mock combat and causes me to wonder whether the game is worth the candle. I will enter the fray from my tradition and mention just a few ways in which people have tried to explain suffering in Christian thought. Most contain moments that make sense, but none of them can entirely explain away the question of suffering. My rendering of them is simplistic, as most involve long and complex arguments. The first goes like this. Evil and suffering exist because we creatures were given a free will by God and we made the wrong choices, choices that caused suffering. This idea explains some suffering, but it does not deal with the suffering of a child dying from some incurable disease unless you believe that we are all tainted by the sins of our forefathers in some punitive way. A variation of the free-will explanation is that our choices lead us into hazardous places and that encountering suffering produces moral and spiritual qualities that equip us to become what we should be — "children of God". Suffering becomes a kind of test, a sort of get-fit routine for life, part of some bigger plan for humanity. But not everyone is "tested" to the same degree, and the amount of suffering in the world is simply too great to justify such an explanation. Why do some people suffer more than others? I do not discount the fact that suffering can lead to greater compassion and enable us to help one another in new ways. It can also build a sense of community. Putting aside differences and pulling together can strengthen relationships between people. Equally, I have seen suffering break people, souring their souls and reducing them to grim shadows of who they truly are, wishing that the world did not exist, ". . . believing that non-being is better than being" in German theologian Dorothee Sölle's words. There are two further explanations for suffering, most commonly found in fundamentalist thinking. The first is rather fatuous. Human suffering is a sign of weakness that serves, by contrast, to show just how strong and powerful God is. We have to be weak and suffering so that God can be strong and powerful. The second is that God "sends" or "causes" suffering, and it is our duty to accept it unquestioningly and to "transform" it into something positive. This is not only misguided, it is theological masochism.

I think it is important to distinguish meaningless suffering from suffering that can be meaningful. Meaningless suffering is unchosen and unredeemed, mindless and destructive like the suffering caused by war, rape, and torture. Suffering can, however, have meaning if one takes it on voluntarily, if it makes us more sensitive to the pain of others and moves us to have greater love for everything that exists. We learn from the suffering of others. I watch you. I long to jump in, to talk, to ask when I see that one of you is just hanging in there. You have taught me to watch and wait, hope and pray, while being grateful for your courage, lack of self-pity and blame.

In tackling conditions that cause suffering, some people find great comfort in the idea of a suffering God who accompanies us in and through suffering. The ultimate argument for this approach is the suffering of Christ on the cross. When we suffer, God suffers with us, as Christ suffered for us on the cross. Throughout the ages countless Christians have taken comfort from this belief. There is, however, a strand in contemporary Christianity that wants a suffering-free faith. Such a faith becomes the religion of the privileged. It downgrades God into a bland apathetic being who will not rock the boat by breathing one word about something as horrid as suffering. Christ suffered on the cross. That is enough for us, and we ourselves are not required to suffer. This kind of attitude does not take the suffering of humanity seriously. It cheapens suffering. It lets Christians off the hook instead of compelling us to take the side of those who suffer. I would rather opt for the idea of a suffering God who is a solace to me in my suffering than this palliated God. Then the question remains: Was God in the gas ovens when Jewish children were thrown into them alive, or with Tutsis slaughtered by machetes or with babies dying slowly of AIDS in hospital wards? Perhaps. I don't know. What is clear to me is that one's affirmation that God is present in suffering must, in Ken Surin's words, be "interrupted" by the stories of the victims. They must speak just as loudly as any affirmations of faith about God's presence in suffering.

As you can see, no rational explanations are really adequate to deal with the problem of suffering. All explanations must proceed from a sense of failure. We simply don't know. We can question and explain, but there are no neat answers. The utter helplessness I feel when one of you has railed at me about the awfulness of suffering has shown me just how fragile my faith is and how my instincts that want to protect you, or find rational answers, are futile. But as soon as I catch my breath, I know that you will find your own way of coping and that all I can do is to share mine.

Let's face it. Suffering is very intractable, yet laced with paradox. Take the story of Job. It is not a highly theoretical account of suffering. It begins with the question: Is it possible to believe in God without expecting rewards? Instead of answering this question, the poet tries to find the right way of speaking about God by relating the drama of an innocent human person's suffering. The "why" of human suffering is not explained or solved. Yet in the literal nakedness of Job's suffering, the bond between humanity and God is never severed. Take the gospel stories of Jesus. Jesus did not try to explain suffering. He was not into metaphysics. He lived through suffering and overcame evil with good. Yet for many, his life and his death is a triumph of hope. The hard truth is that faith must live with unanswered questions and that it has no neat, tidy responses to the dilemmas and paradoxes of life. I am suspicious of accounts of suffering that try to explain too much. Suffering has no point, though good may come of it. I don't see suffering as a theological or a philosophical problem that needs a solution, but rather as a practical challenge that requires a response from a community of people. The above explanations are quite theoretical. As there is no avoiding suffering, I think the better question would be something like: What are we doing about conditions that create suffering? I prefer a practical approach. I also do not see it as a problem that places God's existence at stake but rather a problem of our human fragility and of how we ask the question. I cope simply by asking myself what I can do. If no obvious practical answer is at hand, I know I must take a deep breath, stay in the moment, and wait with tears and resolve until I know.

Should Christians therefore give up on the problem of suffering and evil in the world? I don't think so. The intractability of suffering is with us.

It causes fear. What will happen tomorrow? Whom can we trust? We may not be able to understand all its causes or to end it, but we have to find a way of living with it, hoping to dent its relentless onslaught. My own efforts at doing so are typically ambivalent. On the one hand, I want to shout, "Never again!" On the other hand, I know that we do not choose the conditions of our lives and that suffering and death are part of living. I do not want to be apathetic or mute. I live between the tension of "never again" and "suffering is part of life". I have learnt that we must live with the questions, while getting our hands dirty with the stuff of life. The German poet Rilke says we need to

> . . . be patient towards all that is unsolved . . . and try to love the questions themselves like locked rooms . . . not seek the answers that cannot be given because you would not be able to live with them. And the point is, to live everything. *Live* the questions now. Perhaps you will then gradually, without noticing it, live along some distant day into the answer.

I end here with John Stackhouse's question and answer: "What do you think about God and evil? Your life is your answer."

Finally I am getting to the heart of this letter. I long to tell you about how I have coped with the inevitability of suffering. I have found a language that can lead us out of the temptation to apathy, muteness, and anger, and that does not resort to atheism. Dorothee Sölle writes:

> If people are not to remain unchanged in suffering, if they are not to be blind and deaf to the pain of others, if they are to move from purely passive endurance to suffering that can humanize them in a productive way, then one of the things they need is a language.

My discovery of the ancient tradition of lament has given me this language and this I simply must tell you about. But first a few thoughts on my attempts to sketch a landscape. Throughout the letters in this book I have had a picture of an imaginary landscape of faith in my mind. I have plotted my way through it, marking obstacles and places of rest, putting up signs to mark danger or point the way. How can I possibly mark lament? Tears would do, but more is needed. I think I will draw in some bright red zigzags, like streaks of lightning and some plumes of smoke ascending into the air that meet the flashes of red. Let's see if it will work.

How did I come upon lament? It is not as if the bible, particularly the Old Testament, does not use the language of lament. I knew the psalms, Job's story, and other characters "crying out to the Lord". But somehow I had failed to see the connection between lament in scripture and the South African situation until a secular group, not the church, opened my eyes to its political possibilities. I found public lament in the Black Sash. For nearly forty years this South African women's human rights organization opposed apartheid in very determined and imaginative ways. Their history has still to be told. In the 1950s they began "haunting" Nationalist politicians in an effort to shame them by standing with eyes downcast wherever these men appeared in public. They held vigils outside parliament all night while it was in session to disenfranchise the "coloured" voters of the Cape. A founder member commented: "If they were sitting, we were standing." "Haunts" later became known as "stands", the organization's most characteristic form of public protest. You may remember the sight of Black Sash women lining the streets, wearing black sashes (a sign of mourning for injustice) and holding spirited, pithy placards during the struggle for democracy. In addition to "standing", the women of the Black Sash were running advice offices, monitoring court proceedings, actively putting their bodies on the line by being a visible presence in the townships during times of unrest, keeping vigils at trouble spots, being present when bulldozers demolished people's homes, and running workshops to train and inform people of their rights. Naturally they met with opposition. Their offices were searched by security police and even bombed. Some of their members were forced into exile. Others were harassed and arrested and jailed. They received their highest accolade from Nelson Mandela in his address to the large crowd in Cape Town on the day he was released from jail. He referred to the Black Sash (together with the National Union of South African Students) as "the conscience of white South Africans". I will mark these women on my map with a few sparky black sashes.

I joined the Black Sash in the terrible '80s. At the time I felt increasingly impotent as wave upon wave of repression hit our landscape. I needed a place where I could do something. I also wanted to tell their story and write about their activities. Then, one day, I had an epiphany. The "mourning" of the Black Sash women standing with their eyes downcast in public places and my own grief at what was happening to our country came together. I was outraged at the betrayal of our heritage by Afrikaner nationalism. I revolted against whiteness being a bogey or a burden. I was sickened by the continuous horror of apartheid. In the Black Sash a telling social and political form of lament was being enacted, and I could be part of it. Soon I discovered that lament was not just about mourning political injustice. I found that I too needed to lament my own lost years, those that the locusts had eaten. And, most important, when my heart cracked as you struggled to find yourselves in our changing landscape, I could lament your suffering and my share in it. The connection was clear — political and personal lament were the same thing. After that it was one short step to re-appropriating lament in the bible. I found a language for coping with suffering deep in the heart of my own faith tradition, which was tough enough to deal with all that I could bring to it.

What makes writing about lament difficult is the fact that it is both communal and individual, public and private, and it is the language both of suffering victims as well as of penitent people. It speaks with political, social, and religious voices. It calls God to account and at the same time calls upon God for relief. It accuses and it praises. It complains and confesses. I found that I needed a language that could speak to suffering as well as to penitence. Why? Because, like everyone else, I have a need to lament, personally, for the ways in which my ignorance and lack of insight have caused suffering, while at the same time, as a white, I lament what I left undone during the apartheid years.

By now you are probably wondering what I mean by lament. A friend who heard that I was writing about lament burst out: "Not another white South African breast-beating in public!" That is not how I see it. Lament is not simply a vehicle for emotional release. It is far more than breast-beating. The word "lament" in English fails to capture the provocative relationship in Afrikaans between lament *(klaag)* and accusation *(aanklag)*. Lament is akin to mourning and at times difficult to distinguish from mourning. It is also more. It is somehow more purposeful than mourning. It signals that relationships and circumstances have gone terribly wrong. It is more than railing against suffering, a breast-beating or confession of guilt.

It is a coil of suffering and hope, awareness and memory, anger and relief, a desire for vengeance, forgiveness, and healing that beats against the heart of God. It is our way of bearing the unbearable, as we, in Joel's words, rend "our hearts and not our clothing." It is, in essence, supremely human.

Lament should be generous and not grudging, explicit not generalized, unafraid to contain petitions and confident that they will be heard. Lament is risky speech. It is risky because it calls into question structures of power, it calls for justice, it pushes the boundaries of our relationships with one another and with God beyond the limits of acceptability. It is a refusal to settle for the way things are. It is reminding God that the human situation is not as it should be and that God as the partner in the covenant must act. Lament alternates between complaint and mourning and railing and accusing. Lament is never an end in itself. It is undergirded by the hope that God not only can but that God *will* hear the cries of the suffering *and* the penitent and *will* act with mercy and compassion. How do I know this? Mostly from discovering the tradition of lament in Israel as well as from reading ancient and contemporary literature of lament. And also from the freedom I now have to cry out to God. Let me tell you more.

As I began to delve into lament, I remembered the Greek tragedies. The further I went, the more I discovered that lament has a long and rich history. In ancient times when cities were destroyed, people lamented. When the great cities of Sumer and Ur, which had long held sway over the Babylonians, were ravaged by the Elamites in 2004 B.C.E., the ancient Mesopotamians lamented. Their orchards were "scorched like ovens", while the goddess cried out: "Alas, the destroyed city, my destroyed temple!" In Greece, people lamented in ancient times, and to this day lament remains part of a living folk tradition. Homer describes Achilles covering himself with sooty ash and tearing out his hair, mourning for Patroclus: "Achilles had taken full satisfaction in lament . . . for no good comes of cold laments." In Aeschylus' *The Persians,* the lament is so powerful that it is able to call Darius back to life. Rising from his tomb, the king acknowledges this magical power: "You stood beside my tomb and lamented, and called me piteously to rise up by your laments that lead the soul." People have lamented through the ages. More laments were probably written for the fall of Constantinople in 1453 than for any other single event in history. The loss of the bastion of Eastern Christianity was experienced as the crack of doom. Lament was the only appropriate response. In our part of the world lament at funerals is common. Wailing, keening, and calling upon God is part of African funeral rituals. African American sorrow songs are laments. The tradition of lament continues in the Jewish practices of sitting *Shiva* and saying *Kaddish*.

Once I began to read the bible in search of lament I discovered different kinds of laments. People lamented national as well as personal disasters. David laments the death of Jonathan and Saul, Jeremiah laments for himself and his people. And then there is Job. This incomparable tale of suffering is the best example I know with which to refute the kind of theology that always legitimates life's trials. Job, through terrible circumstances that are much lamented both by him and his friends, refuses to accept his friends' conventional arguments that he is the cause of his own suffering. He raises his voice in pain; he does not flinch from naming the horror of his circumstances and insists that they be transformed. Suffering is in the belly of lament.

When I read that biblical scholar Walter Brueggemann calls Israel's lament an exercise in "enormous *chutzpah*", every grain of my being said "Yes!" These ancient people simply refused to settle for things as they were. They believed that God could, should, and indeed would do something to change unbearable circumstances. Their lament was candid, intense, robust, and unafraid. They complained, mourned, wept, chanted dirges, and cursed. They assailed the ears of God, believing they could wring the hand of God and insisting their petitions be taken so seriously that, in doing so, God is put at risk. *Chutzpah* indeed! I found a language that is honest, that does not shirk from naming the unbearable, that does not lie down in the face of suffering or walk away from God. Reading about lament has been more than just an interest. I found myself unwrapping my own need to lament. I discovered practical wisdom in the way the people of Israel approached suffering, a wisdom as fresh today as it was millennia ago. This sense of discovery is what I want you to hear.

You will, I am sure, not be surprised that I have looked for women's role in lament. Have a chuckle and read on. As I delved into the Greek classics, mediaeval sources, and some modern Irish poetry, it became clear that in ancient times women often led the lament. I remember the joy of finding a large painted urn in New York's Metropolitan Museum of Art depicting a dead warrior lying on his bier. Around him women in flowing robes dance, waving their arms in graceful symmetry, eyes downcast. In Homer, women conduct formal laments both as kinswomen of the deceased and as professional mourners. Describing Hector's death, Homer says: "They put him on the carved bed, and stood singers beside him, leaders of lament, who lamented in grievous song, and the women waited. And white-armed Andromache began their wailing." Later, with the emergence of classical tragedy in the fifth century B.C.E., lament took on new forms. It was channelled into the two great forms of Greek rhetoric, the funeral speech and the tragedy. The role of the chorus in Greek tragedy only became clear to me when I realised that by combining music, dance, and drama, it stood between the world of the play and the world of the audience: angry, vengeful, doleful, and joyous in turn. Until the time of Solon, women were the official lamenters in Greece. They would pull their hair, lacerate their cheeks, and beat their breasts! Then Solon introduced reforms that drastically curtailed these dramatic activities. Women under sixty were, for instance, no longer allowed to lament unless they were related to the dead person, and no woman was allowed to beat herself raw! The state required order, not chaos; cooperation, not vengeance. Public lamenting could be an inflammatory act when blood feuds between families were the order of the day. Consequently the role of women as public makers of lament came to be devalued in classical Greece. Lament was tamed in service of the state. Plutarch says it all: "Mourning is something feminine, weak, ignoble: Women are more inclined to it than men, barbarians more than Greeks, commoners more than aristocrats"! Such are the quirks of a great biographer.

To get back to my point — there are lamenting women in the bible. Jeremiah tells of Rachel's cry: "A voice is heard in Ramah, lamentation and bitter weeping, Rachel is weeping for her children, she refuses to be comforted for her children, because they are no more" (31:15). Her haunting cry echoes down through the centuries and speaks to Matthew (2:18), who quotes Rachel's lament after Herod's massacre of the innocents shortly after the birth of Jesus. Hagar, the abused wife and slave, speaks the dread of every mother, "Do not let me look on the death of the child," while weeping and crying out to God in affliction. God hears her and grants deliverance from her suffering. It is hard to think of a mother who would not identify with these women. Being a mother is finding out that one's skin is paper thin when your children are dealt blows. Love is unguarded. Lament is the language of protest when what is held dear is at risk.

In biblical times, certain women had the professional status of lamenters. Faced with the destruction of Jerusalem, Jeremiah records the public role of women lamenters by calling for "the mourning women to come; send for the skilled women to come; let them quickly raise a dirge over us" (Jer. 9:17, 18a). These professional mourners generally followed the bier of the deceased, lamenting the person's death. A friend of mine, biblical scholar Angela Bauer, finds intriguing possibilities in this text. God not only calls the women to listen, but orders them to teach others how to mourn and be dirge-singers in this time of "terror and tribulation" (v. 19). These women are called to lead the wailing of the people, in "response to the devastation . . . and do the only wise and compassionate thing to do, to mourn themselves and teach others to grieve in the face of death."

And today? Do we hear cries of lament from the mothers of the thirty-five thousand children who die daily from disease and hunger? Or are they too at death's door? The ravages of AIDS call for lament. We have our own history of lament. This we saw at the hearings of the Truth and Reconciliation Commission as victims told their stories and lamented their suffering. Women still lament at funerals in the townships, crying out to God in acts of public mourning. The lament about injustice by the Black Sash has its own history. It scares me when I see headlines like "Dumped HIV Mum's Lonely Death" or "Parents Abandon AIDS kids", because I fear that we are succumbing to numbness or insensitivity. It is a time in which women must lament.

For me the heart of lament is in the psalms. Let me tell you about my first real encounter with the psalms. For years I knew little about them except for the occasional reading of Psalm 23 at a funeral. Then I went on a retreat and was given Psalm 139 to meditate on. With great relief, I realised that there was no one "right" way to speak to God. I read that God has "searched me and known me," that God can "discern my thoughts from far away," and is "acquainted with all my ways." All my decoys, deceptions, and doubts are known. "Even before a word is on my tongue, O Lord, you know it completely." (Sadly there is no promise of a curb on my tongue!) By the time I got to the lines that said: "For it was you who formed my inward parts; you knit me together in my mother's womb. . . . Your eyes beheld my unformed substance, in your book were written all the days that were formed for me, when none of them as yet existed," I gave up any pretense of a cover-up. I could strip away the self-knotted noose of not being up to scratch. With nowhere to hide, there seemed no point anymore in playing hide and seek with myself. From that time onwards the psalms have been the source of many little epiphanies. If you read nothing else in the bible, do read the psalms (and the Gospel of Mark). They give us a language to "say it as it is" to God. When prayer becomes a repetitive chore, I turn to the psalms. When I feel at war with myself, the psalms allow me to question, complain, or rage, to be penitent, depressed, or joyous. As an added bonus, I can immerse myself in the wonder and beauty of their poetry. The psalms are quite simply the truth about the world as it is.

At the beginning of this letter, I raised the intractable problem of suffering. The psalms have an extraordinary and undimmed ability to speak to human suffering. Israel had the gift of seeing that life as it comes along is about trust and betrayal, joy and grief, bewilderment and certainty. The psalms question life itself. Often they blurt out "How long?" and "Why?" This is risky and often very bleak. Psalm 38 is described by Kathleen Norris in *The Cloister Walk* as standing

> . . . on the precipice of depression, as wave after wave of bitter self-accusation crashes against the small voice of hope. The psalm is clinically accurate in its portrayal of extreme melancholia: "the very light has gone from my eyes" (v. 10), "my pain is always before me" (v. 17) and its praise is found only in the possibility of hope: "It is for you, O Lord, that I wait" (v. 15).

Psalm 88, the most anguished of all the psalms, has an unresolved, virtually hopeless tone. The speaker, "one of those whom you remember no more," speaks from "the depths of the Pit in the regions deep and dark", intoning relentless despair and unintimidated by the fact that there may be no resolution. This God must hear. The integrity of the psalms grips me. When the psalmists lament, they shape our experience of despair. Could Jesus have felt the same when he cried out on the cross: "My God, my God, why have you forsaken me?" (Ps. 22:1) God does not promise us a bed of roses, whatever that means. This may not be the kind of God we want. This is a complex kind of God, endlessly fascinating because despite the reality of suffering there is the wonder of life that God has given us. The psalms say it all — God absent, God present, God mysterious, God known, God of wrath, and God of love and mercy.

A last thought about a strange, almost unnatural aspect of the psalms of lament. On the one hand the psalmists complain and lament; on the other, they assure and praise, *in the same psalm!* One voice is insistent, accusing, angry. In effect it says to God: In the face of our suffering, we insist, without embarrassment, that you honour your responsibility to right this wrong, to restore justice, and we know that you can do so. The other is hopeful. It says: We trust you and we honour you to accomplish your just and loving ends and we praise you for so doing. What is happening here? God is often accused of being absent, of not hearing. Praise affirms the certainty of being heard. If God hears, God will act. There is nothing contradictory in this. It is a profoundly serious understanding of the nature of relationship. One can risk making honest statements about despair and grief at the same time one affirms all that is good and trustworthy about the relationship. This unexpected blend of plea and praise acts as a safeguard against censoring our prayers. No language anymore that masks suffering because one imagines that God is too fragile to cope with our painful realities. Complaint and lament, assurance and praise, can come from one mouth. Strangely, the more I lament, the easier it is to praise and feel grateful — the weird and wonderful equations of the life of faith! I long for this paradox to make sense to you. It is part of the practical wisdom of Israel that I mentioned previously — something they tried, tested, and found viable. It works! No beating around the bush. Suffering and the desire for relief are voiced, and God is not let off the hook.

This combination of lament and praise has powerful political implications. When lamenting people assume the power to define reality and to proclaim that all is not well, things begin to change. Complaint asserts that the impossible is possible. The lamenters' voices become subversive. They are, in fact, celebrating God's ability to act in this world, to right the wrongs far beyond conventional notions of the possible. This paradoxical blend of complaint and lament with assurance and praise is hopeful rather than stoical, alive and hard won against all the odds. It recognises the fact that life can move from tragedy to celebration, from displacement to reestablishing of self. Such are the extremities of human experience.

Most often the victims lament. Can those who are not victims also lament, so to speak, "from the other side"? To rephrase the question, can penitent people lament what they have done because they see that their wrongdoing is the cause of grief and suffering and this fact grieves and saddens them? Can we, the beneficiaries of apartheid, like David, lament, from "the other side"? Can we, provided we confess, repent, and acknowledge that God's judgment is just, lament too? Can we, in fact, afford not to lament?

These questions raise even more questions, and you may well react against the idea of being beneficiaries of apartheid. You have in fact inherited a murky past that you had no hand in creating. You are presently living through hard times as adjustments in our society discriminate against you. I know that there are times when you are sick to the teeth of having the past raked up. Through no fault of yours, you were in fact beneficiaries of apartheid. I see a difference between perpetrators, beneficiaries, and victims. Take the Truth and Reconciliation Commission hearings. We now know who a number of the torturers and the murderers are. We have heard the stories of the victims. There are also greyer areas. What about all those who cooperated in oppression? Here I feel uneasy, because despite their willingness to carry out orders, we know that many of them were duped into being the willing cohorts of apartheid. The masterminds, the ones who propagated and legislated the ideology of apartheid and who drew the grandiose plans for "separate development" have gone unpunished and are living in retirement on fat pensions from the state. Perhaps it is more appropriate to make a distinction between victims and beneficiaries. As white South Africans, we benefitted from apartheid. So did some black South Africans. Those, for instance, who cooperated with the nationalist government in running the homelands, grew powerful and prosperous. A minority of white South Africans opposed apartheid. The distinction between perpetrators (and beneficiaries) and victims is not always clear. It is true to say that most black South Africans were victims and most whites were beneficiaries and some whites were perpetrators. The greater reality is that all South Africans were victims of an evil ideology that damaged our humanity in different ways. It is such a mixture of the personal and the political, but when I lament, deep down it feels the same.

As I write this, I find myself being chary of victim speech that does not look at its flip side. I am not denying that being a victim is a reality. But there are times when claiming to be a victim can be a way of buying compassion. I have heard politicians and criminals who do wrong claim that they are victims of history and that they deserve compassion. Good Christian people often fall prey to this kind of appeal because they have not thought through what the links between compassion and justice are. Justice is rather an impulse of compassion. Waiving justice in an effort to be compassionate ends up excusing what is blatantly wrong.

There are conditions attached to lamenting from "the other side". They include the notions of confession, repentance, forgiveness, and reconciliation. Do you remember how we watched perpetrators "confess" before the Truth and Reconciliation Commission, confessions that all too often had their eye on an early release from prison, or the granting of amnesty, or that were manipulative admissions of involvement in nefarious practises that slyly developed into accusations against others? F. W. de Klerk's submission was spoiled when he, in Desmond Tutu's words, "qualified the apology virtually out of existence." I understand genuine confession to say: "I no longer stand by my wrongdoing; I repent of it and side with you in condemning it." We did not hear much of this kind of confession. What about repentance? Literally, repentance means turning around — going in the opposite direction. Does forgiveness require repentance? Not always and not necessarily. We can forgive the dead. This I discovered myself when my father virtually disinherited me. On learning this after his death, I felt angered and rejected, not because of money, but because I was made to feel as if I did not exist. I was unprepared for the effects this had on my relationship with other members of my family. I remember going on a retreat a few weeks after his death. At some stage in the weekend I hurled my bible across the room hoping that God would not duck. I lamented and in time I have learnt that forgiveness is possible. Today I understand; I hold no grudge and even feel loved by my father.

We need to forgive ourselves as much as we need forgiveness. Forgiveness is not a uniquely religious act. We forgive so that we can live with ourselves and with others. Forgiveness is not simply wiping out a wrong, or denying memory; neither is it excusing a wrongdoer. Forgiveness is an active, willed change of heart that succeeds in overcoming naturally felt feelings of anger, resentment, vengeance, and hatred. For me it has a gift-like quality. When confession and repentance meet forgiveness, reconciliation can happen. Relationships can be restored. Whereas forgiveness can happen without reconciliation taking place, reconciliation cannot happen without forgiveness.

A knotty problem raised by forgiveness is whether one group of people can forgive another. Can a representative of a group forgive an offending group in the name of the offended group? And can a wrongdoer receive forgiveness on behalf of an offending group? How far does group identification go? As a mother I know that when you have been wronged, I identify with you. I have struggled with forgiving those who have harmed you. That I have not always been able to do so is not the point. The question is: If it is sometimes right to forgive someone who has wronged a loved one, how far does that circle of identity stretch? Can we forgive the children of those who wronged our forebears and vice versa? The questions are endless.

Talk about forgiveness and reconciliation cannot avoid being caught between a rock and a hard place. On the one hand, there are certain acts that cause such deep moral outrage that forgiving simply seems impossible. Such acts are so evil and so destructive that our very being recoils from all thoughts of forgiveness and reconciliation. We dare not understate the moral significance of anger and retribution. They are legitimate emotions. We cannot bury them. Just think of the abusers of children and women, the perpetrators of genocide, and those who enslave people, to feel what I mean by moral outrage. Premature speech about forgiveness and reconciliation that fails to acknowledge the moral force of anger, hatred, and retribution cannot bring about reconciliation. It is likely to delay it and make it even more unlikely. It is just spiritually and psychologically fraudulent. It does not relate the truth of our lives. While I do not agree with him, I cannot lightly dismiss Nietzsche's searing critique. "[Christians'] inability for revenge is called unwillingness to revenge, perhaps even forgiveness ('for *they* know not what they do — we alone know what *they* do!'). They speak of 'loving one's enemies' — and sweat as they do." So much for mealy-mouthed forgiveness. It reminds me of Dietrich Bonhoeffer's warnings about "cheap grace": "Cheap grace means grace sold on the market like cheapjack's wares. . . . [It is] grace without price; grace without cost!"

On the other hand, living in a state of "unforgivingness" has its own dilemmas. We are caught between legitimate feelings of moral outrage and retribution and the price that there is to pay for not being able to forgive. How do Christians, for instance, deal with the injunction to love our enemies, to forgive those who harm us as God forgives us, if we are not prepared to forgive? And all the more so as forgiveness does not necessarily require repentance. There is no hope of reconciliation without forgiveness. We will have to count the cost to ourselves if we do not forgive. Forgiving requires stepping out of the victims' role. This can be very difficult.

The bible has a tradition of lamenting from "the other side". The psalms that are about penitence are a kind of lament. They combine deep distress, contrition, submission, and pleas for mercy and forgiveness in various ways. Psalm 51 is a splendid example of the lament of the penitent. David, after being confronted by the prophet Nathan for the striking down of Uriah and the taking of Bathsheba as his wife, pleads with God for mercy while lamenting his sins: ". . . blot out my transgressions, wash me thoroughly from my iniquity . . . for I know my transgressions and my sin is ever before me. Against you, and only you, have I sinned. . . ". Psalm 32 knows the burden of guilt: "While I kept silent, my body wasted away through my groaning all day long. For day and night your hand was heavy upon me, and my strength was dried up as by the heat of summer" (vv. 3, 4). It also knows the relief of confession and forgiveness — "Happy are those whose transgressions are forgiven, whose sin is covered" (v. 1).

To return to my theme of lament from "the other side". People like us can lament the misuse of power and privilege and our failure to stand up more courageously against evil and injustice. We can lament the wasted years, the self-destructiveness of sin that destroyed the possibility of true community in our country. Mothers can lament for their sons who were drafted into the defence force and emerged after two years, scarred and depressed, cynical or ready to leave for far shores, while at the same time they can remember and honour other mothers whose sons were tortured, imprisoned, killed, and exiled in the cause of the same ideology of white power. I can also lament my shortcomings as a person and as a mother. Although at times hard to bear, I thank all three of you for being fiercely honest with me and for what you have taught me about myself. Today my lament is more one of sadness than of guilt. I have loved you fiercely but not always wisely. I admit to the refrain "if only . . ." while knowing its futility.

So I have lamented, been humbled by forgiveness offered, have forgiven myself, and I now go on knowing that charity truly does begin at home. I am learning to accept and live alongside my shortcomings, making friends with them instead of allowing them to terrorise me.

You are probably wondering whether lament goes on indefinitely. Lamenting from "the other side" is not unending. As it is primarily part of confession and repentance, it has no need to continue forever. But we know that this side of heaven there will always be something to lament. Ann Weems, who wrote her own psalms of lament on the death of her son, laments:

> In the godforsaken, obscene quicksand of life,
> there is a deafening alleluia
> rising from the souls
> of those who weep,
> and of those who weep with those who weep.

In my letter to Rachel and Jo, I ask, "What makes life worth living?" Lament hardly sounds like a candidate for the good life. Yet it is. Lament is like a hot poultice applied to a festering boil. At first it is painful; it burns, and one application does not do the trick. Gradually, the inflammation becomes localised, the poultice draws the pus out, the angry redness subsides, the pain is relieved and healing begins.

Each one of you sees your future in this part of the world. You love this place with its troubled history and its fraught future. The air has been full of premature talk of reconciliation and is often insensitive to feelings of grief, anger, and revenge. It denies claims for justice as the wrongs of the past are glossed over. I am unable to work out to what extent the waves of criminality that are engulfing us are due to our inequitable past. I suspect a great deal. And then there is AIDS. What will tomorrow be like when today is stricken with infected and dying bodies? How can we be the civil and caring society we hope for when hundreds of people die every day?

I struggle with these kinds of questions because of your future and that of your children. Many of my friends have children and grandchildren living far away. I see how torn some are between their longing for more family contact and their belief that it is somehow more "safe" elsewhere. Laurie and I have been spared this conflict. Hundreds of years of rootedness in this country are our heritage. I also face the fact that I have become an adrenaline junkie. Of course I long for less violence and less sadness. But I am not sure that I know how to live without resisting some adversity while hoping for better days — itself a sad admission. By now I have figured out where I want to put my energies. So let me tell you what the link is to lament.

Despite its many shortcomings, the church (understood in its universal sense) can be an important organ of civil society because it is still the place where many people find community. I know it is not your community of choice, but you will concede that religious institutions have a role to play in the shaping of societies. Unfortunately, the church will have to work hard at shoring up its credibility. It cannot be afraid to be a church that laments suffering. Then it can legitimately challenge political and economic structures that are unjust, oppressive, and uncaring. Experience tells me that eternal vigilance is necessary. There are no guarantees that the oppressions and injustices of the past will not be repeated in some new guise. The upheavals and repressions in countries struggling to be democratic are a fact. The voice of communal lament can be powerful, particularly when it focuses on the dire consequences of empire building, neglect of the poor, corruption, and oppression. At this very moment we have much to lament: the ravages of AIDS, the misery caused by criminal violence, the abuse of women and children. Why is the church not lamenting? Don't we care? Or are we dodging the fact that lament carries the message that social systems can be challenged and changed? Do we instinctively know that lamenting can be politically subversive and therefore dangerous?

The preservation of the status quo can never be the church's true concern. The tragedy of the white Dutch Reformed Church (DRC) is a case in point. For many years I have lamented the fact that your contact with the church as children was through the DRC, with its paradoxical notions of what was right and what was not. Dancing was out. Apartheid was in. Wisely you quit. Its history of complicity in preserving apartheid through its theology and the pledging of its soul to the political power of the *Broederbond* resulted in its isolation from the world community of churches. Brueggemann warns that when the willingness to lament is lost, "justice questions cannot be asked and eventually they become invisible and illegitimate. Instead, we learn to settle for questions of 'meaning' and we reduce the issues to resolutions of love." Biblical faith is relentlessly concerned with the tough questions of justice. If we shelve them because we think them inappropriate for the church, we are unable to lament and we end up offering only feeble niceties as some kind of a sop to God.

I am pleading for a church that laments suffering and injustice. This is my concern more than it may be yours, because I believe that the church can and does play a role for many people in making life worth living. The church should draw contemporary political and social concerns into its rites. It need not shy away from lament. Instead of worship services that are unremittingly positive in tone, there is room for mourning and protest — not as an end in themselves — but as a holding together of loss and hope. Lament does not end in despair — it ends in affirmation and praise that are hard won. Why? Because it has grappled with radical doubt about God's presence in the world; because it is compelled by the belief that God can be worshipped despite the reality of human suffering; because it comes "out of the depths"; because truth is at the heart of the prayer of lament. Can you see why I am passionate about lament?

Yesterday in church I listened to the baptismal vows of a group of parents and godparents gathered around the font. Every time this happens, I am stricken by a strange mixture of remorse and hope. I repent and lament afresh my own failures to honour more fully the promises I made at your baptisms. I am also moved by the meaning of baptism. The unknowing infant is brought in trust to be accepted into the community of faith. From that moment on the baptised have a new identity and a new family. How satisfying it would be if the church were to act like a loving family. Instead we are all able to list our alienations. The bigoted Sunday school teacher who tells small children that dancing is a sin, or the one who resorts to no more than religious clichés — "Just take Jesus into your heart", to which you, Tess, with the devastating logic of a six-year-old replied: "Then I'll get a hole in my heart!" The centuries of denigration suffered by women at the hands of male clerics. The disillusionment with conversion experiences that promise only sunshine and fail to grapple with despair and suffering; or simply having one's trust in members of the clergy betrayed when they behave badly. These are causes for lament. Strange, isn't it, that such a fractious, unfaithful body of people are, in some inexplicable way, God's hands in the world?

More of the language of lament and less of the language of pious rectitude can make relationships in the church more authentic and more durable.

To end where I began — I have found that the language of lament makes for a more intimate and authentic relationship with God. We live in a world of displaced people, of war, exile, devastated communities, abuse and poverty, depression, anxiety and abandonment. These situations raise legitimate questions about God, about justice and about God's presence and power in a suffering world. Is God's justice reliable and where is it? There is much cause for lament, yet its loss stifles our questions about evil in the world. Instead we settle for a God who is covered with a sugar-coated veneer of religious optimism whose omnipotence will "make everything right in the end". Religious optimism differs deeply from a life of faith that is unafraid to examine suffering but is nonetheless grounded on hope. Religious optimism prefers to sanitize God by removing God from the ugliness of evil and suffering. This is a God whom we dare not approach with our genuine grief and with whom we are in a relationship of eternal infantilism. The language of lament is direct and truthful about suffering; it names the unnameable to God and in so doing helps to heal our doubts and to restore our faith in our power to call on God to act on our cries. This makes life worth living.

What does the sketch of my landscape look like now? You are at the centre of my sketch. The red flashes and plumes of smoke meet over your heads and the heads of lamenting people. You are looking at those with outstretched arms and bowed heads, some weeping and others letting out loud cries. The air crackles. Voices mingle in the smoke. Something is about to happen.

Much love as always,
Mom

NOTES

My children are, I am sure, chary of further comments about them. Briefly, Lise, who is a caterer by profession, likes gardening and handiwork.

She is Rachel's mother and they live together in Cape Town. Lourens is married to Liesa; their children are Seth and Jo and they live in Windhoek, Namibia, where Lourens does developmental work for an engineering firm. His passion is writing, matched by his love of the outdoors, fishing and hunting. Liesa works as a commissioning and copy editor for a publishing house. Tessa, a clinical psychologist and psychotherapist, is married to David, a textile technologist and a potter in his spare time. Tessa enjoys various creative pursuits like making artefacts when she and David are not hiking in the mountains or camping in the veld, and she is expecting to be the mother of twins.

I have deliberately steered clear of the term "theodicy" in this letter to avoid theological jargon and because I think that theodicy is not a purely theoretical or scholarly matter. My approach is practical and historically conscious. "Theodicy" is in fact the word used in English to describe attempts to vindicate the justice or righteousness of God in the face of the reality of evil and suffering. It was coined by the German philosopher Leibniz in his work *Théodicée,* from the Greek *theos* (God) and *dikē* (right or justice).

The Black Sash is a women's human rights organization that was established in 1955 in opposition to efforts by the Nationalist government to change the constitution of South Africa and to remove the "coloured" inhabitants of the Western Cape Province from the voter's roll. Today it continues its advocacy work as the Black Sash Trust.

Theological works on evil and suffering are plentiful. I have chosen to use Dorothee Sölle's work, simply titled *Suffering* (Philadelphia: Fortress Press, 1975); Jürgen Moltmann's *The Crucified God,* trans. R. A. Wilson and J. Bowden (London: SCM, 1974); and French philosopher Simone Weil's *Waiting for God,* trans. E. Craufurd (New York: Harper & Row, 1951). I also recommend Paul S. Fiddes, *The Creative Suffering of God* (Oxford: Clarendon Press, 1988); John G. Stackhouse Jr., *Can God Be Trusted? Faith and the Challenge of Evil* (New York: Oxford University Press, 1998); and Kenneth Surin, *Theology and the Problem of Evil* (Oxford: Blackwell, 1986).

On forgiveness, a work edited by Everett L. Worthington, *Dimensions of Forgiveness* (Philadelphia: Templeton Foundation Press, 1998), is particularly useful as it examines forgiveness from psychological and religious perspectives. For a legal philosophical view on forgiveness, see Jeffrie G. Murphy and Jean Hampton, *Forgiveness and Mercy* (Cambridge: Cambridge University Press, 1988).

Much has been written on the psalms and there are a number of works that connect the psalms with the theme of lament. For further reading I suggest the following:

Kathleen D. Billman and Daniel L. Migliore, *Rachel's Cry: Prayer of Lament and the Rebirth of Hope* (Cleveland: United Church Press, 1998).

Walter Brueggemann, *The Message of the Psalms: A Theological Commentary* (Minneapolis: Augsburg, 1984).

Walter Brueggemann, *The Psalms and the Life of Faith* (Minneapolis: Fortress Press, 1995).

Gustavo Gutiérrez, *On Job: God-Talk and the Suffering of the Innocent* (Maryknoll, N.Y.: Orbis Books, 1987).

Patrick D. Miller, *They Cried to the Lord: The Form and Theology of Biblical Prayer* (Minneapolis: Fortress Press, 1994).

R. Kelvin Moore, *The Psalms of Lamentation and the Enigma of Suffering* (Lewiston, N.Y.: Edwin Mellen Press, 1996).

J. David Pleins, *The Psalms: Songs of Tragedy, Hope and Justice* (Maryknoll, N.Y.: Orbis Books, 1993).

Claus Westermann, *Praise and Lament in the Psalms,* trans. K. R. Crim and R. N. Soulen (Atlanta: John Knox Press, 1981).

I am indebted to Margaret Alexiou's classic work on lament, *The Ritual Lament in the Greek Traditions* (Cambridge: Cambridge University Press, 1974). For the particular role of women's lament in the Greek tradition, see Gail Holst-Warhaft, *Dangerous Voices: Women's Laments and Greek Literature* (London: Routledge, 1992).

The references to Homer are from the *Iliad* XXIV, 720f., and to Plutarch from his *Letter to Appollonius.* Piotr Michalowski's *The Lamentations Over the Destruction of Sumer and Ur* (Winona Lake, Ind.: Eisenbrauns, 1989) documents the laments of the Mesopotamians.

A great deal more can be said on the subject of lament. Scholars have debated whether Israel's laments are essentially different from those of their surrounding cultures. Most agree that although they are not precisely identical, there is a high degree of formal similarity between them. What is more problematic is the use of the term "lament" when referring to the psalms. The Hebrew *kinah* (lament) occurs only nineteen times in the bible, never in the psalms, and refers mainly to dirges for the dead or songs lamenting the fall of a city. While some Old Testament scholars prefer the term "complaint", "lament" is now also accepted as a descriptive term for the complaining, mourning, and calling upon God found in the psalms. Communal laments are found in psalms 44, 60, 74, 79, 80, 83, and 89. Individual laments occur in psalms 6, 13, 22, 27, 35, 38, 42, 43, 88, 102, and 109. For lament from "the other side," refer to the penitential psalms 6, 32, 38, 51, 102, 130, and 143. As a last comment on penitence and confession it is interesting to note that the older prayer books in the Anglican Church state: "We acknowledge and bewail our manifold sins and wickedness, which we from time to time most grievously have committed" instead of "we confess that we have sinned against you."

Other works consulted are:

Angela Bauer, "Tracking Her Traces: A Literary-Theological Investigation of Gender in the Book of Jeremiah" (Unpublished Ph.D. thesis, Union Theological Seminary, 1993).

Dietrich Bonhoeffer, *The Cost of Discipleship* (New York: Macmillan, 1959).

Gregory Jones, *Embodying Forgiveness: A Theological Analysis* (Grand Rapids: Eerdmans, 1995).

Tim Trengove Jones, *Who Cares? AIDS Review 2001* (Pretoria: University of Pretoria, 2001) for quotes from headlines of newspapers.

Immanuel Kant, *On the Failure of All Attempted Philosophical Theodicies* (1791), trans. as appendix in Michel Despland, *Kant on History and Religion* (London and Montreal: McGill-Queen's University, 1973).

Antjie Krog, *Country of My Skull* (Johannesburg: Random House, 1998).

Peter Levi, *The Lamentation of the Dead with the Lament for Arthur O'Leary by Eileen O'Connell,* trans. E. Dillon, inaugural lecture as professor of poetry in the University of Oxford, given on 25 October 1984 (London: Anvil Press Poetry Ltd., 1984).

Alasdair MacIntyre and Paul Ricoeur, *The Religious Significance of Atheism* (New York: Columbia University Press, 1969).

Friedrich Nietzsche, *On the Genealogy of Morals,* trans. W. Kaufmann and T. J. Hollingdale (New York: Vintage Books, 1967).

Rainier Maria Rilke, *Rilke on Love and Other Difficulties,* trans. J. J. L. Mood (New York: W. W. Norton, 1931).

S. Paul Schilling, *God and Human Anguish* (Nashville: Abingdon, 1977), to whom I owe the quote from Darwin that was cited in L. Charles Birch, *Nature and God* (London: SCM, 1965).

Donald W. Shriver, *An Ethic for Enemies: Forgiveness in Politics* (New York: Oxford University Press, 1995).

Ann Weems, *Psalms of Lament* (Louisville: Westminster/John Knox Press, 1995).

For my own writing on the topic of lament, see "Lamenting Tragedy from the Other Side", in James R. Cochrane and Bastienne Klein, eds., *Sameness and Difference: Problems and Potentials in South African Civil Society* (Washington, D.C.: The Council for Research in Values and Philosophy, 2000); "Tales of Terror and Torment: Thoughts on Boundaries and Truth-Telling", *Scriptura* 63 (1997): 425-33; "On Hearing and Lamenting: Faith and Truth-Telling", in H. R. Botman and R. M. Petersen, eds., *To Remember and To Heal: Theological and Psychological Reflections on Truth and Reconciliation* (Cape Town: Human and Rousseau, 1996); "'Take Up a Taunt Song': Women, Lament and Healing in South Africa", in Leny Lagerwerf, ed., *Reconstruction: The WCC Assembly Harare 1998 and the Churches in Southern Africa* (Zoetermeer: Meinema, 1998). Some of the material in this letter appears in several of these articles. My doctoral thesis, "Liberating Praxis and the Black Sash", was a theological effort to find a model for the church's praxis of justice in the actions of this secular women's organization.

And a final thought: Paul Joyce drew my attention to how many musical settings are generated by the book of Lamentations, including those of Gregorio, Allegri, William Byrd, Marc-Antoine Charpentier, François Couperin, Giovanni Pierluigi da Palestrina, Thomas Tallis, and Alessandro Scarlatti. Elaine Pagels lent me an interesting book, *Lutheranism, Anti-Judaism and Bach's St. John Passion* by Michael Marissen (New York: Oxford University Press, 1998), and suggested that I look at the chorales as vehicles for lament. She is right. Besides Marissen's fascinating confrontation between Bach and Judaism, this book contains an annotated literal translation of the libretto of the Passion. The chorales indeed contain powerful motifs of lament.

CHAPTER 5

To Francis

on a Bag of Holy Tricks
for the Journey

I will repay you for the years
  that the swarming locust has eaten,
the hopper, the destroyer, and the cutter,
  my great army which I sent against you.

You shall know that I am in the midst of Israel,
  and that I, the Lord, am your God and there is no other.

In that day
the mountains shall drip sweet wine,
  and the hills shall flow with milk,
and all the streambeds of Judah
  shall flow with water;
a fountain shall come forth from the house of the Lord
and water the Wadi Shittim.

JOEL 2:25, 27; 3:18

Dear Francis,

Years ago I heard someone quote (or misquote?) a biblical phrase that stayed with me: "The Lord will restore unto you the years that the locusts have eaten". I have no idea where or when I heard these words, but I never forgot them. I longed for healing, my own and that of the land I love. As the years passed, I read the prophet Joel and saw that despite the destruction wrought by the great army of locusts that attacked the land of Judah, the mountains would one day "drip sweet wine" and the "hills would flow with milk." I held on to this promise of restoration without having any idea of the strange paths I would tread in search of healing. You will not mind being called a "strange path". Perhaps it is more apt to describe you as a person who looked like Merlin the magician and who had a bag full of holy tricks that played havoc with my defences.

I remember how we met. I went to the Irene Convent outside Pretoria to hear some Anglican priest speak about spirituality. You were that someone. I can still see you clearly, lost in a large chair at one end of a room, a very small old man with a large head and big white beard, pink cheeks, and clear blue eyes, speaking in a deep, resonant voice without a single note. Your talk was full of humour, anecdotes, and something I recognised at once as wisdom. You were explaining spiritual direction, the need for silence in the life of prayer, and you spoke about a spirituality that balanced activity and involvement with times of withdrawal. At the end of the afternoon, with a *chutzpah* born of need, I asked you to be my spiritual director without having any idea whatsoever of what it would entail. For more than fifteen years, until your death, you helped me to find life after the locusts.

Your faith was contemplative yet involved. An Anglo-Catholic by inclination with a deep love for your church, you showed me that holiness is ordinary, yet extraordinary. You were no pious saint removed from the hurly burly of life. You lived a down-to-earth kind of holiness, one that knew a hazelnut in the palm of the hand is "all that is made". In Julian of Norwich's incomparable metaphor, the hazelnut "lasts and it will go on lasting forever because God loves it". Holiness is seeing the world and everything that is in it, including a hazelnut, as touched, indeed transformed by God's love, while at the same time being utterly aware of one's dependence on and trust in this all-enfolding love. As ordinary as a hazelnut, yet quite extraordinarily all-embracing.

Like me, you were a news junkie. You listened to the news several times a day. You read the papers. You wanted to know what was happening and where. At the same time you rose at four in the morning so that you could get through your prayers. Would it be fair to call you a democratic socialist with roots in the Oxford Movement? You were much more than labels can portray. We shared the moral outrage, anger, and guilt that came from living with apartheid. We talked, prayed, argued, worked, marched, taught, travelled, and read the mystics together. Getting the Institute for Christian Spirituality off the ground at Bishop's Court, Cape Town, so that Desmond Tutu's urgent vision of "getting the clergy back at prayer" could be realised, was your last task for the church you loved. The years I spent as part of your team still give me a sense of having been involved in something truly worthwhile. All kinds of people came to see you about their journeys: the powerful and the poor, disaffected church members, those who disdained the church. Nothing I could bring to you shocked you. I remember you saying: "Sin is so boring. Find me a new sin and make my day." At the same time that I was assigning my own personal locusts one by one to the pit, things came to a head in our country. Despite the terror of the 1980s, we sensed change in the air. The swarming, hopping, and cutting pests had had their day. We marched, not once, but in growing numbers, until the police's water cannons and purple dye became badges of pride. I have a vivid picture of you sitting on the curb in Adderley Street in the middle of Cape Town confronting an irate burly young policeman who did not quite know what to do with this little old man who smiled at him beatifically as he tried to hustle him into a police van. After the first democratic election in 1994, we shared a sense of euphoria. Democracy at last! We could hang up our "struggle clothes". Our marching days were over. (Today, the neglect of AIDS sufferers by the state health system is cause to march again. I know you would be there in the front line.)

I want to give account of life after the locusts. It has taken a lifetime to get here. Your bag of holy tricks, so full of surprises, helped me towards the freedom and the wholeness I long for. Sadly, you were no longer here to share the moment when I crushed my last pesky locust under my heel. How can I describe being touched by the indescribable? At the birth of each of my children I experienced moments of intense astonishment, elation, and gratitude; astonishment at having survived their birthing, elation at being part of the miracle of life, and gratitude at their perfection — gifts after many miscarriages. The death of my last locust was, however, different. I was on a short retreat when suddenly, quite unobtrusively, I heard a question: "Why do you judge yourself more harshly than I do?" At that very moment the "whys" and the "wherefores" melted away. A sensation of sweetness in which I lost myself came over me. Love, lightness, and peace took hold of me. I lost all fear. Everything that the locusts had stood for in myself shrank to nothing. I felt light, almost buoyant, assured of the freedom to be "me". I crossed over my self-imposed restraints in one divine moment. This feeling lasted for days and then gradually wore off. The memory is indelible. The sense of wholeness is lasting. Freedom is being responsible for who I am and what I do. No longer am I a slave to fear or chance. My history, the pain from childhood, the adult burdens of failure, are in their place — a place in which I can recognise them, wave a greeting to them occasionally, and move on. I have no desire to analyse this moment any further other than to say that I perceived truths that I had not known before but that finally made sense of my longing. I now know that every idea we have of God fails God.

The themes in this letter are about what I learnt from you along the way; how spirituality is about relationship, what spiritual direction and prayer can be, how thinking about death is fruitful, and lastly, how the wisdom of those who have gone before us, like Julian of Norwich, has helped me along the way. I have marked my landscape of faith with questions, tears, and snares, with ailing and lamenting bodies. Now I want to find signs of hope and new life. Looking across the landscape, I see that everything I have sketched thus far is, in some way or other, related to our conversations over the years; the ups and downs, the injustice and violence as well as the hope for newness. Spirituality and the work of justice were never separate issues for you. They were simply all of life. I would complain: "My inner noise will never cease." And you replied: "Don't worry, God hears the noise. Just give it to God and wait." Or I would ask impatiently: "When will we get beyond poverty and need?" You would say: "I don't know, but it is in our hands to hasten their end."

The word "spirit," like many other religious words, conjures up images rather than concepts. Mostly spirit evokes the image of a breeze, of the air being stirred, or of a deep sigh-like breath. Like the wind, "spirit" cannot be seen or touched; it is invisible yet palpable. Ancient people meditated on the fact that in the blowing of the wind and the breathing of human beings there was something incomprehensible but nonetheless divine and mysterious. They knew, as should we, that we are physical spiritual entities. I have come to see that my unquenchable, often incomprehensible longing is a matter of the spirit. Augustine's much-quoted ". . . you have made us for yourself, and our heart is restless until it rests in you" sums it up. (You quoted Augustine liberally, often with a roguish smile, saying "You can attribute anything to Augustine. No one has ever read everything he wrote!")

Like "feminism", the very word "spirituality", derived from "spirit", evokes different reactions. Unlike "feminism" it is in vogue and has become somewhat of a buzzword. To some it suggests an in-house clubby piety in which people are wrapped up in their own inward condition. To others it feels spooky and wraithlike, an existence in which the spiritual, in contrast to the material, is removed from the grime of everyday life. To yet others, the word is simply baffling. When I first heard it, I had no idea what it meant. This was not surprising, as it is a quite ambiguous term that can describe a host of different spiritualities: Pentecostal fervour, evangelical Protestantism, New Age enthusiasm, different forms of Eastern religions, Anglican, Roman Catholic, Islamic, and Jewish traditions of spirituality, and so on. Broadly speaking, spirituality is the reaching out of human beings to God in an infinite variety of ways. All variations of spirituality incorporate a dimension of transcendence, and theistic spirituality has a personal God as its subject. Sandra Schneiders has helped me to sort out the different ways in which the term is used. She points out that "spirituality" can refer to a fundamental dimension of every human being. It can also mean the actual lived experience of that dimension, and it can refer to an academic discipline that studies that experience.

I fell into spirituality, because I, like many others of this age, experienced an inextinguishable longing. I was not bothered by the ambiguity of the term. I just wanted "to know" the source of my longing. So I started to read about spirituality. Had I not sat in the chair opposite you, my reading could have been nothing more than an intellectual pastime. Instead I was connected to a rich vein in our traditions. You introduced me to the English mystics. I read *The Cloud of Unknowing,* Julian of Norwich, William Hylton, and then, later, Hildegard of Bingen and Teresa of Avila. I devoured Thomas Merton, Evelyn Underhill, Maria Boulding, Kenneth Leech, and Esther de Waal. Simone Weil and Dorothy Day helped me to bring contemporary issues into dialogue with spirituality. Looking back on our years together, I wish your love for the mediaeval poets had rubbed off on me more. You liked to quote William Langland's *Piers Ploughman* and from Richard Rolle's spiritual treatises. But I had not recovered enough from being forced to read Chaucer and Beowulf when I was seventeen to appreciate their wisdom clothed in strange-sounding English! Your memory was prodigious. You once told me that you had memorised the Gospel of John when you were a boy in order to earn a watch. You quoted reams of Shakespeare with ease. You knew the bible inside out. You helped me make sense of what I was reading and how it was related to life in the awful '80s in South Africa.

Later, when I became involved in the work of the Institute for Christian Spirituality, I had to come to grips with the term "spirituality". I found a thousand definitions. Anything from the most circumscribed description ("spirituality is the life of prayer") to the most encompassing ("spirituality is all of life") were on offer. I remember liking Kenneth Leech's description: "The spiritual life is the life of the whole person directed towards God." I warmed to the fact that Rowan Williams rejected the idea that spirituality is merely about private experience: ". . . it must now touch every area of human experience, the public and social, the painful, negative, even pathological byways of the mind, the moral and relational world". The simplicity of Bernard McGinn's understanding that "Christian spirituality is the lived experience of Christian belief" was helpful because it saw spirituality as more concerned with experience than with doctrine.

I want to record Anne Carr's more detailed description of spirituality to remind myself of its many facets as I write this letter.

> Spirituality can be described as the whole of our deepest religious beliefs, convictions, and patterns of thought, emotion, and behaviour in respect to what is the ultimate, to God. Spirituality is holistic, encompassing our relationships of all creation — to others, to society and nature, to work and recreation — in a fundamentally religious orientation. Unlike theology as an explicit intellectual position, spirituality reaches into our unconscious or half-conscious depths. And while it shapes behaviour and attitudes, spirituality is more than a conscious moral code. In relation to God, it is who we really are, the deepest self, not entirely accessible to our comprehensive self-reflection.

She continues by pinpointing a particular emphasis in feminist spirituality.

> A specifically feminist spirituality . . . would be that mode of relating to God, and everyone and everything in relation to God, exhibited by those who are deeply aware of the historical and cultural restriction of women to a narrowly defined "place" within the wider human (male) world.

Relationship is at the core of a spirituality and can make the heart sing in anticipation of a love that is mutual. I am who I am through others coming into my life and opening me up to the possibilities of the "not yet". As Hildegard of Bingen knew, "Everything that is in the heavens, on the earth and under the earth, is penetrated by connectedness, penetrated with relatedness." Two experiences have made me certain of just how vital relationship is for spirituality. First, the experience of apartheid, the very antithesis of relationship, showed me over the years how ghastly it is to deny relationship as essential to being human. Second, I have come to see that relationship is related to my longing. I can, with my head, identify aspects of my longing — justice, freedom, harmony, peace, healing all come to mind. My ultimate hope is to be in loving relationship with God, with myself, with others, and with all of creation. But I know that my longing is more than a wish list about relationships. It is like a longing for what the Sufi poet Rumi calls a "dance inside my chest". It is wanting to be washed in crystal clear water, to emerge seeing with new eyes, to hear new refrains, and to taste a new sweetness.

My newfound freedom from the locusts has made my longing less raw and more exciting. I still hunger for a vibrant, all-enfolding love in a relationship of trust and dependence. Symeon, the New Theologian, knew this longing: "Come, for your self is the desire within me, come, for you are my breath and my life." This is not head stuff. It is about love. Spirituality is about the struggle to hold together my inner longing with my outer realities. Dag Hammarskjöld wrote in his journal: "On the bookshelf of life, God is a useful work of reference, always at hand but seldom consulted." I want to "dust" God off, no more a work of reference but a relationship at the centre of my being. I want a new relationship with the world, "one that has borrowed the eyes of God" in Dorothee Sölle's words.

Before I move on, a comment on the place of spirituality in the academy. You taught mediaeval English and English literature and witnessed the beginning of academic tensions around subjects that were not considered "useful". Things are worse today. Classical languages, philosophy, ethics, and theology are among the disciplines under threat as we bow to the modern version of the educated person — someone who can crunch numbers, understand technology, practice "pure" science, or predict with monotonous inaccuracy what will happen to the world's economies, and above all else, produce money. Rhetoric, the origins of world languages, universal questions and concepts, morality and ethics are dispensable in our less than "brave new world".

Spirituality cannot be divorced from theology. Some of my favourite theologians like Dietrich Bonhoeffer, Letty Russell, Gustavo Gutiérrez, Rosemary Radford Ruether, Dorothee Sölle, Edward Schillebeeckx, and Karl Rahner share the conviction that, in Schneiders' words: ". . . only a theology that is rooted in the spiritual commitment of the theologian and oriented toward praxis will be meaningful in the Church of the future." I have watched friends and colleagues lose that commitment, and I have seen how it has affected their students and the relevance of their work. In recent years I have taught courses on spirituality. I am sure that it is an autonomous discipline worthy of study in the academy. It investigates spiritual experience and traditions of spirituality and how they cut across disciplines, in a descriptive way. I have as little doubt that the study of spirituality should be an ecumenical and cross-cultural enterprise as I have that its aesthetic, political, and social dimensions are also worthy of study. To tap its riches truly, the teaching of spirituality should allow students to investigate the experiences that are part of spiritual traditions in a practical way. Reading about traditions of silence, for instance, needs to be accompanied by the practise of silence. Reading about justice calls for involvement in the restoration of justice. This tension between our theoretical study of spirituality and our practises has caused the respectability of spirituality as an academic discipline to be questioned. I understand this kind of mistrust because I know that it comes from a particular separation of the so-called rational from the non-rational, common to Cartesian thought. In the academy the starting point should be the historical texts and the different traditions of spirituality. This could then be followed by a critical analysis of these texts and traditions and by finding the links between them and contemporary spiritualities that are rooted in the events of everyday life. Finally, knowledge and experience are brought together and appropriated by the students within their own traditions, where they can either make them their own or reject them. Is this so much different from the study of psychology, for instance?

I have not found my quest to deal with the longing inside me easy. It has taken years of sifting and probing, laced with intervals of lazy neglect and succumbing to the temptation to busy myself with other things. In the process of sifting, I have identified the roots of my spirituality. Once again I am a hybrid. My mother had me baptised an Anglican. I married in the Dutch Reformed Church, but I subsequently left it and returned to the Anglican Church when I could no longer take communion in a church that practised apartheid. I could have joined another reformed church, but I was drawn back to Anglicanism because there was no apartheid at the communion rail. In the midst of states of emergency, it became a compelling need to take the bread and the one cup together with the very people who were being oppressed. Today I am an Anglican with reformed roots. These roots stretch way beyond my baptism and my experience of two different churches to the French Reformed Church of the sixteenth century.

How much of my Huguenot heritage is still in my bones? I often wonder about my forebears, about their circumstances and how they were compelled to leave their homeland after the repeal of the Edict of Nantes in 1687 which signalled the end of religious freedom in France. Originally from Lille in northern France, they fled to the Netherlands and appear to have had relatives in Leyden. They could have become citizens of Amsterdam. Holland and Friesland also offered Huguenot refugees twelve years free of taxes and rights fully equal to those of the native-born residents. Why then did they accept the offer of subsidized travel to the Cape of Good Hope instead of staying in the Netherlands? What did they know about this remote, virtually unknown settlement at the southern tip of Africa? What made them brave the long voyage and years of hardship at the Cape? Did they long to return to where they had come from when times were difficult? Why did most of them eventually forsake their heritage of radical resistance, their independence of spirit, their principle of equality for all undergirded by a belief in the priesthood of all believers and a desacralizing of political power, and eventualy embrace an unquestioning loyalty to the Afrikaner state and its repressive policies? Michael Walzer, who defines ideology as "a kind of mental and moral discipline", sees Calvinism as an ideology that is

> . . . marked by its critical view of the patriarchal and feudal world, its political realism, its bold suggestion for social reconstruction and its extraordinary capacity for organizing men and sending them into battle against Satan and his allies — even when these allies turned out to be kings and noblemen.

This is a heritage of resistance, not of capitulation to nationalist ideology. Did this ingrained tradition of resistance turn back on itself and prompt so many of the descendants of these French refugees in South Africa to support the cause of white minority rule on a black continent? History shows that the French Huguenots at the Cape were forced, fairly shortly after their arrival, to integrate into the existing Dutch community in a number of ways by the policies of the Dutch East India Company. Did this enforced community with the Dutch settlers and authorities explain the course so many of them took? Yet, something remained, a certain pride in the history and tradition of resistance. Laurie's grandmother used to tell him about his foremother Marie Durand, who "had been imprisoned for her faith for forty years". He took this story with a pinch of salt until one day his grandmother was redeemed. On a trip through the Camargue we came across the Tour de Constance in Aigues-Mortes. There, on the second floor, was a small museum to honour Marie Durand, who had in fact been imprisoned for thirty-seven years for her faith. Her crime was having a Protestant minister as a brother. Carved on the stone floor of the tower was the word *Résistez*. I was moved by this encounter and remembered snippets of stories my father had told me about my Huguenot heritage. I had paid scant attention to them because I felt they were being imposed on me. His favourite occupation was to spend his holiday going through the baptismal register of some French village, tracing Huguenot ancestry. His passion after his retirement was the Huguenot Museum in Franschoek where most of the Huguenot refugees to the Cape had settled in the 1680s. It was all too much for me because I could not separate the Huguenots from Afrikaner nationalism at that stage. Yet, despite his Afrikaner pride, my father was never a "joiner" of political parties or secret societies. He remained at heart a French resister with a recalcitrant spirit.

But you, dear Francis, allowed me to be what I had to be. You helped me to channel the inherited spirit of resistance into ways that were life-giving. You gave me the best of Anglicanism while I knew that ministers of the Dutch Reformed Church were coming to you for spiritual direction. So what does it mean to be an Anglican with reformed roots? I have had a highly ambivalent relationship with the Calvinist tradition. I have no truck with Calvin's teachings on predestination and feel aversion at some of his actions. I am attracted by the power of his intellect and by the depth and probing quality of his theology. I am not a Calvinist. But I do have a love for scripture as central to all that I believe. I know that in some indescribable way believers are in union with Christ, the *unio mystica*. (So does Julian of Norwich, but more about that later.) When Calvin writes, "Not only does Christ cleave to us by an indivisible bond of fellowship but with a wonderful communion, day by day, he grows more and more into one body with us until he becomes completely one with us", I say "amen". That this union begins with baptism may be disputed by some, but it is an assertion you taught me to value. Through baptism we are offered all the gifts needed for community. You showed me that one's baptism was worth celebrating. After you were gone, I went to St. Saviours, the stone church in Claremont, Cape Town, where I was baptised. To my astonishment my original baptismal certificate was found within ten minutes. Now, on 5 May when my baptismal day comes around, I think of you with gratitude for what you taught me. You were certainly no Calvinist, but when Calvin says that ". . . baptism assures us that we are so united to Christ himself that we become sharers in all his blessings", you would say "amen" too.

Two of my other reformed roots have remained. The first is rather problematic. There is a particular ethical demand that comes out of the reformed tradition. At its best, it insists that although we are justified by faith alone, faith must produce works. One cannot claim a relationship with Christ and not be involved in a style of life that such a relationship demands. According to Calvin, a good conscience is "nothing but inward integrity of heart". My father, who was reared in this tradition, applied it to his children, albeit in eclectic ways. We were not allowed to use pencils

that belonged to the government, and children of diplomats were not entitled to be transported in government cars. If you promised to do something for someone you never let them down. If you owed three cents, you
paid three cents. At the same time he did not condemn what was being
done to our fellow citizens in the name of apartheid. Was this not a betrayal of his much-loved tradition of radical resistance, which was based
on the freedom to choose your religious affiliation and the belief that all
human beings are equal in the sight of God? Works are not only about personal morality but about the well-being of one's neighbour. I mention this
because my life has been a struggle to live out the ethic demanded by my
faith — with startling failures along the way! This is very common, but it
has an added edge when Calvin lurks in the background!

The second reformed hold-over I live with is the longing for the
preached word in which Christ comes to us and enlarges our understanding, strengthens our commitment, and deepens our assurance. The reading of the word and the preaching of the word should be one single indis-
soluble event. Now Anglicans certainly do read the word regularly — at
least three parts of scripture at every worship service. But sermons in our
Anglican churches are too often rambling, pleasant chats with vague and
unreflected connections to the texts of the day. Preaching should be an
event in which Christ comes to us in the word. This requires probing the
text, grappling with its meaning, and proclaiming its truth in new ways.
We used to talk about this. Your own sermons were usually short, gems of
deeply considered truths, illustrated with stories that all could relate to. In
short, my reformed roots have not been without blessing, an awareness
that is subliminally part of my spirituality. I know too that my longing is in
essence part of the Reformation cry of *semper reformanda*. Never letting go
of the desire to reform means that one yearns for the church to be true to
its calling to be God's hands in the world by proclaiming the Good News,
by taking the side of the poor and the needy — all this because the longing
for God to be in our midst has to be translated into deeds.

My experience of Anglican spirituality has been less qualified than my
brush with Calvinism. I do know that Anglicanism has its own share of
woes. It participated in the colonial outreach of the British Empire. For a
long time it perpetuated the British class system with all its iniquities. Today the Church of England is caught in the historical trappings of its
founding. The matter of "establishment" is in urgent need of reformation.

A church that has the right to twenty-four seats in parliament, whose titular head is the monarch, and whose bishops are appointed by the prime minister is an anachronism in need of change. The Anglican Communion has members in one hundred and sixty-four countries. The leader of this group of disparate Christians, the Archbishop of Canterbury (so-called "the first among equals" — a description that reminds me of "separate but equal"), can surely not continue to be drawn from the kind of closed shop perpetuated by British history and the days when the king wanted a primate loyal to the crown of Britain and not to Rome! Lastly, an episcopal church needs to be reminded constantly that the role of the bishop is that of an overseer. The bishop's prime task is to take care of the clergy. Too many clergy feel neglected by their bishops or frustrated by the abuse of episcopal authority. No one should be a bishop who yearns to be one. We need more reluctant bishops, humbled by the magnitude of their task. Thanks to you, I have, however, been able to find much that is worthwhile in some of the enduring traditions of Anglicanism: spiritual direction, silent retreats, the liturgy of the word and sacrament, and quite unexpectedly, a vocation. I also know that the Anglican Church has been an agent for social reform in different parts of the world, and its educational and charitable work come from an understanding of the social relevance of the gospel.

What it means to be an "Anglican" is not easy to describe. In South Africa, Anglicans belong to every class and race and are described alternately as "high church" and "low church". Some like the smells and bells. Others prefer simple services with as little ritual as possible. In 1998 I spent three weeks in Canterbury at the Lambeth Conference. This confirmed the fact that being an Anglican can mean almost anything; you can be conservative or liberal in your approach to scripture, you can subscribe to church authority and pomp or to simple egalitarianism, you can read the bible to condemn homosexual practice and women's ordination (yes, even today) or to affirm both. I saw how different cultures and traditions influenced Anglican worship in ways that differ in texture and colour. I saw that being Anglican means belonging literally to every race in creation. Despite our differences there is something cardinal that holds Anglicanism together. Harvey Guthrie describes this something as "simply participating in what the Church does as Church". This, he points out, is both a strength and a weakness. Its weakness lies in the church being overly concerned about pragmatic questions, such as valid ordination and who should preside at the sacraments. Its strength lies in the fact that it is not narrowly sectarian, and at best, it is inclusive and truly catholic.

You showed me that "Anglican spirituality" should be grounded in the corporate life of the church. It is not just about God and me, but about God, me, and my neighbour. And I don't get to choose my neighbour. When we participate in "what the church does as church" we, as a band of very diverse people, sing, listen, pray, eat bread, and drink wine as one. Liturgy means "the work of the people". Worship is *our* work, not the work of the liturgist, the theologian, or the cleric. The sermon may not be memorable, the singing ragged, the readings no lesson in elocution, but it is we, the people, who make it our work. All are welcome. Worship must be hospitable enough to make place for someone like me — critical, confused, and crying out "I believe, help my unbelief!" With the *Book of Common Prayer* in our hands, the liturgy takes shape. Whether one is in Polynesia, Panama, or Pretoria, the *Prayer Book* is comfortingly familiar. It is not the exact words that are important. It is the drama itself that is essential, in "what the church does as church". Your *Prayer Book* was well used. You prayed the daily offices, and your spirituality echoed the rhythm of the church calendar. Whether Advent, Lent, Easter, or Pentecost, feasts or saints' days, you invariably had some or other interesting comment drawn from the traditions of the church.

I find Anglicanism doctrinally rather laid-back. I don't mean that there are no reputable Anglican theologians. I read Sarah Coakley, Rowan Williams, and Kathryn Tanner with relish. I have enjoyed working on theological projects with a diverse group of theologians such as Kwok Pui-Lan, Ian Douglas, Jenny Plane Te Paa, and Christopher Duraisingh. In South Africa, biblical scholar Gerald West is breaking barriers and Luke Pato blends African traditions with his Anglican beliefs. What I mean is that Anglicans are usually not dogmatic about what we believe. When we do take to theology, we like to think about the Incarnation. This means that the fact that God took on a human face in the person of Jesus has implications for how we understand our relationship with God and with one another. God is not just Other, God is among us and the divine is in all aspects of creation. God wants every creature to be redeemed, and there is no split between the sacred and the secular. Nothing, no person, no issue, no condition, no circumstance does not have a claim on the redemptive work of the gospel.

This means that social justice is an indispensable component of religious practice. Take the issue of poverty. Lambeth '98 debated the issue of third world debt at length, looking at how this debt continues to impoverish countries in the developing world, and it recommended that a year of the jubilee be declared to eradicate third world debt. At its best (and I have seen it at its worst) Anglicans are just another human community trying to be the church of Jesus Christ across a myriad of differences, but held together by the *Common Book of Prayer* and by a need to try and understand what the gospel asks of us in a world of poverty and suffering.

When all is said and done, spirituality for me is the lived experience of relationship with God, with people, and with creation, fed by a longing for justice and wholeness and a resistance to all that thwarts well-being. On my faith landscape I mark spirituality with figures reaching out to one another, some joining hands, others touching tentatively, and yet others not making contact but looking on with longing, all knowing that they will be repaid for the years that the swarming locusts have eaten. You are in my picture as my spiritual companion. So I draw two figures walking on the road to Emmaus. There is no third figure that I can see, but around them there is a Presence, impossible to pinpoint, yet visible and quite beautiful.

The phrase "spiritual direction" is unfortunate. I know you agreed. Both words carry hidden meanings. "Spiritual" could mean something related to the soul at the expense of the body, something abstracted, even ephemeral, removed from issues of bread and body. "Direction" sounds prescriptive, formal, and top-down. Directives are to be obeyed without questioning. Personally I don't like either words when taken on their own, but I cannot abandon the phrase "spiritual direction." It has an ancient history and as a concept it is still useful today. Sometimes spiritual direction is misunderstood as suggesting that our relationship with God requires the mediation of a spiritual director. Nothing could be further from the truth. Spiritual direction is about a relationship entered into with another person with the intention of mutually seeking God's revelation in Christ. It is about having a friend for the journey. It is based on the conviction that relationship with God is at the centre of being and that relationship with God is intrinsic to our relationship with others. It is about the search to quench a longing within the context of a relationship of trust and strenuous honesty. Its aim is freedom in the love of God.

I put you to the test. Did you know yourself? Was your life rooted in penitence and prayer? Would you stay the course with me? I became impatient when you refused to be directive. I remember being frustrated by the pace of our times together. I felt that you were not seeing the urgency of my need. We disagreed, mostly about strategies to change the church. You were hurt because I would not drive with you. I like to drive fast when I am behind the wheel, but your speeding made me nervous. When I finally understood that our relationship was not what Bonhoeffer calls a "wish dream", in other words, it was not some ideal we had in mind for spiritual direction, that it was in fact God's reality and God's time, my tensions evaporated. You prayed for me unceasingly. You were patient because you trusted God in the process. You understood that for too long the central metaphor in my life had been survival — a bare and often dreary existence. There are no shortcuts in the shift from years of practising self-reliance to reliance on God. Being remade is hard work. I may have quit before seeing Emmaus had it not been for your belief in a "me" I had not yet met.

Looking back on our years together I find it hard to describe what we actually did. I talked and you listened. You talked and I listened. Our talk ranged from the latest madness of the state to my struggles with prayer. We did not only talk. We worked together, we marched in the streets, and we worshipped together. All we said and did was encircled by our common need to know God. Alan Jones, after quoting W. H. Auden who said somewhere that life is a very grand opera played by a tenth-rate touring company, continues: "There is a double truth there which helps me understand the art of spiritual direction. It is, at once, sublime and ordinary, even funny. It requires a breadth of vision informed by a strict regard for reality." So it is: a combination of humour, the ordinary, confrontation, nurture, and tears. You had a nice sense of the ridiculous. I remember a trip on the indescribable roads of Mozambique in a rattletrap van. A large shabby red chair was put in the back of the van facing the tail. Looking every bit the mediaeval sage, you sat on your perilous red throne, graciously acknowledging the children waving to us along the road, intoning English mediaeval poetry. What kept me going back for spiritual direction over so many years? Quite simply, your compassion and empathy. You had the capacity to be in the inner world of the other as if it were your own. You helped me to wake up by making me more aware. "Christian companion-ship is often the alarm clock that wakes me up to the fact that my life is rooted in God who reveals himself as a friend," writes Jones. Sometimes waking me took a huge shake; at other times it was subtle and indirect. Through it all, you honoured all the fragments of my life and helped me to befriend them.

There are many quick fixes on offer in the marketplace of spirit-ualities. How can one discern what is life-giving from what is not? Discern-ment in faith requires companionship in faith that is, in turn, immersed in the life of the larger community of faith. If you had been a sham, our com-mon membership of a church with a long tradition of spiritual direction would have rung alarm bells. The Spirit-led common sense of a commu-nity that worships together should be able to help discern what is false from what is authentic. However, the possibility of being misled, even ex-ploited, is always present. There are plenty of self-styled gurus and spiri-tual fads around. The only check I can think of for keeping one's footing on the risky journey to wholeness is one that taps into the discernment of the worshipping community of faith. Nagged by uncertainties, dogged by questions, frustrated by the unquenchable longing, we cannot go it alone. We need companionship along the way. So it is not surprising that talk on the road to Emmaus raises questions and expresses fears. I want to recall now how we talked about despair.

In the biblical story, the figures on the road to Emmaus are talking "about all these things that had happened" since Jesus' death. Two thou-sand years later, we are still talking about things that have happened. This talking is often about bad news. Not surprisingly, terrorism, rampant pov-erty, HIV/AIDS, the tragic intractability of the Israeli/Palestinian conflict, the bombing in Afghanistan, and the war in Iraq are on the agenda. But apart from particular cases of human intransigence there is a sense today that something uncontrollable and evil has been let loose upon the world. This is nothing new. I am sure the prophet Joel felt despair as the locusts consumed his land. So talk along the road to Emmaus turns to Paul's letter to the Colossians (1:16): ". . . for in him all things in heaven and on earth were created, things visible and invisible, whether thrones or dominions or rulers or powers — all things have been created through him and for him." Does this mean that both good and bad are created in Jesus? We look for clues in Romans where Paul writes: "For I am convinced that neither death, nor life, nor angels, nor rulers, not things present, nor things to come, nor powers, nor height, nor depth, nor anything else in all creation, will be able to separate us from the love of God in Christ Jesus our Lord" (8:38, 39). Who are these dominions, powers, rulers? Will understanding these confusing verses lessen the despair that comes from an awareness of evil and our powerlessness? It seems as though we are being thrown back onto the well-used language of spiritual warfare. I find myself resisting metaphors of war. I simply hate war talk. I do not want to be a Christian soldier pressing on into battle! But I am curious about these dominions, rulers, powers, and what they may mean for the sense of helplessness I admit to feeling when faced with evil.

I try to place myself in the shoes of the writers of the biblical texts and then find that most of the references to "powers" in the New Testament consider them as fallen. "Fallen" implies that this was not always their lot. When people of ancient times tried to explain why there was evil in the world they resorted to a simple but vivid cosmology. God sits on high in the heavens, creating and ruling with a council of heavenly beings. Originally all was good and all "powers and principalities" were part of God's good creation. Then members of God's heavenly council become power hungry. They disobey God; they rebel and take matters into their own hands. They become the "powers and principalities" (that Paul speaks of) whose aim is to separate the world from the love of God. They thwart human efforts to live a life that is full and free. Despite their fallen condition these powers cannot escape God's providence. God can use them for good and will ultimately redeem all of creation. This explicit account of the origin of evil is simple enough for a child to understand. It has a certain archaic charm. I can, with relative ease, find different enlightened, modern categories to explain evil. Evil is perpetrated by human beings, encased in evil structures, surrounded by evil intent. Evil is all about power, bad power, and of course, greed. We certainly are capable of great evil, and so the arguments go. But I reach a stage when I am at a loss to explain the pervasiveness of evil convincingly. My efforts are as esoteric as Paul's and not half as charmingly graphic. So the conversation about despair at evil in the world continues unabated on the road to Emmaus.

As we talk, I find that the New Testament offers some comfort. It is, in fact, clear and forthright. God's love in Christ liberates us from slavery to the powers of fate. Whatever ambiguity there may be in understanding the "powers and principalities", Paul has no doubt about the outcome of the world. We need not despair. He tells the Colossians that Christ's death "disarmed the principalities and powers and made a public example of them, triumphing over them by the cross" (2:15). Disarming means taking away their weapons; making an example of them in public means shaming them; triumphing over them is quite simply the concrete event of the resurrection. This sounds like a resounding victory — a more than comforting prospect! Ultimately all will be reconciled to God, including the powers, rulers, things to come or whatever, because all relationships will be restored to their true and proper integrity. So our talk along the road settles for the fact that we are in an "already, not yet" situation. The "powers" are so patently still with us, but whenever Christ's love is spoken about, a limit is set to their working until the end time when all will be reconciled to God. In Hendrikus Berkhof's words: "This limit is the sign and the promise of their defeat." Emmaus talk does not "solve" problems, but it does air them and lighten them as new understanding seeps into our moments of despair.

Bad news does not have the last word. There is beauty, love, courage, and truth if one looks for it. I learnt from your bag of holy tricks to look for the good. No one is more certain of the existence of good than Desmond Tutu, the man we call the Arch. His belief that the universe is ultimately a moral one, with God in charge, enables him to say:

> And in this moral universe nothing is useless. The sighs and groans of the persecuted and tortured, the courage and fidelity of the unremarked, the generosities and compassion that happen unsung, the heroism often hidden — these do not just evaporate into the ether. No, they impregnate the atmosphere. When you enter a happy home you do not need to be told — it is in the air you breathe, in the fabric. As when you enter a church that has been hallowed by much praying, you know it; it is in the bricks and the mortar, it is unmistakable. Nothing is lost, all make a contribution, even the seeming failures; and in the fullness of time, it all comes to a head and others enter into the labours of their predecessors. It is God's work, who watches patiently as it all unfolds, writing straight with crooked lines, adjusting God's plans according to our response, our waywardness and recalcitrance.

To find the "straight lines" takes attentiveness. Being attentive is like tuning in on a new wavelength with a quivering antenna catching up new sounds, or like putting on new spectacles that see sharply, even at night. Being attentive is to recover wonder and amazement. Attentiveness, awareness, or what Buddhist monk Thich Nhat Hanh calls "mindfulness" is "keeping one's consciousness alive to the present reality". It is a kind of sharpened hearing and seeing. I remember looking through a small field magnifying glass for the first time and exclaiming: "A whole new world." I saw lichen that looked like a moonscape. A perfectly ordinary little veld flower turned out to have silvery hairs on its stem, glistening petals that were no longer white, but shaded pink and yellow with a cheeky pistil nestling at the centre waiting for a friendly insect. We can and should be seized by wonder. You once made me meditate on a potato! After forty-five minutes of squirming about, I began to understand what you wanted from me. Attentiveness is about discovery. It means that we no longer edit our experiences, tailoring them to fit the experiences of others. Is it very different from the amazement that Plato experiences at the beginning of philosophy? Attentiveness is basically a spiritual quality. It gives new eyes to see and ears to hear God in oneself and around one. It is waking up to the origin of being-in-relation. Dorothee Sölle comments that

> The soul needs amazement, the repeated liberation from customs, viewpoints, and convictions, which, like layers of fat that make us untouchable and insensitive, accumulate around us. What appears obvious is that we need to be touched by the spirit of life and that without amazement and enthusiasm nothing new can begin.

Seeing with new eyes enables us to let go. The trivia that have taken up energy and time, the guilts long confessed but not let go of, the envy that saps gratitude, begin to wilt before the new gaze. We become receptive because we are flooded with gratitude for seeing what was hidden and hearing what was just a whisper.

Awareness can elude us. I can choose not to give up the preconceptions that blunt my awareness and keep me on unfertile soil. I can prefer to stay with the known and miss a heartbeat. I can resist heightened awareness because I know instinctively that it comes with a price. I may long for the healing breath of God, I may think I can inhale it at will, but I find that

God is beyond my grasp, beyond what I can control. Instead of trusting God in new ways I settle for staying within my comfort zones. "Better the devil I know," says my one inner voice. "I know its face. Why stir the pot? New devils may emerge." "Let go. I want to be free," says the other voice in me. The first voice is the "observer" voice that watches, comments, and analyses. The second is a dampened "gut" voice that is closer to the centre of what I feel than what I think. For years these voices would not stop their competing inner noise. They disappeared after I crushed my last locust. Anne Lamott says, "Awareness is learning to keep myself company." Yes, it is. It also helps to have a companion along the way.

Hearing attentively needs silence. For a long time the story of Mary and Martha left me feeling inadequate. By nature I am a Martha. I can be distracted by mundane things, burdened by a sense of responsibility to "provide" and resentful at others like Mary when I feel that they are free-wheeling on my willingness to keep the pots cooking. Yes, I admit, I used to be envious of Mary and wondered what Jesus might have been saying to her. What might I have heard had I been still? So I consoled myself by the fact that Martha could say, "Yes, Lord. I believe that you are the Messiah," despite her bubbling pots. Now I know that Mary and Martha are both needed to serve Jesus. As Teresa of Avila says, "Believe me, Martha and Mary need to be together to host the Lord and keep him with them forever, or else he will be badly hosted and be left without food." Mary and Martha portray two aspects of the spiritual life, the active, involved side and the listening, contemplative side. My problem has never been with action. It is the inner listening that scuttles me. You showed me how important silence is for listening. You loved to quote Revelation (8:1): "When the Lamb opened the seventh seal, there was silence in heaven for about half an hour." I saw that attentiveness, awareness, and mindfulness are composted in beds of silence and that being willing to try silence is an aspect of letting go.

I remember you saying: "There are different kinds of silence: listening silence, resting silence, and prayerful silence." You also said, "There is the silence of the body, of the mind, and of the spirit." At first I did not understand. But not for long. You encouraged me to go on a retreat. Undaunted by my ignorance, I was an enthusiastic novice and went off on my first nine-day silent retreat. Soon I realised that I was in for the long haul. My struggles with silence have not ended to this day. You taught me how to quiet the body, to focus the mind, and to meditate by using the imagination. You assured me that I was a contemplative person, something I still struggle to believe. I began to understand that silence is not something apathetic and boring. It is in fact active. I should have known this. The silent protest of the Black Sash women spoke volumes. The Quakers sit in silence as an act of worship. Silence is more than taking a holiday from words. Body and mind are tuned into awareness, in a flutter of expectation. Being impatient, I complained. Thankfully you reminded me a thousand times, "just acknowledge the thoughts as they come, don't try and suppress them, just acknowledge them and let them go". Now I know that silence is rather like listening to a cello. Words are not uppermost as the music haunts one's being.

Growing quiet is not merely leaving the chatter and the noise of life behind. One of my favourite stories in scripture is about what happens in the silence. God tells Elijah to go out and stand on the mountain "for the Lord is about to pass by". A great wind comes up, so strong that it splits mountains and breaks rocks, "but the Lord was not in the wind". Then comes an earthquake, and after the earthquake a fire, but the Lord is not in either. After the fire comes "a sound of thin silence". "When Elijah heard it, he wrapped his face in his mantle and went out and stood at the entrance of the cave" (1 Kings 19:11-13). I want to hear that voice of "thin silence" and wrap my cloak around myself as the Lord passes by so that all sadness and need can be washed away.

My years in the Institute and my own experience have both shown me that Christians experience more problems with prayer than with anything else in the life of faith. We get bogged down by ideas about what prayer *ought* to be instead of getting on with what our prayers *can* be. You had a mantra about prayer that you repeated countless times: "Pray as you can, don't pray as you can't." Authenticity is the touchstone of all prayer. C. S. Lewis described the essence of prayer as follows: "May it be the real I who speaks. May it be the real Thou that I speak to." He also said: "The most blessed result of prayer would be to rise thinking, 'But I never knew before. I never dreamed,'" as every idea we form of God, "God must in mercy shatter." Such is the awesomeness of authentic prayer.

Sölle says, "If there is a verb for the life of mysticism, it is praying."

Borrowing from her, praying is the verb for spirituality. It is probably the most difficult aspect of spirituality to write about because most prayer is intensely personal. It is of course also institutional as part of the communal life of the church. I like the prayers of the Anglican liturgy because they have the power to connect me to millions of others praying the same prayers all over the world; because they are supremely indifferent to my moods; because they are ancient and uncluttered; because they express the movements of the life of faith, from adoration through confession to affirmation and praise; because they have become part of my being and will probably be the only phrases I will remember at my end. The prayers of the church keep me in touch with the teachings of the church and jog my memory about what I should be doing and asking. They also provide an element of the ceremonial that carries me along when I feel dry and cold and on the outside.

Personal prayers are offered in many guises. Some prayers are thinking prayers — one might say left brain prayers. When we need to understand something or are grappling with a problem or with a decision, or when we are struggling to understand, we pray. Other prayers are meditative, prayers of the senses, right brain prayers. Chewing on a piece of scripture — imagining the place, the people, the events, the smells and sights, and allowing the text to become alive and contemporary — is right brain praying. A prayer that comes from the wonder and surprise at being alive, or from fear when a loved one is late, or from tears caused by the swelling chorus in a Bach Passion, or from the marvel of the horizon meeting the sky at sunset in the south Atlantic, is an experience of the senses that then gives voice spontaneously to a "Help!" or a "Thank you!" There is also contemplative prayer, prayer beyond words, just a simple "being" one with God. Was it you who told me the story of the elderly French peasant who came to church every day and sat there quietly for hours? When asked why he just sat in silence, he replied: "I look at God and he looks at me, that is all."

Words and more words about prayer are really superfluous. What really matters is intention. You were fond of quoting William Law, one of the well-known Caroline divines of the Anglican tradition, who found himself unable to swear the oath of allegiance to George I, and who left Cambridge to become a private chaplain and writer on the spiritual life. Prayer, he said,

. . . is not silence, or simple petition, or a great variety of outward expressions that alters the nature of prayer, or makes it better, but only and solely the reality, steadiness and continuity of the desire; and therefore whether a man offers this desire to God in the silent longing of the heart, or in simple short petitions, or in a great variety of words is of no consequence. But if you would know what I would call a true and great gift of prayer, and what I most wish for myself, it is a good heart that stands continually inclined towards God.

I suspect you agreed with Law.

The essence of prayer is relationship. Without a relationship of love, desire, and dependence, praying to God would be a mere formality. We pray because God has first called us by name into relationship. We pray because it is in God that "we live and move and have our being." Relationship assumes reciprocity. After the woeful tale of how Adam and Eve get themselves into trouble, there is a wonderful snippet in the creation story: "They heard the sound of the Lord God walking in the garden at the time of the evening breeze . . ." (Gen. 3:8). I imagine the Creator God enjoying the beauty of the garden, looking forward to conversation with the man and the woman. Instead, they hide themselves from God's presence and the moment of holy conversation is scuttled. Prayer is our effort at re-establishing holy conversation. Dorothee Sölle tells how Thomas Müntzer underscored one of his manifestos with the words:

Thomas Müntzer will pray to no mute God,
but only to a God who speaks.

Fortunately God does speak, not always when and in the manner we want conversation, but often unexpectedly and softly. Bernard Häring said: "Love desires to be loved." So God speaks. Love and desire woo us without end. You knew that God speaks. You taught many of us that God is heard in the silence. To paraphrase a well-known line: I believe in the sun when it rains, in love when I see hate, and in God when God is silent. It is about being faithful when locusts are wreaking destruction.

I remember your first remark at workshops on prayer for the clergy: "Prayer is standing naked before God." You then proceeded to explain the layers of nakedness that have to be stripped off for authentic prayer. Here lies the rub. We don't know how to unwrap the coverings of the years. We know intuitively that our prayers are not right, but we don't know how to become naked. Praying is often intensely frustrating. No voices, no hot lines, no awesome moments. Too often it seems to be only distraction, monotonous repetition, and a sense of failing God. Some of my holy tricks on prayer are from your bag; others I picked up on the way. I can no longer sort out what came from whom or from where, so I offer them with apologies to you, to authors not quoted, and to friends not acknowledged.

– *We don't know how or what to pray.* This is the most important realisation in the life of prayer. It is also the most comforting. Fortunately the "Spirit helps us in our weakness, for we do not know how to pray" (Rom. 8:26).
– *Pray as you can, don't pray as you can't.* I acknowledge you and thank you for this wisdom. Frankly I don't think any prayer is worth making unless it is authentic to who and where I am. Prayer is not performance. Our only audience is God. This the Spirit knows.
– *Pray briefly and frequently.* As Benedict counsels, "So prayer ought to be brief and pure, unless you are moved by the inspiration of divine grace to prolong it." Augustine warns us only to pray as long as "fervent intention" lasts. Thomas Aquinas in much the same vein says that when we cannot go on praying without getting bored, it is time to stop. Too often we pray as though God is deaf or as if we are on a treadmill of pious phrases. Praying frequently means learning to live our whole lives with God.
– *Be modest; do not aim at more than placing yourself ready for prayer.* Just be willing to grow quiet and to wait. Put aside the "oughts" and be willing to wait in trust. Aquinas said that the minimum requirement for prayer is intention, not attention.
– *Acknowledge distractions, don't fear them or try to suppress them.* My most common experience when trying to pray is a mind that jumps about like the proverbial cat on a hot tin roof. I make my most efficient lists at prayer, I remember things I have tried to dredge up all day, I wander into speculations about tomorrow. Soon I am exhausted and frustrated. It helps to acknowledge each distraction as it appears and to let it go. Laugh about them with God. Even when our minds are dis-

tracted we can still be present bodily. I read somewhere that the apostle James had knees like a camel because he knelt so much!

- *Use repetition in times of drought.* You taught me this. You showed me how repeating the Jesus prayer — "Lord Jesus Christ, Son of God, have mercy on me" — can become the prayer of the heart and not just a mouthing of words that becomes meaningless and repetitive. The Lord's prayer and the prayers of the *Prayer Book* are always there in lean times.

- *Prayer is not pitting our feelings against our thoughts.* Prayer is not experience versus doctrine. Anselm knew this. He said: "Make me taste in love what I taste by knowledge, may I perceive in my affections what I perceive in my mind." Aquinas knew the danger of excluding the affective when he said of his own theology: "It reminds me of straw." Perhaps this a trap for those with a theological training. (I am not sure I share the optimism of Evagrius Ponticus, who said, "If you truly pray, you are a theologian, and if you are a true theologian, you will know how to pray"!)

- *Praise, confess, petition, and thanks in prayer.* I have no recipes or five-finger exercises here. I do know that Evelyn Underhill is right when she says that confession should be done ordinarily, not as "spiritual spring cleaning". Repentance is making room for God's compassion. Petition often rattles nonbelievers. What is the point of asking God for anything since your assumption is that God knows everything anyway? Yes, God hears our desires long before we articulate them. We bring them nonetheless. It's a matter of honesty. Prayer is after all talk from the heart. Praise and thanks are easy when things are going well. They require tough talk when things are going wrong. It's a question of perseverance. Anthony the desert father cried out: "I psalmed down the devil!" Enough said.

The Eucharist was central to your spirituality. You took me there. I saw how the bread and the wine are food for life and the source of my hope. What fun to discover that Calvin himself shared your view! One wonders what he would have said about some of the vapid liturgies in present-day reformed churches. How aching is the need for *semper reformanda!* For Calvin, Christ was present in the preached word and the Supper. Touchingly he wrote in his fourth book of the *Institutes*:

In his sacred supper Christ bids me take, eat and drink his holy body and blood under the symbols of bread and wine. I do not doubt that he himself truly presents them and that I receive them.

I wonder how many times you presided over the Eucharist in your more than fifty years as a priest? We celebrated together in many strange places. Never once did I see your gentle mixture of sadness and joy waver. I was always moved.

I remember that night in Maputo. We had just motored down from Chambone in northern Mozambique, a hair-raising trip on a road with holes the size of baths. I was resting when the bishop invited us to his chapel for the Eucharist. I was tired and demurred, but he insisted. We were a handful of people in front of the altar. Twelve-year-old Candida was to be baptised and given communion. Two years previously she had been sent by parents to visit a relative in the rural area. There she was kidnapped by Renamo, the opposition force in the civil war. For two years she disappeared. That morning she had reappeared out of the bush, strips of cotton wrapped around her small pubescent body to ward off evil. Her parents contacted the bishop. "You were about to baptise and confirm her two years ago. We are bringing her today." Candida stood between her parents wearing a pink dotted dress and broken blue plastic sandals, her legs dusty, her body rigid. I looked at her and saw only trauma. My mind raced — rape, AIDS, medication, therapy, long-term therapy. In those times no such remedies were available. So her parents did the only thing they could do — they brought her to the altar to be baptised and to receive the bread and the wine, the only means of grace available to them.

Our traumas, failures, and losses do not have the last word. I take comfort from putting those I pray for into the cup when I take communion. I know that deep in the wounds of Christ are all the wounds of this world, including Candida's hurting body. Our hope is in Jesus Christ, the embodiment of our faith, whose life, death, and resurrection we celebrate in the Eucharist.

Ageing and the prospects of dying were part of our conversations. These days I think a great deal about getting old and about death. This is not an exercise in morbidity, but rather a mixture of curiosity and discovery. I am curious about the signs of ageing as I find my priorities changing. You worked until the end of your life. I had to retire at sixty-five, an age that strikes me as rather arbitrary. I wonder who determined that sixty-five was time to go? Did the age-limit bureaucrats know that Michelangelo (1475-1564) was appointed architect of St. Peter's in Rome at the age of seventy-two and worked on its dome until he died at eighty-eight? Or that Carl Jung (1875-1961) completed his autobiography *Memories, Dreams, Reflections* in the year he died, at eighty-six? Or that pianist Arthur Rubenstein (1887-1982) was still performing at eighty-eight and wrote his autobiography *My Many Years* at ninety-two?

Undoubtedly comedian George Burns was right when, at ninety, he quipped that ageing has a bad reputation! Augustine is tough on old age: "an inferior age, lacking lustre, weak and more subject to disease . . . and it leads to death". Contradicting himself somewhat in a sermon, he says rather piously: "In humility, seek; and when you have found, you will come to heights that are free from danger. Innocence will be your infancy; reverence your childhood; patience your adolescence; courage, your youth; merit, your manhood; and nothing other than venerable and wise discernment, your old age." Simone de Beauvoir in *Coming of Age* writes: "The vast majority of mankind looks upon the coming of old age with sorrow or rebellion, and it fills them with more aversion than death itself." For her, death was ever present as mutability. "I could not bear to think of myself as finite and ephemeral, a drop of water in the ocean; at times all my endeavours seemed vanity, happiness became a false lure, and the world wore the mocking illusory mask of Nothingness."

Why this negativity? Are we the products of societies that think only about ageing as a political or an economic issue — How much will the welfare state be affected by the growing numbers of old people, or how will the "grey vote" swing political outcomes? Or do we see ageing as a state punctuated by the loss of meaning? Or is ageing simply an exhausting stage we must stave off as long as we can by substituting things that are disguised to assert youthful values? Or is fear of impending death the reason for such melancholy?

In the Old Testament, old age is seen as a blessing of God. "Grey hair is a crown of glory; it is gained by a righteous life," say the Proverbs (16:31). Leviticus instructs the Jews: "You shall rise before the aged, and defer to the old" (19:32). But little or nothing is said about ageing in the New Testament. The early church seems to focus on hope and the life after death rather than getting old.

Someone told me that the process of ageing was like rusting. I picture how, slowly, but inexorably, creaking joints and much-used organs are rusting away while knowing that the biology of ageing remains a mystery. Why does the common mayfly live for a day and the giant sequoia tree have the promise of reaching two thousand four hundred years? Why do hamsters live for three years and dogs for sixteen? Some fish, like sharks and sturgeons, don't age, they just add years to their life span. Despite these mysteries it is clear that ageing is about time and about irreversible change. It is both a process of loss and of gain. It can be both despair and hope, decay and maturity, fate undergone and chance embraced.

Place, class, and circumstance all play a role in weathering age. More well-connected people may find that their status is enhanced by age. Resources help to cushion some of the unpleasant aspects of ageing. But being poor and old is to be neglected and dishonoured in my country. Old people walk miles to get their pensions, wait with dogged fatalism in long lines, are often disappointed, and have to return again as inefficient or dishonest bureaucrats disregard their plight. Failure of the social welfare system results in too many elderly barely surviving on meagre pensions shared among unemployed relatives. Their fate is compounded by the spectre of disease. As HIV/AIDS decimates the lives of so many South Africans, grandmothers are having to find the energy and the means to rear their orphaned grandchildren with no support from the state. Being old and poor is an unenviable lot in South Africa.

As I said, ageing is both loss and gain. Some losses are obvious; loss of balance, failing sight, forgetting your friends' names, finding that your old jeans are no longer your favourite item of clothing. In the last few years I have lost friends who are my age. One was ravaged by Alzheimer's, others have succumbed to diseases like breast cancer. Bereavement is part of ageing. I expect to grieve as time passes. The ability to face loss does not come easily. What does surprise me is to find that ageing is trivialised. Don't misunderstand me. I am not for a gerontocracy. I just want a creative and respected place for all ages in society, one in which self-worth is less dependent on economic productivity or social roles. I resist the bias that favours males in regard to ageing in most cultural traditions. King David takes the beautiful young virgin Abishag to lie in his bosom and to keep him warm (1 Kings 1:1-4). Old women are not encouraged by society to take young virgin males into their beds to serve as hot pads! Despite notable exceptions, our history is riddled with dignified patriarchs and too many old crones and hags. I do not feel a victim of age, neither do I feel redundant in life. While my body is slowly decaying, my sense of myself is not. I want to experience my body's ageing with understanding and realism. I want ageing to have a human face and a spirit that dreams. George Bernard Shaw in *Back to Methuselah* wrote, "You see things: and say 'Why?' But I dream things that never were: and say 'Why not?'" I still dream of dancing with Fred Astaire.

Ageing is not the end but the beginning of another reality. It is not all loss. I don't want to go back in time. So what are the gains? Growing old is pay-back time. Hurts, joys, lessons learnt on the way are harvested to make sense of who one is and who others are. There is a turning inward. The "is" becomes central in one's life rather than the "ought". Meaning is sought in the dynamics of one's previous history that help to meet the challenges of today. It is a process of moral becoming. Fredrica Thompsett reminds us that "growing old is still *growing*". Ageing is the discovery of creativity that is less hampered by expectations. Perhaps I will paint or pot or write some more. Etty Hillesum writes: "I do believe it is possible to create, even without ever writing a word or painting a picture, by simply moulding one's inner life. And that too is a deed." The one indispensable blessing for ageing is a sense of humour. The absurdities, contradictions, and foibles of life are not only inherently funny, but the fact that I took them so solemnly is a lark! There is joy in recalling the humorous family anecdotes, the well-worn jokes, the *faux pas*, embarrassing moments, the traps one has fallen into and survived. Gaping at and groping for the names of those close to me leaves me with two choices: either I sweat, or I laugh. The laugh that starts in an ageing belly should be fruity and forgiving, affirming — "So be it."

Memory, sorely taxed as it slips and frustrates, becomes vital in new ways. I want to recover the past but find that large chunks of my life are simply missing. What remains is a sense of what was worthwhile and what was not, and with it the urge to pass this on. I am not sure whether this is succumbing to the arrogance of wanting to leave a legacy or some primal urge to hold on to the interconnection of the generations. I do know that with increasing age, biography becomes important and that life is seen more as a continuation than an end in itself. K. Brynolf Lyon writes, ". . . the consummation of hope in old age is made possible through the contribution older adults can make to the lives of others." Even a most modest sense of being able to make a difference will do. How blessed you were that your work went on to the end, dispensing wisdom from your bag of holy tricks.

Hope is essential for remembering. I hope that who I have become can allow me at this stage of my life to continue to realise the values that are important to me even in the midst of bodily decay and increasing closeness to death. I hope daily for greater closeness to God. I recall God's blessing, mercy, and forgiveness throughout life. This supports my faith that God makes available the potential for realising the greatest value of every moment and condition of our lives. God's blessing is present in every moment in all circumstances. You showed me that being open and aware of the blessings in the humdrum things changes the day. Even in your worst moments of anxiety and pain, you found holy tricks to live by in the most unlikely places. Of course, God's blessing is unconditional. Our realisation of the fruits of blessing is not. To speak of blessing is not to say that the world is devoid of hardship, loss, or disease. But it does say that God provides the potential to realise the greatest value even in these circumstances. Meaninglessness is done away with. Everything is taken into God. This is the blessing of age. God takes the venture of getting old seriously and becomes my confidant as I age.

Whilst writing this letter I visited an exhibition of Pieter Breugel the Elder's drawings at the Metropolitan Museum of Art in New York. I was drawn to a piece titled "The Triumph of Time", a startling drawing depicting two versions of time. In the foreground is a horse-drawn cart on which Time, depicted as an aged male figure, devours an infant. The victory of time over the ordinary things of life shows the cart crushing the symbols of daily life: plates, urns, spades, and spoons. Behind the cart is Death, a skeleton wrapped in a sheet, carrying a scythe. In the distance figures dance around a maypole, lovers walk hand in hand, and birds swoop over the sky. The entire drawing is one of contrasts. One black and one white horse draw the cart, one with the symbol of the sun, the other with the symbol of the moon. I gazed at this drawing for some time, wondering why it fascinated me. The disturbing figure of Death, the contradictions, the paradoxes, the ordinary and the extraordinary, all crowded into one drawing, depicting the fragile joy of life and the fearsome face of death. "Bruegel's world, like ours, showed a gaping divide between the monstrous and the magnificent, between freaks and demons and hellish fantasies out of Hieronymus Bosch and landscapes near paradisal in their impervious splendor," writes John Updike in his review of this exhibition. The remainder of this letter is about an aspect of this gaping divide. On the one hand thoughts about death can be full of dread; on the other death can be a friend in the business of living.

Psychoanalyst Ernest Becker in his wonderful book *The Denial of Death* vividly describes the paradoxical dilemma of life and death. We humans have minds that can speculate, imagine, and create symbols. We roam the cosmos, we have a sense of history. Yet, at the same time, we are food for worms. In Becker's words, we are housed in a "heart-pumping, breath-gasping body that once belonged to a fish and still carries the gill-marks to prove it." We are aware of our uniqueness, yet we go back to dust. We think about death and reflect on its meaning, something animals are spared. For them there may be a few minutes of fear, a few seconds of anguish and it is over. Søren Kierkegaard thought a great deal about anxiety or what he called "dread". In his work *The Concept of Dread* he wrote:

> If man were a beast or an angel, he would not be able to be in dread. [That is, if he were utterly unself-conscious or totally un-animal.] Since he is a synthesis he can be in dread . . . man himself produces dread.

We are neither animals nor angels. Our anxiety, dread, or fear is a result of our ambiguity. Death is our peculiar and greatest anxiety, says Becker. This is what I saw in Bruegel's drawing.

The Christian existentialist Paul Tillich distinguishes between fear and anxiety. Fear knows a definite object, such as physical pain, rejection, or the loss of a loved one. Fear can be faced, analysed, and endured. Anxiety on the other hand is "ultimate non-being". Anxiety threatens us with nothingness. It cannot be met with courage and is always unendurable. "It is impossible for a finite being to stand naked anxiety for more than a flash of time. People who have experienced these moments, as for instance some mystics in their visions of the 'night of the soul' . . . have told of the unimaginable horror of it," writes Tillich in *The Courage to Be*. Although fear and anxiety are different, they are closely related and often intertwined. Tillich applies his distinction between fear and anxiety to the ultimate example, namely, fear of death. Death is not only unknown but *absolutely* unknown. This most basic of anxieties is anxiety about one's "ultimate non-being". The dread, the fear of non-being, drive us to find means to lull the dread — drugs, drink, sex, holidays, fast cars, even shopping. Anxiety is the result of the perception of the truth of one's condition. Knowing "the dread" and the anxiety is to admit to possibility. We have to face up to our natural impotence and our death. Edgar in King Lear says:

> What, in ill thoughts again? Men must endure
> Their going hence, even as their coming hither;
> Ripeness is all; come on.

Dr. Johnson said that the prospect of death concentrates the mind. Mortality is a constant companion of ageing. The death of friends and my own ageing are no doubt focussing my mind on death and dying. I have friends who are HIV positive. Five hundred South Africans are dying daily of AIDS-related causes. Ongoing wars are giving death a rich harvest. The reality of death is ever present whether one sees it or not. Death has its dark side, what H. L. Mencken called the "engulfing impenetrable dark". We fear it and we can surrender to despair, withdrawal, or even passivity when thinking about death. We are fragile creatures who experience emptiness and terror. But death is not all darkness; it has an en-lightening side. I like to think of death as a friendly shadow, contrasting light and dark, ever present, marking our moments. Death is the basis for our being and doing in the world. The more we refuse to contemplate our own death, the less able we are to find new possibilities for living. As we are all going to die, living with the acceptance that our lives are moving to that sure end effectively clears the mind of false props and empty assurances. Befriending death like Francis of Assisi, who called death "sister", helps us to recognise its many guises and to unmask its terror so that we too can call it "sister", Then death can become a companion and a counsellor, a salutary presence. "The willingness to live with the knowledge of our inevitable death enables us to face, more and more, both the freedom and responsibility that life offers," writes Alan Jones. The willingness to walk with the friendly shadow of death is in fact life-affirming. It is not easy. Sickness has taught me just how much I cling to life. With my mind I assent to God's gift of death: "You have died and your life is hid with Christ in God" (Col. 3:3). This means that the "I" that I hang onto so desperately is already dead. I half believe this. I cannot take what it means in large helpings. At the same time I know that only God knows the "I" in me and that something positive happens when I look my death straight in the eye.

Alan Jones, in paraphrasing one of my favourite theologians, Karl Rahner, writes:

Death puts my whole existence into question without being able to answer the question. I have to surrender to the uncertainty of death, and this surrender can be simply an act of despair in the ultimate futility of being. On the other hand, my act of surrender can prepare me for the possibility that the answer may come from a totally unexpected quarter. It is, then, not a surrender to despair, but to the Unknown. Finally, my surrender can be an act of faith that a radical rescue is at hand. I am caught in all three responses; and to be thus caught is, in some sense, to be a participant in a great passion (the believer in me would call it *the* Passion). I want to be a believer with both passion and intelligence and my longing always brings me into a desert place — a place of emptiness and death. And it is there that I begin to love.

Humans have to thrash around in our finitude in order to see beyond it. Our impotence exists over against a living God for whom everything is possible. We have to face the fact that we are from dust to dust, yet full of inner longings and authentic talents. Our deepest feelings of uniqueness and our longing for ultimate significance take us to the very ground of creation. We reach out for hope so that life can be worthwhile. You showed me how Easter gives meaning to mortality. At the heart of the Easter story is the dying and the rising of Jesus Christ. Through faith in this event, we are initiated into the new life of the risen Christ. This gives us a different way of looking at the undeniable paradox of being human. Instead of the pessimism of an André Malraux, who wrote in *The Human Condition* that it takes sixty years of incredible suffering and effort to make something of ourselves and then we are only good for dying, we see life and death through new spectacles. We hope, and hope gives the right focus to the reality of dread and death. I can't escape writing to you about death, because I saw how you lived with the reality of your own mortality. I am grateful for your gentle end.

Throughout the letters in this book I have been trying to answer the question: "What makes life worth living?" My answer is simple: Faith makes life worth living. How do I know this? When one falls in love, one knows pretty well how different the "before" is from the "after". So it is in the life of faith. I can only say that I know what I saw, thought, and believed before I had faith and how different it has been living the "after". I believe my own experience. I see it in the lives of others. If the "after" is so worthwhile, why write about injustice, suffering, lament, sickness, ageing, and death? I write about these things because they are the reality of much of life. By grace, the story does not end here. Suffering and pain do not have the last word. Faith sees all of life touched by the breath of the Holy One. Patches of composted earth appear in my landscape. Holy breath brings new growth to the veld, comfort to the lamenting, vitality to the despairing, and hope that transcends the dread of death.

You helped me to navigate the landscape of faith, stopped me from taking the shortcuts I favour so readily, and held out hope of healing when I saw only wounding. You combined utter realism about the world with an unshakeable faith in God's promise of redemption for all. I found the same quality of realism and faith in Julian of Norwich. She has been a silent partner along the road to Emmaus. Born in 1343, this extraordinary English mystic had a virtual death experience at thirty, an event that gave rise to her series of revelations or "showings". She records visions of Jesus on the cross, voices, conversations, teachings, confrontations with evil, experiences of abandonment and despair, and what can only be described as out-of-body experiences. What draws me to Julian are her straightforward and down-to-earth descriptions of these weird events. I do not feel conned. Her style is simple, her theology refreshing and unique. The first woman to compose a book in the English language, she was an exact contemporary of Chaucer's and a lot easier to read. She is not a mystic because she has visions. She is a mystic because her faith flows from her lived experience of God's grace and presence throughout her life. Julian is no simple pietist. She actively longs for God, wanting enlightenment and understanding. Thomas Merton is unstinting in his assessment of Julian. "There can be no doubt that Lady Julian is the greatest of the English mystics," he wrote.

We talked about Julian and what she meant for our lives. You loved to read her in the old East Anglian dialect; I stuck to the modern version. In memory of these conversations, I want to record how Julian has helped me sort out the theological knots that get in the way of the life of faith. Kathleen Norris observes: "The problem of theology is always to keep it within its bounds as an adjunct and response to a lived faith." She points out:

> Since the earliest days of the Christian church, there has been a curious tension between Semitic storytelling, which admits a remarkable diversity of voices, perspectives, and experience into the canon, and Greek philosophy, which seeks to define, distinguish, pare down. It is the latter most people think of when they hear the word "theology," because at least in the Christian West, it is the tendency that has prevailed.

Julian is no mean theologian. But she is not caught in the trap of "rational inquiry into religious questions", one of the stock ways of defining theology. She tells us that she experienced her "showings" in three ways: through bodily sensations, through spiritual visions, and through intellectual enlightenment. Out of these experiences she writes her Revelations, which C. S. Lewis describes to Bede Griffiths as follows: "I have been reading Lady Julian of Norwich. A dangerous book, clearly: I'm glad I didn't read it much earlier." A dangerous book indeed because Julian weaves her theology from her reflections on her visionary experience, something that is not subject to control. We either accept the validity of her writings or we dismiss them as eerie and unnatural. I have described moments in the letters in this book that defy "rational inquiry". I consider myself a rational person. I strive to think coherently when I write theology. I cannot deny that my faith experiences, both those that defy rational explanation as well as the humdrum aspects of being a Christian, all feed my theology. When theological precision becomes exclusionary, when the simple faith of people is highjacked by orthodoxy, I want to quit as a theologian. Then Julian's way of bridging the divides between the genuine theological questions and the experienced life of faith becomes my guide. You led me to Julian. I now want to tell you how she continues to check my efforts at doing theology.

Take the perennial question of evil and sin, one that Julian does not avoid. Her well-known words "Sin is necessary, but all shall be well. All shall be well; and all manner of thing shall be well" are not simply wishful thinking, but are arrived at after twenty years of reflection on the enigma of sin. Julian understands that one cannot think about the nature of sin and evil apart from thinking about the nature of God. Her visions leave her with a new appreciation of the love of God and life itself. With absolute certainty she proclaims that love of God is identical with the being of God. Love is not something that God does. It is not a virtue or a property of God's. It is simply what God is. And God loves "all that is made." Brant Pelphrey points out that Julian is intensely aware of existing hierarchies of believers in which the "beginners" are separated from the "perfects." She was not having any of this spiritual elitism. Pelphrey continues:

> For Julian, the message of love which she received was intended from the start for those poor and uneducated who would have been most troubled by the questions of divine wrath, the judgment, of death and suffering and how to live a decent life in the midst of a world full of turmoil and uncertainty.

It is true that most Christians believe that God is love. What is unique about Julian's views is that God's love is shown in terms of humility or what she calls "kindness". God's love is shared with humanity and we in turn share the divine nature, which is always to love. God is "kynde". Julian does not mean that God is kind in an affectionate yet distant way. Kindness is inherent to God's disposition. True kindness involves relationship. There is nothing patronising about kindness, no superiority — just a deep charity and understanding. So God cannot withhold love or kindness — God simply *is* both loving and kind. It is impossible for God to be unkind. "It is impossible for God to be wroth." Through all her visions she never saw God angry. What a comfort this must have been for the poor folk who consulted her in her anchorite's cell and who were being threatened with fire and brimstone for their sins. Julian's idea of God's love was neither psychological nor romantic. It was based on the very being of God. We are meant to share in God's nature — in this sense love is also inherent to our being human. God's love is immediately present in everything that *is*, simply because it exists. This means that every person who loves, "regardless of cultural or religious background, and whether conscious of it or not, has come into contact with God and indeed is experiencing something of God," writes Pelphrey. We are "knit" to divine nature, whether we know it or not.

Against this understanding of the nature of God as inherently loving, Julian wrestles with the reality of sin and the fact of evil. Earlier in this letter I quoted Tillich, who said that "some mystics in their visions of the 'night of the soul' . . . have told of the unimaginable horror of it". Julian's convictions about God's love are not an airy fairy optimism about God that shows no knowledge of evil and suffering. Julian understands the reality of sin and of evil. She confronts "the fiend" "with his heat and his stink . . . so vile and so painful, frightening and hard to bear . . .", who holds her by the throat and tries to strangle her. She also lived in hard times. Repeated plagues of the Black Death, famine, the brutal suppression of the church in her later years, and the burning of Lollards at the stake all happened during her lifetime. She was no stranger to suffering. Her life as an anchorite did not cut her off from the plight of the world.

Julian describes a "soft dread [that] came over me", and asks: "What is sin? For I saw clearly that God does all things, even the very least . . . that nothing happens by chance or accident, but all is by the foreseeing wisdom of God." How does she reconcile a God who knows all, who is wise and loving, with the irrefutable fact of evil and sin? To begin with, she does not resort to a common solution — imputing the origin of sin to a source other than God. She does not buy into the orthodox solution that attributes evil to the free will of creatures who deliberately choose to disobey God. She simply cannot. For God "is in the midpoint of all things and he does all things: yet I was sure he did not sin". We are inhabited by God's love. Sin is not inherently part of being human. But she cannot resist wondering ". . . why in God's great foresight and wisdom sin had not been forestalled in its beginning?" Julian's answer is unambiguous: Sin and evil are non-being — they have no substantial reality. We cannot understand evil because evil is non-being. As God is in everything, sin cannot be something that exists. Sin is known only in the absence of joy and love and what is good. To say that something *is* without having any real being appears contradictory. In order to explain this paradox, Pelphrey points out that a similar idea exists in modern science. The recent discovery of black holes offers a sobering parallel to Julian's seemingly contradictory statement. "Sin is like these pockets of darkness whose existence cannot be positively measured, but which paradoxically are dense concentrations of mass focussed entirely upon themselves. . . . They emit no light; they are not "there" though their presence is absolutely destructive," explains Pelphrey. Julian is concerned that evil and sin do not have ultimate power. There is only one God and that God is good and loving. Sin is hateful to God but it can be useful to us as we struggle to work out God's love and compassion in our lives. I can't help wondering if she knew that Augustine had come to the same conclusion: "Therefore, whatsoever is, is good. Evil, the origin of which I had been seeking, has no substance at all; for if it had substance, it would be good."

Julian finds her answer to the problem of sin in Christ's atonement for all. Through Christ's act of atonement "all shall be well." I simply understand this to mean what Paul's great hymn to the Philippians (2:5-11) tells us. "Let the same mind be in you that was in Christ Jesus", begins Paul, and then goes on to describe in lyrical terms how Christ "though he was in the form of God . . . emptied himself" and became human, humbling himself to the point of death on a cross after which he was exalted by God, who "gave him a name above every name." You loved this hymn and saw the emptying of Jesus as a paradigm for our lives. Going through the suffering is part of the journey from life to death, as we "work out our salvation with fear and trembling." The journey does not end there. "But God, who is rich in mercy, out of the great love with which he has loved us even when we were dead through our trespasses, made us alive together with Christ — by grace you have been saved — and raised us up with him in the heavenly places in Christ Jesus" (Eph. 2:4, 5). Julian helps me to make sense of Jesus' emptying of himself and becoming a servant. For Julian, Jesus is both fully human and fully divine. For it is in God's nature to be self-emptying; such is God's kindness. Therefore it is natural for the Son to empty himself and become the servant of all. Because Jesus is the true human being, he is our nature, and through him we are "knit" to God. "This 'knitting' took place before we ever knew of it, and even before we were born, and so it involves much more than our own decision or faith, or even the event of the crucifixion itself," writes Pelphrey. Our salvation is a process that has been ongoing before time and into time. It is cosmic and includes the creation of the world. We are in process of what Julian calls "oneing" — becoming one in God and in the fulness of our humanity. "Oneing" is a process of union with God, Julian's version of *unio mystica*. Quite literally this means at-one-ment. We remain who we are, creatures made by God, yet God does not separate us from Godself. No wonder all things shall be well!

Julian understands the reality of sin as a distortion of our nature. Sin is what is unkind and unnatural, a distortion of our true nature. We are made for God's love. We know this instinctively — after all, we love our children and we "fall in love". Sadly, we lose sight of our true nature and cloud our vision with sinful acts. But sin is useful, because it helps us to know ourselves and to know God. It is a "sharp scourge" that we all experience, and in our falling into sin we encounter the "wonderful love of our Creator" in whom "all shall be well and all manner of thing shall be well".

Just a last thought about Julian and her visions. Julian declares: ". . . I saw that God rejoices that he is our Father, God rejoices that he is our Mother, and God rejoices that he is our true Spouse and our soul his beloved wife. And Christ rejoices that he is our brother, and Jesus rejoices that he is our Saviour." I warm to her use of human relationships to describe God. This is nothing new. Anselm could say, "And you Jesus, are you not also a mother? Are you not a mother who, like a hen, gathers her chickens under her wings?" Julian's views on the motherhood of God are quite in keeping with the bible, which also describes God's "mothering" — a fact that is overlooked all too often today. Julian's understanding is carefully developed. God is the creator giving birth to us, like a mother. Christ is our mother because he gives birth to us as we are reborn in him. As a mother bears the pain of birth, Christ takes upon himself the pains of death to bring us to spiritual birth. In the Eucharist we are fed with Christ's blood that pours from his side like milk from a mother's breast. Like a true mother he seeks to take away our sin and our pain. These metaphors are simple but extraordinary and quite daring for her time. I don't think that Julian's theology is arrived at through playing mind games. Her visions of God's love and of Christ's passion, her bodily experience of these visions and decades of reflection on them, shape her theological insights. Julian, as Grace Jantzen points out, is an integrated theologian, ". . . for whom daily life and religious experience and theological reflection are all aspects of the same whole." She laboured long and hard to understand her visions. "She would settle for neither undevotional theology nor for untheological devotion," says Jantzen. Apart from the profundity of her theological insights, I like Julian's simplicity, her earthiness, and her joyful hope. She is positive, full of light and joy. She often speaks of the delight in knowing God — of bliss, cheer, joy, blessedness. She knows experiences of doubt and temptation and separation from God that are "murky as night", but she does not stay there. While aspects of her theology are a challenge to the church of her day, she takes great care to say that she is a loyal daughter of the church and has no desire to take away from the teachings of the church. Julian is, in Pelphrey's words, on a "joyful pilgrimage — a journey of the soul into the heart of God." When I am tempted to fall back on orthodoxies or clever arguments, when I find my theology parting company with my hard-won beliefs, when jargon gets the better of me, I turn to Julian. She is the kind of theologian I would like to be.

I have written letters that have been about life with and life after the locusts. I have learnt that the God who says ". . . that I, the Lord, am your God and there is no other" can repay us for the years the locusts have eaten. The road to Emmaus has not been without obstacles and pitfalls. I am grateful to have had you as a companion on the way. I can't help imagining you chuckling at my efforts to recount some of our times together — a gentle chuckle because that was your way, kindly, firm, and affirming.

> With thanks and the
> certainty of blessing,
> *Denise*

NOTES

Francis Cull was born in Standlake in Oxfordshire, England, in 1915. He came to South Africa in 1958 to work in a parish in Maseru, Lesotho. Subse-

quently he was a parish priest in Chatsworth near Durban and then, for a number of years, taught at Rhodes University and the University of the Wit-
watersrand. An interesting snippet about Francis is the fact that he did his
doctorate on "Love and Marriage in the Novels of Henry James". After returning to parish ministry, he took up the challenge of establishing the Institute for
Christian Spirituality at the request of Archbishop Desmond Tutu. A few years
before his death in 1998, he celebrated the fiftieth year of his ordination to the
priesthood.

My use of the phrase "holy tricks" has nothing to do with deception or
trickery. It is used to describe certain skills with a touch of humour at their unexpected nature. Other terms that need explanation are "the Arch", a term of
affection used by those of us who have worked with Archbishop *emeritus*
Desmond Tutu over the years. It is one he enjoys and uses himself. An anchorite, from the Greek *anachoreō* meaning "to retire", was a type of recluse. Julian
was an anchoress, a reclusive nun. Anchorites vow never to abandon prayer and
can counsel those in need. The word "contemplative" has different meanings.
Martin Thornton in *Spiritual Direction* writes: "Contemplation used to be a
frightening word, and it is one which comprehends a vast range of prayer and
experience. But if its root meaning indicates an integrated, intuitive, experien-
tial approach to prayer instead of a discursive intellectual one, then it has not
become the norm." The term "mysticism," not to be conflated into contemplation, also has different meanings. Evelyn Underhill, a remarkable scholar of
mysticism, writes in her book *Mysticism:* ". . . mysticism is no isolated vision, no
fugitive glimpse of reality, but a complete system of life carrying its own guarantees and obligations. . . . It is the name of that organic process which involves
perfect consummation of the Love of God. . . ". In a later work called *Practical
Mysticism* she describes mysticism as ". . . the art of union with Reality".

The Institute for Christian Spirituality is now known as the Centre for
Christian Spirituality. With a small but dedicated staff it continues to give spiritual direction, to train spiritual directors, and to run retreats and workshops
on aspects of Christian spirituality.

Much has been written about the history of the term "spirituality". Its origins lie in its Latin root *spiritualis,* itself an attempt to translate the Greek noun for
spirit, *pneuma*. The adjective of *pneuma* is *pneumatikos,* a term first used by Paul.
According to Sandra Schneiders, ". . . the adjective 'spiritual' was coined by Paul
to describe any reality (charisms, blessings, hymns, etc.) that was under the influence of the Holy Spirit. Most importantly he used it in 1 Cor. 2:14-15 to distinguish
a 'spiritual person' *(pneumatikos)* from the 'natural person' *(psychikos anthrōpos)*."

I have labelled Francis Cull an Anglo-Catholic with roots in the Oxford Movement. This needs explanation. In the nineteenth century a group called the Tractarians (so-called because they published *Tracts for the Times*) stressed the importance of social ministries and emphasised the roots of the church in the earliest days of Christianity. They also emphasised the importance of social ministries, inspiring Anglo-Catholic priests to minister to the poor out of the belief that the church was catholic and had to be inclusive in its ministry. The Oxford Movement originated in England immediately after the Reform Act of 1832 as part of a wider movement that protested the government's interference in the affairs of the church. One of the characteristics of this movement was its devotion to spirituality and a renewed interest in the ritual of the church. The Oxford Movement was also intensely aware of the need for social action and service to the urban poor. Quoting from John Newman's *Arians of the Fourth Century,* in William George Peck, *Social Implications of the Oxford Movement* (New York: C. Scribner's Sons, 1933), ". . . the Church was formed for the express purpose of interfering or (as irreligious men would say) meddling with the world." This combination of a zeal for holiness with a dedication to social action characterised Francis' ministry.

The etymology of the word "Huguenot" is controversial. According to the *Oxford Dictionary of the Christian Church* (1997), the German for those admitted to the Swiss Confederation was *confederates,* which was later Gallicised in Geneva as *eigenots.* Roughly 200,000 Huguenots left France after the repeal of the Edict of Nantes on 22 October 1685, some 50-70,000 to the Netherlands. The Edict of Nantes, signed on 13 April 1598, improved the lot of Protestants in France. Although it did not place them on a par with the Roman Catholics, it guaranteed certain religious freedoms. At its repeal, all pastors had to leave the country, all temples were to be destroyed, all Huguenot schools were closed, all children were re-baptised and taken to mass, and emigration was forbidden. The era of toleration in France had ended. The initial group to leave the Netherlands for the Cape numbered some 180 people, among them my forebears, the du Toits. I have been interested to discover that in Calvinist resistance literature such as the writing of Théodore Béza, Calvin's designated successor, history, reason, and scripture are used to defend the Huguenot engagement in the resistance movement in France. (Today Anglicans base their faith on scripture, tradition, and reason.) For reading on the French Huguenots in South Africa, see C. Graham Botha, *The French Refugees at the Cape,* 3rd ed. (Cape Town: C. Struik, 1970); Maurice Boucher's *French Speakers at the Cape in the First Hundred Years of Dutch East India Company Rule: The European Background* (Pretoria:

University of South Africa, 1981); and Manfred Nathan, *The Huguenots in South Africa* (Central News Agency, 1939). There is a vast body of literature on the French Huguenots. For background reading on the religious and economic factors that preceded the horror of the St. Bartholomew Massacre (24 August 1572) and the persecution of the Huguenots, see Mack P. Holt, *The French Wars of Religion, 1562-1629* (Cambridge: Cambridge University Press, 1995). G. A. Rothrock's *The Huguenots: A Biography of a Minority* is an easy read for those interested in the history of the Huguenots up to the time of the repeal of the Edict of Nantes.

A useful reader on spirituality is edited by Kenneth J. Collins, *Exploring Christian Spirituality: An Ecumenical Reader* (Grand Rapids: Baker Books, 2000). Sandra Schneiders' article "Spirituality in the Academy" from which I have drawn for understanding the concept spirituality, is reprinted in this volume as well as Anne Carr's piece from which I have quoted. Martin Thornton's *English Spirituality: An Outline of Ascetical Theology According to the English Pastoral Tradition* (London: SPCK, 1963) is an excellent reference work on the type of spirituality in which Francis Cull was rooted. Thornton's chapter on the *Book of Common Prayer* discusses at some length how its origins lie in Benedictine spirituality, the pastoral and spiritual undercurrents of the fourteenth century, and the historical situation of the Carolines. Martin Thornton's *Spiritual Direction* (London: SPCK, 1984), *The Christian Ministry of Spiritual Direction* edited by David L. Fleming in a series "The Best of the Review — 3" (St. Louis: Review for Religious, 1988), and Kathleen Fischer's *Women at the Well: Feminist Perspectives on Spiritual Direction* (London: SPCK, 1989) are useful works on spiritual direction. Thich Nhat Hanh's *The Miracle of Mindfulness: A Manual of Mindfulness* (London: Rider, 1992) is a little gem on the practise of mindfulness by one of the leading Buddhist teachers living in the West. Dietrich Bonhoeffer's *Life Together*, trans. J. W. Doberstein (New York: Harper & Brothers, 1954), describes life in the Christian community of Finkenwalde near Stettin and contains penetrating insights into Bonhoeffer's own spirituality. Philip Sheldrake in *Spirituality and History: Questions of Interpretation and Method* (London: SPCK, 1995) gives a lucid account of the development of the concept spirituality and sets it in its historical context.

Works consulted on ageing from theological, philosophical, and medical perspectives are: Theology and Pastoral Care Series, ed. Don Browning (Fortress Press); Sally Gadow, "Recovering the Body in Aging and Ethics," in Nancy S. Jecker, ed., *Philosophical Problems in Gerontology* (Totowa, N.J.: Humana Press, 1991); K. Brynolf Lyon, *Toward a Practical Theology of Aging*

(Philadelphia: Fortress Press, 1985); Carol LeFevre and Perry LeFevre, eds., *Aging and the Human Spirit: A Reader in Religion and Gerontology* (Chicago: Exploration Press, 1981); and Fredrica Harris Thompsett, *Courageous Incarnation: In Intimacy, Work, Childhood and Aging* (Cambridge, Mass.: Cowley Publications, 1993). Thompsett, p. 61, points out that the term "ageism" was first coined in the United States by Robert Butler in his 1968 study *Why Survive? Being Old in America*. Psychiatrist Gene D. Cohen's *The Creative Age: Awakening Human Potential in the Second Half of Life* (New York: HarperCollins, 2000) is informative and easy to read. On death and dying the following works have been consulted: Ernest Becker, *The Denial of Death* (New York: The Free Press, 1973); Jonathan Dollimore, *Death, Desire and Loss in Western Culture* (New York: Routledge, 1998); John Donnelly, ed., *Language, Metaphysics, and Death* (New York: Fordham University Press, 1978); and Norbert Elias, *The Loneliness of Dying*, trans. E. Jephcott (Oxford: Blackwell, 1985).

Thinking about ageing and the diseases we fear because they rob us of our rational minds (like Alzheimer's or certain terminal conditions associated with dying of AIDS), I have found psychiatrist Oliver Sachs' views (see his works *Awakenings* and *The Man Who Mistook His Wife for a Hat*) valuable for understanding that people's innate worth is not determined by their ability to communicate with us. His writings and his documentaries have shown that no matter how delusional or even demented a person is, there is still a struggle to hold on to a sense of personal identity.

A last thought on ageing — Plato reminds us that true philosophers are always occupied in the practise of dying. While I am not sure that Plato describes the philosophical life accurately, I know that theologians think about death because we cannot think about life without contemplating death. Plato was certainly occupied with Socrates' death. Charged with heresy and corrupting the minds of the young, Socrates was condemned to death. In his final address to the court, he says that death is not to be feared for it contains one of two things, immortality or annihilation. Neither is to be feared. The first for obvious reasons, the second because we will have no consciousness of anything ever again. For Socrates the latter would be preferable — akin to a dreamless sleep in which "the whole of time . . . can be regarded as no more than a single night" (Plato, *Apology*). (Nietzsche, the irrepressible sceptic, is unequivocal in his view of Socrates' choice: "Socrates *wanted* to die — it was not Athens, it was *he* who handed himself the poison cup, who compelled Athens to hand him the poison

cup. . . . 'Socrates is no physician . . . death alone is a physician here. . . .
Socrates had only been a long time sick. . . .'")

Paul uses a variety of terms to refer to forces at work, e.g., principalities,
powers, thrones, dominions; see Hendrikus Berkhof, *Christ and the Powers,*
trans. J. H. Yoder (Scottdale, Pa.: Herald Press, 1977). I have used this work as a
basis for the discussion on the question of evil around us, as well as John
Howard Yoder's *The Politics of Jesus* 2nd ed. (Grand Rapids: Eerdmans, 1994),
which draws on Berkhof's work.

The original manuscript of Julian of Norwich's "Showings", written in
East Anglian dialect, was lost for a long time. In 1670 a version was printed by
the English Benedictine Serneus Cressy based on what is known as the Paris
manuscript, which surfaced at the Bibliotheque Nationale. Works consulted
on Julian of Norwich are: Christopher Abbott, *Julian of Norwich: Autobiography
and Theology* (Cambridge: D. S. Brewer, 1999); Denise Nowakowski Baker,
Julian of Norwich's Showings: From Vision to Book (Princeton: Princeton University
Press, 1994); Grace M. Jantzen, *Julian of Norwich: Mystic and Theologian*
(New York: Paulist Press, 1988); Joan M. Nuth, *Wisdom's Daughter: The Theology
of Julian of Norwich* (New York: Crossroad, 1991); and Brant Pelphrey, *Christ
Our Mother: Julian of Norwich* (Wilmington: Michael Glazier, 1989). For Julian's
text I used John Skinner's translation, *Revelation of Love: Julian of Norwich* (New
York: Doubleday, 1996).

Other quotations in this letter are taken from the following sources:

Augustine, "To the Seekers of Baptism", *Sermons on the Liturgical Seasons,*
    trans. Sister M. Muldowney, vol. 38 of *The Fathers of the Church,* 1959.
Augustine, *Confessions,* trans. H. Chadwick (Oxford: Oxford University
    Press, 1991).
Calvin, *Institutes* (1559), III,xix,16.
Simone de Beauvoir, *The Coming of Age* (New York: Putnam, 1972).
Harvey Guthrie, "Anglican Spirituality: An Ethos and Some Issues", in
    William J. Wolf, ed., *Anglican Spirituality* (Wilton, Conn.: Morehouse-
    Barlow, 1982).
Dag Hammarskjöld, *Markings* (New York: Alfred Knopf, 1971).
Alan Jones, *Exploring Spiritual Direction* (New York: Seabury Press, 1982).
Alan Jones, *Soul Making: The Desert Way of Spirituality* (San Francisco:
    Harper & Row, 1985).
Søren Kierkegaard, *The Concept of Dread,* trans. W. Lowrie (Princeton:
    Princeton University Press, 1957).

William Law, taken from Robert Llewelyn and Edward Moss, eds., *Fire from Flint: Daily Readings with William Law* (London: Darton, Longman and Todd, 1986).

Kenneth Leech, *Soul Friend: A Study of Spirituality* (London: Sheldon Press, 1977).

C. S. Lewis, *Letters to Malcolm: Chiefly on Prayer* (London: Geoffrey Bles, 1964).

Wilhelm Niesel, *Reformed Symbolics* (Edinburgh: Oliver and Boyd, 1962).

Friedrich Nietzsche, *Twilight of the Idols,* trans. R. J. Hollingdale (Harmondsworth: Penguin, 1968).

Kathleen Norris, *Amazing Grace: A Vocabulary of Faith* (New York: Riverhead Books, 1998).

Rumi, *The Essential Rumi,* trans. C. Barks (San Francisco: HarperSanFrancisco, 1995).

Dorothee Sölle, *The Silent Cry: Mysticism and Resistance,* trans. B. and M. Rumscheidt (Minneapolis: Fortress Press, 2001).

Paul Tillich, *The Courage to Be* (Glasgow: Collins, 1952).

Desmond Tutu's extract is taken from the Oliver Tambo Lecture, given at Georgetown University on 1 November 2001; see http://www.wfn.org/2001/11/msg00087.html

Michael Walzer, *Revolution of the Saints: A Study in the Origins of Radical Politics* (New York: Atheneum, 1970).

CHAPTER 6

A Postscript for Seth

Do not fear, O soil;
be glad and rejoice,
for the Lord has done great things!

JOEL 2:21

Dear Seth,

A couple of years ago we walked up Lion's Head in Cape Town. Normally this walk would take a comfortable hour and a half. It took us three hours to get to the top. We spent time looking at lizards, beetles, butterflies, and lichens and had a lot of fun. You spotted the tiniest creatures, you hunted in the crevasses for signs of life, and you asked dozens of questions. I marvelled at your ability to see truly and with wonder the small and unobtrusive objects. I have written a great deal in the letters in this book about how I have followed my longing. I know that all my life I have longed to know the hand of the One who writes the history of life. I have wondered a lot about the Author of creation. I am a scientific ignoramus who collects rocks, small fossils, and stone-age implements, simply because I feel awe when I hold them in my hand. I hope that, as long as I am able to do so, we can enjoy the ability to wonder at the unpretentious details of creation together.

This postscript to you is about wonder at the miracle of the minutiae about us. At the outset let me say that I am not romanticising nature. Nature has its own rules, its own inevitabilities, and its own surprises. My interest in the small things does not mean that I am not filled with awe when the whales sport their giant flukes in the bay below our place at Hermanus, or that I do not wonder at the majesty of an elephant moving almost noiselessly through the African bush. It simply means that the small things move me. They make my world infinitely enthralling and delightful. Wonder is feeling the joy of recognition. Suddenly something quite unexpectedly sparks a connection inside me and opens me to something new. You once asked me what I thought about God. I think you were actually asking me, "Who is God?" So let me tell you what I know. I think that, as Joel says, ". . . the Lord has done great things." I also think God is to be found in the grandeur of creation, that God is to be found within us, and that the bible tells us more about God than anything else. In this postscript, however, I want to tell you about finding God in the detail.

One of my favourite books about the history of life, called *Wonderful Life,* was written by the late Stephen Jay Gould, the well-known paleontologist and science writer. This remarkable work, which I hope you will read one day, tells the story of the wonders of the Burgess Shale. In a shale formation high in the Canadian Rockies in British Columbia, the world's most important animal fossils were found in the early part of the twentieth century. Preserved in exquisite detail, these small fossils are precious because the soft parts of these tiny creatures — like their gills and guts — have been preserved. They represent a fascinating range of diversity of ancient animal life. Imagine a puzzling event that happened some 570 million years ago. Suddenly an explosion in the number of different living creatures on this planet took place, containing the greatest variety of anatomical designs ever known. We may have more actual species on earth today, but nothing can equal the variety of designs found in the Burgess Shale. That is why Gould, an acknowledged agnostic, can say:

God dwells among the details, not in the realm of pure generality. We must tackle and grasp the larger, encompassing themes of our universe, but we make our best approach through small curiosities that rivet our attention — all those pretty pebbles on the shoreline of knowledge. For the ocean of truth washes over the pebbles with every wave, and they rattle and clink with the most wondrous din.

Relatively few people know about the Burgess Shale. We are, as Gould points out, much more awestruck by the sheer size of *Tyrannosaurus* or the feathers of *Archaeopteryx,* which you know all about. We get excited at every scrap of fossil human bone discovered in Africa. But none of these has taught us anywhere near so much about the history of life as have the little creatures of the Burgess Shale, many of which are less than one centimetre in length.

I pore over the drawings in Gould's book. Imagine a small wormlike creature with a nozzle that ends in a claw and has five eyes on its head! It is so bizarre, so different from all known living creatures, that the scientists realised they were looking at a whole new view of the history of life. Another really wacky-looking creature looks like a worm with a bulbous head balanced on seven pairs of sharply pointed spines with seven tentacles on its back! It took years of detective work to sort out exactly what these weird little creatures really looked like. Imagine fitting together a crustacean without a head, a curved feeding appendage, a jellyfish with a hole in the middle and a squashed section of something, to eventually find the largest of all the Cambrian animals — nearly two feet of it! It needed scientists who could think against the mainstream and *who could see the details in new ways.*

I am fascinated by the small things in nature. To my unscientific mind one thing is clear — in the history of life, the small creatures seem to have the edge in most mass extinctions. We probably owe our existence to them! The ability to see beyond the obvious and discover worlds that have hitherto been glossed over starts in our backyards. I remember a remarkable film called "Metamorphosis" — a silent, visually dazzling account of life in a meadow. No lions, tigers, buffalo, or elephants — just snails, moths, butterflies, and worms, feeding, mating, changing, dying, and new life emerging.

The wonder in the details, the sensation of the minutiae, originates for me in the natural world. It calls me to look at all of life in a new way. Take justice. Justice is not just an abstract concept — something for philosophers and lawyers to debate. Justice trickles into the smallest of our dealings, the insignificant action, the thought glossed over. I remember when I was small often feeling and sometimes saying: "That's not fair!" You know when you think things are not fair — and so does Jo even though she is much younger than you are. And many of the things that we find unfair are not big issues but are about seemingly less significant things that happen every day. We want justice in the small things as much as we need it in the big issues that govern our lives. Take our relationships. What are the small things that are important? Noticing when someone's voice has a tremor as they tell a story, or when a friend avoids looking you in the eye, or being aware of the hidden and unsaid parts of a conversation — all help us to understand more about the difficult, often messy, business of living together.

I am quite sure that God is interested in the small things, like small acts of kindness and generosity and small beginnings. There is a story in the bible's New Testament about a widow who, after rich people put large sums of money in the treasury, comes and gives "two small copper coins, which are worth a penny" (Mark 12:42). Seeing this, Jesus remarks: "Truly, I tell you, this poor widow has put in more than all those who are contributing to the treasury." These small coins are all she has. God's reign has small beginnings. It is compared to a mustard seed which is, as you may know, quite literally a tiny dark speck, the smallest of all the seeds. But when sown it grows into "the greatest of shrubs and becomes a tree, so that the birds of the air come and make nests in its branches" (Matt. 13:31-32). In a previous letter I mentioned a hazelnut. What could be more insignificant than a little hazelnut? Yet Julian of Norwich, a great mediaeval thinker, saw in this hazelnut "all that is made." That may sound strange, but what she was really seeing was the meaning of the small hazelnut within the greatness of creation. Insignificant, yes, when compared to the giant oak or a granite boulder, yet so important that it will "last and will go on lasting forever because God loves it." This is more than just God's interest in the detail. God invests in the small things. God actually loves the detail.

That's what I think about God. I hope you will never stop wondering at the little things and that you will pursue the small curiosities that rivet your attention. You may well find the answer to your question in the details. In the meantime I will scatter mustard seeds and small copper coins on my landscape and try hard to draw a few of those weird little creatures from the Burgess Shale in a corner of my sketch.

With my love,
Denise

NOTES

Seth Musker is the son of my daughter-in-law Liesa. Our "ready-made" Jewish grandson, truly a gift, is eleven years old and lives in Windhoek, Namibia, with his family where he attends the international school.

I am an avid reader of Stephen Jay Gould's writing. The work referred to in this letter is *Wonderful Life: The Burgess Shale and the Nature of History* (New York: W. W. Norton, 1989). In this fossil bed in British Columbia, scientists have found early representatives of all four major arthropods, the dominant animals on earth today. But, more importantly, they have identified "the remains of some fifteen to twenty organisms so different one from the other, and so unlike anything now living, that each ought to rank as a separate phylum." (For the uninitiated like myself, a phylum is the basic unit of differentiation within kingdoms — plant, animal, fungi, etc. — and represents the fundamental ground plans of anatomy.) Many of these fossils can be seen in Washington's National Museum of Natural History at the Smithsonian Institution. Other favourites of mine by Gould on natural history are *Ever Since Darwin* and *The Flamingo's Smile: Reflections on Natural History*. I also recommend Gould's *Rock of Ages: Science and Religion in the Fullness of Life*. This book sets out the dilemma that has plagued people since the Renaissance, the idea that one has to choose between religion or science. Gould suggests a golden mean that accords dignity and distinction to each realm.